Bear's Boys

Eli Gold

With MB Roberts

THOMAS NELSON
Since 1798

NASHVILLE DALLAS MEXICO CITY RIO DE JANEIRO

Published in Nashville, Tennessee, by Thomas Nelson. Thomas Nelson is a registered trademark of Thomas Nelson, Inc.

Thomas Nelson, Inc., titles may be purchased in bulk for educational, business, fund-raising, or sales promotional use. For information, please e-mail SpecialMarkets@ThomasNelson.com.

Page Design by Casey Hooper

ISBN 978-1-59555-315-7 (TP)

Library of Congress Cataloging-in-Publication Data

Gold, Eli, 1953-
Bear's boys / Eli Gold with MB Roberts.
p. cm.
Includes index.
ISBN 978-1-4016-0324-3
1. Bryant, Paul W. 2. Football coaches--United States. 3. Football players—United States—Anecdotes. 4. University of Alabama—Football—History—Anecdotes. 5. Alabama Crimson Tide (Football team)—History--Anecdotes. I. Roberts, M. B. (Mary Beth) II. Title.
GV939.B79G65 2007
796.332092--dc22
[B]

2007021884

Printed in the United States of America
09 10 11 12 RRD 6 5 4 3 2 1

CONTENTS

FOREWORD

By Keith Jackson

There was a time several years ago, and I do mean *several years.*

I was helping with a series of video stories having to do with college football. It was a pleasant adventure because I was working with good people on a subject that reached right to the core of me: *The Coaches of the Game.*

Well, you don't write or talk about those people without putting a man like Paul William Bryant right in the center of it.

We were working on the campus at Tuscaloosa on a soft warm day, nearing the end of the project, and I was not satisfied that we had the right closing attitude for a video about the Bear.

We went looking for a small pond, found it, and scratched around it to find some pebbles of the right size. For some time we pitched those pebbles into that small pond, several times changing the location of the cameras so we had just right image to make our point.

And voila! We had it!

Now I know there is a funny image here: an ole Georgia Cracker on the University of Alabama campus standing by a little pond pitching rocks at it, looking at the videotape, shouting, "Voila!"

But by gum, we had the video to carry the thought that defined the man. The Leader. The Coach.

Each ripple on that pond represented a generation, and generation after generation those ripples spread, each carrying the teachings, the philosophy, and the meaning of the man, the leader, the coach, carrying to thousands of people.

This book from Eli Gold gives voices to those ripples—direct commentary from those who knew the Bear the best. Some played for him and some worked with him. They knew him on good days and bad days, through great victories and lashing losses, but it is in that environment in which people experience life in such a way they never forget it.

They are part of a massive fraternity that had its birth on the Bermuda grass on the football fields of the University of Alabama.

They are BEAR'S BOYS!

And when you have finished the book, try to remember the last time you heard one of Bear's Boys say something bad about the Coach.

Well done, Eli.

ACKNOWLEDGMENTS

Start digging into the history and lore that is Alabama football and one name will always rise to the surface: Paul W. "Bear" Bryant. It has been said many times, "Coach Bryant is Alabama football." Despite the fact that he has been gone since 1983, this is still true today.

Fans, players, and coaches still aspire to his standards. And why shouldn't they? He defined what it meant to be a winner—in football and in life.

Ultimately, we have Coach Bryant to thank for this book. He inspired and influenced many, many people and that is why we have these great stories to tell.

First, the authors would like to thank a very dear friend, Bob Baumhower, for lighting a spark that became an idea and finally, this book. Also, we sincerely appreciate every one of Bear's boys (and wonderful people such as Linda Knowles and Jack Rutledge) who agreed to be interviewed for this book. Your stories and sincere affection for your former coach and the University of Alabama blew us away.

We could have not done this book without the incredible knowledge and hours of assistance from everyone at the Bryant Museum in Tuscaloosa, especially Coach Clem Gryska, Brad Green, Erik Stinnett, and Ken Gaddy.

Thanks also to Neely Portera in The Alumni Association office for helping track down players and to Barry Allen in the university's Media Relations department for assistance in verifying stats. Thanks also to Eli's cohorts at the Crimson Tide Sports Network who were hugely supportive, just as they are of *Crimson Nation.* Also, the advice and background information offered by author David Briley and the transcription work done by Jessica Senorin are both truly appreciated.

A special thanks goes to Larry Black, the producer of the Alabama Football Legends Reunion, for giving permission to quote from the DVD. The DVD is a must-have for Alabama fans and is available at www.sportsreunion.com or 800/410-9877.

Thanks also to everyone who took the time to gather and send pictures for the book, especially photographer Ron Modra, who photographed several subjects, contributed historical photos, scanned all the prints, and also provided major inspiration for this project.

We are very grateful to Mal Moore and our editor Geoff Stone who helped us make good on our wish to create a scholarship fund from a portion of the proceeds of this book. We appreciate the opportunity to give back to the University that has given us so much.

Finally, thanks to legendary Hall-of-Fame broadcaster Keith Jackson who was so kind to contribute the foreword. The subject matter of the book is impressive enough, but Keith's "seal of approval" has made the project that much more special.

INTRODUCTION

"Give everything you've got in everything you do."

—PAUL W. "BEAR" BRYANT

EVERYBODY KNOWS WHAT COACH PAUL W. "BEAR" BRYANT ACCOMplished on the football field. He won games. Lots of games.

When he retired as head coach of the Crimson Tide in 1982, he was the winningest college football coach in history with 323 wins. Although Penn State's Joe Paterno and Florida State's Bobby Bowden have since passed that mark, people will forever associate Coach Bryant with one word: *winner*.

True, he's been gone from the sidelines a long time, but Bryant is still well remembered and exceptionally revered. He is still a huge presence in Alabama and is considered an icon among sports fans everywhere.

There have been literally dozens of books published (not to mention a few movies made) about the man, his philosophies, and his winning ways. During football season, Alabama fans erupt into thunderous applause every time his

Photograph by Ronald C. Modra. Used by permission.

There was only one Bear.

image and voice appear on the jumbotron before Crimson Tide home games. In Tuscaloosa, his name graces Bryant-Denny Stadium, Bryant Drive, Bryant Hall, and the Bryant Museum. Students still wear houndstooth hats on game day and parents still name their kids after him.

There is no denying his presence or his winning record. At Alabama, Bryant brought home six national championships and thirteen SEC titles. During the Bryant era, no other college team won more games or played in more bowl games than Alabama. But Coach Bryant didn't just care about winning. He cared about the people doing the winning. And that, as it turns out, has been his lasting legacy.

As he saw it, his job was to take young men and show them how to be part of a team and reach their full potential as players. And although they didn't know it at the time, while they were tackling and hitting and running and studying their *X*s and *O*s, he was giving them the tools to be successful in life.

"I can't think of a player that played for him that didn't go on to become successful," said Dennis Homan, Crimson Tide receiver from 1965 to 1967. "It's amazing. There are coaches, attorneys, doctors, and businessmen. Coach Bryant used to say, 'it doesn't matter if you go on to be the President of the United States or a garbage collector, be successful at it.' He was not only concerned with us being better football players and winning games and winning championships. He was interested in whatever endeavor we took up after football."

Ray Perkins, who played for Bryant in the sixties and followed him as Alabama's head coach in 1983, agrees. "The people who had the success, winning games and winning championships, went on to become highly successful," he said. "Afterwards, what we did later, was what mattered to him. If you could cope with what they dished out on the practice field you should be able to cope with life."

Even though they didn't like it at the time, players would come to appreciate his lessons later.

"I think there is no question he affected every player who came through here in a positive way," said Mal Moore, his longtime assistant coach and current Alabama Athletics Director.

So, when Coach Bryant pushed a player to his limit, he wasn't just teaching

Photograph by Ronald C. Modra. Used by permission.

Coach Bryant directs on-field traffic.

Photograph courtesy of Paul W. Bryant Museum/The University of Alabama

Bryant fires up Dennis Homan, Ken Stabler, and Ray Perkins (1967 Sugar Bowl).

him not to quit in the fourth quarter of a football game. He was showing him how to reach down and get that little something extra during tough times (bankruptcy, divorce, a child's illness) that everyone encounters in the real world.

When he hollered at a player who just made a successful block but then failed to pick up another man, he wasn't just teaching a player to go the extra mile on the field. He was showing him that in life, you do your job then go see how else you can help.

When he failed to compliment a star player on an awesome performance, he was teaching him to stay humble. When he pumped up an average player he was pushing him to achieve beyond his talents.

When he walked through the cafeteria and asked a player, "Did you write to your mama this week?" instead of posing a more coach-like question ("What happened on the reverse?"), he was showing his team that some things are more important than football.

"Coach Bryant always said football was number one but that it is a very small part of your life," said seventies Crimson Tide lineman Bob Baumhower.

"He talked about principles we should take away from the field. Take care of your mom and dad. Go to church. Give 100 percent in everything you do."

No question, Bear Bryant would ache with pride if he could see what many of his former players achieved and the kind of people they have become. And there is no doubt, these guys we call Bear's boys, acknowledge his continued presence in their lives.

"Whenever two or more of us get together, his name will come up," said Sylvester Croom, who played center and later coached for Bryant's teams.

"There is probably not one player who played for him that doesn't think of him in some way every day. He still pops up in my dreams. I still think about him and remember things he said and did. When I am confronted with certain situations, I often find out that he prepared me for it years ago."

During his long coaching career, Bryant touched a lot of lives. Or as the punter from the 1978 championship team, Woody Umphrey, puts it, "He touched a lot of hearts."

And it wasn't just players he reached. Part of his success was his ability to reach all kinds of people in all walks of life. Sylvester Croom, who traveled with him extensively as an assistant coach, was continually amazed at how he would treat hotel workers the same way he would treat a university trustee. "He would take off his hat and say 'yes ma'am,' to a hotel maid," Croom said. "He walked with kings but never lost the common touch. Very few people can do that."

Coach Bryant impacted many, many people over the years. But it was the players who got his undivided attention. Dozens of young men played for Coach Bryant at the University of Maryland, the University of Kentucky, and at Texas A&M; but for this book, we focused on players and a couple of coaches from Coach Bryant's Alabama teams from 1958 to 1982. Obviously, there are hundreds of stories we could have told, but we were limited by space and time. Plus, we were unable to locate some potential subjects and a few people chose not to participate. Please know that it was our goal to put together the best possible list of players who were great on the field and continued to carry themselves with pride and class after their playing days were done.

Still, we realize there are some gaping holes in this book. Looking back at the sixties, it would be easy to include every player from the national championship teams of '61, '64, '65, and the undefeated season of '66. There were so many great players such as Billy Richardson, Tommy Brooker, Jimmy Carroll, Steve Bowman, Bobby Johns, Darwin Holt, and the great Cecil Dowdy, who died in a tragic hunting accident in 2002.

What about Billy Johnson, Les Kelley, Bruce Stephens, Wayne Trimble, Dicky Thompson, or Wayne Cook? Looking at the seventies, we'd like to have told the story of John Croyle, the defensive end (and Brodie's dad) who runs the Big Oak Ranch for disadvantaged kids in Springville, Alabama. Robin Parkhouse, Buddy Brown, Jim Krapf, Gus White, Jeff Rutledge, Robert Fraley, Leroy Cook, Mike Washington, Terry Rowell, Major Ogilvie, Rich Wingo, Murray Legg, Tony Nathan, Byron Braggs, and David Hannah would have made great subjects. So would have players on Bryant's last few teams such as Thomas Boyd, Mike Pitts, Jesse Bendross, Walter Lewis, and many of their teammates.

As for the dozens of other guys who weren't stars or even starters, but who contributed season after season by playing on scout teams, it would have been very satisfying to show how they carried Coach Bryant's lessons with them as they went on to succeed in business and in life.

We just hope these stories are read with appreciation and that Alabama fans know we acknowledge the tremendous players and coaches who worked for Bear Bryant but are not included in these pages.

One thing every Alabama fan can agree on: Coach Bryant's influence was vast and continues to this day. In the mid-eighties, he was still on players' minds. Cornelius Bennett grew up watching the great Bryant-coached teams and said he made his decision to play for Alabama when he saw the picture of The Goal Line Stand on the cover of *Sports Illustrated.* Jay Barker, who led his team to a national championship in 1992, said he grew up wanting to play for the Bear. John Copeland, who never met the coach, said he loves hearing Bear Bryant stories. "He's kind of like Elvis around here," he said. "They won't let him die."

Mal Moore tells a great story about a letter Coach Bryant once received. It was postmarked "Baton Rouge, 1976," and was addressed simply to "The Bear." The letter got to him. The reason for that is obvious. There was only one Bear, but the number of people that he influenced, and continues to influence, is incalculable. With *Bear's Boys,* we have attempted to scratch the surface.

BOB BAUMHOWER

"I wanted to be great at something."
—BOB BAUMHOWER

SOME PEOPLE CALL IT AN "A-HA" MOMENT. YOU KNOW, WHEN SOMEthing happens to you that shapes your life forever? Bob Baumhower remembers such a moment. It was the fall of 1974, Bob's sophomore year. He had just quit the University of Alabama football team and was sitting on (or sinking into) the infamous low-slung couch in Coach Bryant's office.

Things had begun well for Bob at Bama. He started his freshman year as an offensive lineman but moved to defense and was a starter by the following spring. So, in the fall, Bob assumed he would automatically be a starter again. He assumed wrong.

"I didn't do a whole lot between spring and fall ball because in my mind, I'd already arrived," Baumhower said. "When I got back, I wasn't in great shape. Then I got my jersey. I was last string. I was wondering what was going on. So, after three or four days, I quit."

Photograph courtesy of Paul W. Bryant Museum/The University of Alabama

A lean and mean Bob Baumhower

Then, Coach Bryant summoned Baumhower and Baumhower's dad to his office. When the Baumhowers arrived, Coach Bryant greeted Baumhower's father warmly. Then he turned to Baumhower and said, "What the hell are you doing here? I don't talk to quitters."

Then he mumbled something in a low growl along the lines of, "Well, as long as you're here. . . ."

Coach Bryant then proceeded to explain to Baumhower what every other player ahead of him on the roster had done over the summer to improve. One guy lost weight. Another got stronger. A third got faster.

According to Baumhower, Coach Bryant told him, "I don't think you're a quitter; I think you're frustrated. But it doesn't mean enough to you. To have someone on the starting line, I have to know this is their number-one priority."

By the end of the meeting, Baumhower was begging to come back. Eventually, Coach Bryant gave the nod, but he also warned him it wasn't going to be easy. The defensive coordinator, Ken Donahue, had a reputation for being an extremely tough and demanding extension of Bryant.

Again, the low growl: "Donahue is probably going to kill you," Bryant said. "But we'll see what you've got."

Baumhower was off and running. Being singled out by Coach Bryant was just the kick he needed. "He cared about me enough to turn the light on for me," Baumhower said. "He made me believe I had the opportunity to do something special."

Baumhower went right to work. He not only regained his starting position, but over the next three years he became one of the best defensive players the Crimson Tide ever produced, racking up 246 tackles in his career. He was a two-time all-SEC performer and played in the Senior Bowl, where his coach was the Miami Dolphins' Don Shula. Coach Shula apparently liked what he saw: at the end of Baumhower's senior year, he was drafted by Miami in the second round of the NFL Draft. He played there for ten years.

From the get-go, Baumhower was in sync with the attitude and the goals of his pro team.

"At Alabama we played for the national championship," Baumhower said. "In Miami we played for the Super Bowl. That was our goal. Not just to have a winning season but to go for the top."

Baumhower was also shocked to discover that although it wasn't going to be a cakewalk, he was more than prepared to play in the pros.

"We hit the field, and before I knew it someone said, 'Practice is over,'" Baumhower remembered. "I hadn't broken a sweat yet! At Alabama, we practiced three or four hours. I thought, *Man, I'm gonna love this!*"

One thing Baumhower didn't love at first was his new position—nose guard.

"It's a really tough position," Baumhower said. "You're getting nailed from every direction. The guys who came in with me said, 'You poor SOB—I wouldn't play the middle for nothing.'"

But another light went on for Baumhower when his defensive coach told him he could be a *good* defensive back but he could be a *great* nose tackle. "I wanted to be great at something," Baumhower said. "So I jumped on it."

Baumhower's Dolphins career was outstanding! He was named Defensive Rookie of the Year in 1977 and would go on to win the honor of 1983 NFL Defensive Player of the Year. He played in 125 consecutive games, five Pro Bowls, and two Super Bowls, all for Don Shula. Baumhower has often been asked to compare his two legendary coaches.

"Both Coach Bryant and Coach Shula were extremely organized," Baumhower said. "They were both extremely focused, had great vision, and did a good job communicating that vision to their teams. But college and pro ball are two very different animals. In the pros, more of how you perform is up to you. In college, things are more regimented. In that way, Coach Bryant was more like a dad."

Like children who grow closer to their parents as they get older, many of Bryant's players got to know him as a person and even sometimes as a dear friend after they left the university. Baumhower counts himself in that group.

"I was shocked at how much he knew about us and kept up with us," Baumhower said. "I'd get little notes from him saying, 'Hey, I watched you on *Monday Night Football.* Great job. I should have had you there—that's your best position. Shula knows what he's doing.' He would call me and his secretary would say, 'Got a minute for Coach Bryant?' Yeah. I think so!"

A few times Coach Bryant came to Florida to visit. As much as Baumhower loved spending time with him, he still couldn't completely relax in the coach's company.

"I'd borrow my teammates' nicer, bigger cars before I picked him up," Baumhower said. "Then they'd tell everybody that Coach Bryant had ridden in their car! These are guys who didn't even go to Alabama!"

Coach Bryant confided things to Baumhower as they drove around visiting players in South Florida. These included his top-secret discussions with Dolphins Owner Joe Robbie regarding possibly becoming the Dolphins head coach. (Obviously, he stayed put.)

Baumhower talked about many things with Coach Bryant too. But one thing he never mentioned was that they had something in common: bear-wrestling.

As Bama fans know, Paul Bryant famously wrestled a black bear at the Lyric Theater in downtown Fordyce, Arkansas, when he was just thirteen years old. This was after being promised a dollar for every minute he stayed in the ring. Even though the bear bit young Paul's ear, he lasted three full minutes. The promoter stiffed him. But he had earned the nickname that followed him his whole life.

When Baumhower was seventeen, his dad entered him in a bear-wrestling exhibition at a West Palm Beach boat show. The bear was enormous—450 pounds—but Baumhower was cocky. He also had a plan.

"I was going to go low and try to get one of his legs," Baumhower said. "But he hit me with his paw and I went scattering across the floor. I got him in a headlock. Here was this big ol' bear head sticking up! All of the sudden he puts me down, gets on top of me, and starts licking me with that big ol' tongue!"

And that's why Baumhower was never known as "Bear Baumhower."

Baumhower's bear-wrestling era coincided with the start of his football career. Partly because his family moved a lot (he was born in Virginia and lived in Ohio, Michigan, Florida, and Alabama), Baumhower never played football until he was a junior at Palm Beach Gardens High in Florida. His family moved to Alabama his senior year, and he played well at Tuscaloosa High School, although he never managed to catch the eye of the coaches from the famous university down the road.

Baumhower's big break came late in the recruiting process, when coaches were watching film of their signees. "A top offensive prospect was having a hard time, and it was me giving him the hard time," said Baumhower.

Taking notice, Bryant told his coaches to "go get that kid." They got him just in time. He was in Nashville, ready to sign with Vanderbilt when he called his mother.

"Don't do anything yet," she said. "The coaches from Alabama called."

Baumhower told Vanderbilt Coach Charlie Bradshaw that he wanted to talk to Bryant before he made a decision. Bradshaw, who knew the Bear well said, "Good luck. We won't be seeing you again."

Baumhower says he met with Coach Bryant and that the coach apologized for not giving him the respect of signing him earlier. Then Coach Bryant told him Bama wanted him.

"I get chills thinking about it," said Baumhower. "I think I was the last person to sign!"

Years later, as a pro player at the top of his game and loving life as a football star in South Florida, Baumhower was called on stage to sing "Jump!" during a Van Halen concert! The evening was also significant because he met a gorgeous blonde named Leslie who later became his wife.

Having struggled with several serious injuries, Baumhower knew his pro career wouldn't last forever. To prepare for a career after football, he began seeking other business opportunities while still playing with the Dolphins.

In 1979, Baumhower, together with former Bama-teammates-turned-NY-Jets-stars, Joe Namath and Richard Todd, opened a restaurant in Fort Lauderdale, Bachelors III.

"It was a lot of fun, but I learned everything you don't do in running a restaurant," Baumhower said. "It didn't make money because it wasn't a top priority for any of us. You can't just put your name on it. Customers and employees want to know you're going to do what it takes to make sure your business is run right."

Right around that time, one of Baumhower's Dolphins teammate, Steve Towle, took him to Wings & Things for lunch. Baumhower, like much of America at the time, had never heard of buffalo wings. He liked them. And he liked what he saw at the restaurant—a line out the door. He met the owner and after promising he would never compete with him in South Florida, picked his brain about the wings business.

Next stop: Tuscaloosa, where Baumhower partnered with an old high school buddy and opened Wings & Things on campus in 1981. His first logo? A chicken with a houndstooth hat!

Meanwhile, Baumhower returned to his other job, making bruising tack-

Photograph by Ronald C. Modra. Used by permission.

Baumhower was a natural in Miami.

les for the Dolphins. In late 1984, an ankle and knee injury sidelined him for a while. But being one of Bear's boys, he refused to quit.

"I kept going, but I never felt like I played 100 percent that year," said Baumhower.

After playing in the 1985 Super Bowl, in which San Francisco knocked off the Dolphins, 38-16, Baumhower needed help hobbling off the field. Knee surgery was inevitable. After the operation, Baumhower couldn't walk for two months. He missed the entire 1985 season.

Photograph by Ronald C. Modra. Used by permission.

Indulging his other passion: deep sea fishing in Florida

"The frustrating part was that it took away what I loved so much so quickly," he said. "That aspect was tough to take. But life's not fair, and you have to make the best of what you've got."

So, Baumhower moved back to Alabama to become a full-time restaurateur. His next venture was Wings & Whiskers, in Northport, Alabama, featuring catfish fingers as well as chicken wings.

"What a horrible name!" Baumhower laughed. "People thought we were a pet shop."

Baumhower even got into the catfish-farming business for a while. His sister Debbi and soon-to-be-wife Leslie helped with the operation.

Soon, Baumhower got out of the counter service business and began his full-service Wings restaurants. When he expanded the sports-themed element, things really took off.

Today, Baumhower has eight Baumhower's Wings restaurants and plans to add a Cuban-Creole-themed restaurant to his empire, Aloha Hospitality

International, in the near future. His Tuscaloosa location is the undisputed hub for Bama fans who gather to watch the weekly live coach's show during the football season or just enjoy the mountains of Bama (and other sports) memorabilia while eating really great food.

"I'm a student of the restaurant game," Baumhower said. "I want to learn everything I can about it. I don't want to just be an ex-jock. I want to make a mark in the hospitality business."

No question, the restaurant biz is Baumhower's top priority. OK, maybe it takes a slight backseat to his family. He and his wife, Leslie, have been married for seventeen years and live in Fairhope, Alabama, with their four kids, Spencer, fourteen; Katherine, twelve; Allie, ten; and Wesley, seven. Their bustling home is full of critters that include a ferret, rabbits, birds, and two labs named "Coach" and "Bear."

His kids know all about Bear Bryant.

"He made such a huge mark," said Baumhower. "That man really walked the walk."

JIM BUNCH

"To me, the seventies was like the Camelot of college football."

— JIM BUNCH

NO ALABAMA PLAYER EVER FORGOT HIS FIRST CONVERSATION WITH Coach Bryant. That gravely voice and the choice words he spoke never failed to leave a lasting impression.

Jim Bunch vividly remembers his first exchange with the legendary coach. It was two o'clock in the morning. Bunch was a senior at Fork Union Military Academy in Virginia. He was asleep in the barracks when the messenger from the gate woke him and said, "Coach Bryant called and wants you to call him back right away."

Bunch could hardly believe it. He was hoping to sign with Virginia Tech or N.C. State. Although he'd had some contact with Alabama, he had been given no promises. Playing football for the Crimson Tide was a dream, and he'd just woken up to find out Coach Bryant had called him in the middle of the night.

"I looked at the 205 area code and figured the number was legit," Bunch said. "Still, I wasn't sure what to do at that time in the morning. But I figured if he was calling that late, it must be important."

Because there were no phones in the barracks, Bunch walked almost a mile in the dark to a pay phone down the road.

"All the lights were out, so I had to scramble," Bunch said. "I called the number—collect. I'll never forget hearing that voice when he came to the phone. I knew I woke him up. I said, 'Sir, this is Jim Bunch at Fork Union Military School, and I'm returning your call.'"

The coach paused for a moment and said, "I didn't call anyone."

Then he said, "Someone's playing a joke on us, son. I'll have one of the coaches here contact you tomorrow."

Bunch was mortified. But he was impressed that even being rousted from a deep sleep, Coach Bryant knew what was going on. To this day, Bunch thinks the culprit was someone from Virginia Tech. (By the way, he'd love to know whodunit.)

Photograph courtesy of Jim Bunch

Bunch strikes Coach Bryant's famous goal post pose.

The joke (or the intended sabotage) backfired because Coach Bryant wasn't fooled, and he was a man of his word. One of his coaches did call Bunch the next day to invite him to Tuscaloosa for an interview. Then Bunch, who would go on to play offensive tackle for the Crimson Tide from 1976 to 1979, says he caught another break courtesy of his military school's tight budget.

At Fork Union, they put all their football films on one reel instead of splitting them into two (one for offense, one for defense). Alabama assistant coach Ken Donahue was checking out a defensive back on one particular film and noticed Bunch on offense. He shared the films with other coaches, and soon Bunch was trading in his white gloves and brass polished buckles for a helmet and pads.

Bunch's brief military training served him well when he got to Tuscaloosa. He was used to rising by 5:45 AM, making his bed (complete with crisp hospital corners), and obeying orders. Discipline was not an issue for Bunch. But even though he was accustomed to tough superiors, he was still impressed with his new head coach in a big way.

"You could hear yourself breathe when you walked into a meeting room," Bunch remembered. "Everybody just respected Coach Bryant so much. You could hear your own heartbeat."

Bunch's first year at the Capstone was a very good one. In 1976 he was the only freshman to break into the Crimson Tide's starting lineup and ended up being named first team Freshman all-SEC. The following spring he won the Paul Crane Most Improved Offensive Lineman Award.

His on-field excellence continued for the next three years. He played alongside Dwight Stephenson, Vince Boothe, Buddy Aydelette, and Mike Brock protecting the likes of quarterbacks Steadman Shealy, Don Jacobs, and Jeff Rutledge.

"As Crimson Tide fans know well, in 1977, Alabama, the defending champions, finished undefeated. Then, despite their 35-6 Sugar Bowl victory over Ohio State, Alabama finished third in the polls."

"That still bugs me," said Bunch. "But we won 12 that year. That's incredible in itself."

Bunch's teams finished on the highest note possible, winning the national title in both 1978 and '79. Bunch was named all-American in 1979 and finished his college career as a three-time all-SEC player.

Life was good for a kid who had endured a lot of hard knocks growing up. His dad had died when Bunch was nine years old, and his mother struggled to take care of the family, including Bunch's disabled grandfather. "She did a heck of a job raising me," Bunch said. "She got us through."

It was a long way from his hometown of Mechanicsville, Virginia, to the roar of Bryant-Denny Stadium. The first time he heard it, it was a little scary.

"You walk out, and there are all these people!" Bunch remembered. "You feel kind of like a rock star. Then after we won, forget it. All I wanted to do was go back to the dorm and take a nap. But fans were everywhere!"

After graduating from Alabama in 1980, Bunch joined Coach Bryant's staff as an assistant for one year while attending graduate school. Some players-turned-coaches found their relationship with the coach changed when they became a colleague. For some, this meant they grew closer to Coach Bryant.

Bunch had a bit of a different perspective.

"To me, the seventies was like the Camelot of college football," Bunch said. "And Coach Bryant had his round table. We had meetings at 5:30 in the morning, and he'd go around and ask the coaches to talk about what they'd seen the day before. Once, when it was my turn, I said something about a player who I thought would play for us in the future. Well, he lectured me for about an hour, basically telling me why this guy would never be a player. He turned out to be right."

In other words, no slack. You had to know your stuff. Or the head coach would call you on it.

Photograph courtesy of Jim Bunch

Bunch delivers the game ball (2006).

"I think the coaches were more afraid of Coach Bryant than the players were," Bunch said. "I really do!"

After leaving the university, Bunch went into the restaurant management business. His first job interview, with an ownership group opening Quincy's Family Steakhouses, was his only interview, and he stayed with the company for twenty-five years. He retired from that position in 2005 and recently became vice president of operations for Drane Enterprises in Scottsboro, Alabama, which operates Hardees restaurants.

These days, Bunch, his wife Leslie, and son Jeb split their time between Valley Head and Fort Payne, Alabama, where Jeb plays high school football. (He got his nickname, "the Governor" when a local reporter praised his performance in a game but mistakenly called him "Jeb *Bush*.") Bunch's daughter Kelly is a law student at Syracuse University.

Bunch and Leslie, a teacher, also are involved in another hospitality-related business: Winston Place Bed and Breakfast in Valley Head, Alabama. The charming southern home, with its sprawling wrap-around porch, was built in 1831 and later occupied by Union troops during the Civil War. Leslie's grandfather bought the home in 1944. After she and Bunch moved to Valley Head in 1992, she ran the B&B for a while. Now her parents run the place, but Bunch and Leslie help out on weekends.

Many of the guests are Alabama football fans who enjoy browsing through the memorabilia (including four Christmas cards from Bob Hope addressed to all-American Jim Bunch) and photographs (of the team synonymous with "the Goal Line Stand") in the home. They also enjoy hearing stories of Bunch's playing days.

One story he tells is of the day he took his turn on Coach Bryant's infamous couch. Many players over the years (such as Stabler, Baumhower, and Krauss) tell stories of being called into Bryant's office when they had done something wrong and then being made to feel as low as possible as they sat on his sinking couch.

Bunch's situation was different. He wasn't in trouble. It was he who asked Bryant for the meeting. He wanted to get married, and in those days players had to ask the coach's permission first.

"I walked in his office and sat on his couch," Bunch remembered. "That thing engulfs you! You only had to sit on it one time until you realized you had to sit on the edge of it. So, Coach Bryant is getting larger and larger in front of those huge bay windows he had, and you're just getting smaller and smaller. He had the most penetrating eyes you've ever seen in your life. It was just incredible.

"You felt like he could just look right down into your soul. When you sat on that couch you had to tell him everything, and it had to be the truth. It was like he had his own lie detector there!"

But although Bunch heard stories of past players having their nuptial requests denied, he was pleasantly surprised when the coach gave him the nod.

"He said OK," Bunch remembered. "He said it helps some players, and it hurts some players. And that was it."

Over Sunday brunch at the B&B, Bunch tells other stories, several of them involving practical jokes. There is, of course, the story of his middle-of-the-night phone call to Coach Bryant. Then there was the time a group of offensive players were warming up on the field, when one of them spotted Coach Bryant's unattended golf cart.

"When he used to get in that thing, he would floor it and head for the tunnel," remembered Bunch. "So this guy gets in it and puts it in reverse. We're out there stretching, and we see Coach Bryant come out. He gets in the golf cart and just floors it. He almost falls out of it. It scares him a little bit. We were just rolling on the ground laughing. He just smiled."

Months went by. Nothing was said about the incident.

Bunch continued: "Then one day after practice, our offensive line coach says, 'Coach Bryant wants everybody back on the field now. He says you're getting fat and lazy.'

"We go back out there, and he just about killed us. We're doing grass drills. He says, 'Up! Back! Right! Left!' We could barely hear him. We're falling down, going all different directions. He's laughing the whole time, having a ball."

Many people ask Bunch and other guys who played on the late seventies and early eighties teams if they played for a "kinder, gentler Bear" than guys from the fifties and sixties knew.

Bunch says yes and no.

"If I compare him to myself, I don't know if I'm more mellow at fifty than I was as twenty-two, but I have a better understanding of life. I would say with all the experiences he had that he probably handled things better when I played for him than he did when he was younger."

Bryant passed away just three years after Bunch left the university. But a lasting image of his coach remains in his head.

"He leaned on the goal post before the game," Bunch said. "One time, the first guy on the team we were playing came out of the tunnel looking right at Coach Bryant and he fell. Then everyone else fell right after him. Coach was always good for a touchdown."

JEREMIAH CASTILLE

"I have had a great career, and that's because of great men like this man right here, Jeremiah Castille."
— PAUL W. "BEAR" BRYANT

DURING THE FOUR YEARS HE PLAYED DEFENSIVE BACK FOR THE CRIMSON Tide, Jeremiah Castille didn't say much. Basically, he kept quiet and did his job.

His friends used to ask him, "Why are you majoring in communications? You don't even talk!"

So it stunned everyone—including himself—when prior to the 1982 Liberty Bowl he stood up in the locker room to address his teammates and Coach Bryant.

"It was Coach Bryant's last game as head coach, and it was my last game as a player at Alabama," Castille said. "I was a shy, quiet player. It took the prompting of the Lord for me to even get up there. I was nervous to get up in front of the whole team.

"But before that game I realized all the things Coach Bryant had done were for my benefit. He cared about me. So I had the opportunity to share that with him and the team. It was nothing I planned on doing. It was really impromptu, but I think sometimes that makes the best speeches."

Photograph courtesy of Paul W. Bryant Museum/The University of Alabama

Jeremiah Castille at the ready

His rapt teammates and coaches agreed.

"I said, 'Coach, with all my heart, I appreciate what you've put me through. The ups and downs. All of the tough times. The bleeding, the times I may have felt like quitting. I'm glad I stuck with what you told me and believed in it. Look at where we are right now. I came to the university as an eighteen-year-old boy and I'm leaving a twenty-two-year-old man."

Castille also inspired his teammates by declaring, "There is no way we are going to lose this game." He contributed greatly to Alabama's 21-15 Liberty Bowl victory over Illinois by intercepting three passes. When he was named game MVP, Coach Bryant gave him a nod saying, "I have had a great career, and that's because of great men like this man right here, Jeremiah Castille."

"That was the best game of my career," Castille said. "What a way to finish as a player at the university, and it being Coach Bryant's last game."

As emotional as it was to see Coach Bryant retire, no one expected him to be gone a mere twenty-eight days after he coached his last game.

"His death was so shocking," Castille said. "I was looking forward to coming back and visiting him over the years, and I didn't get a chance to do that."

Photograph courtesy of Paul W. Bryant Museum/The University of Alabama

Castille let his actions do the talking.

Of all the magnificent honors Castille received as a player (he was named all-SEC in 1981–82 and all-American in 1982, and later he was selected to the Tide's Team of the Century), nothing came close to being asked to serve as one of Bryant's pallbearers at his funeral.

"That was probably the greatest honor I've had," Castille said. "During the sixty-mile ride [from the service in Tuscaloosa to the cemetery in Birmingham], there were people lined along the highway and they are crying. They didn't know him like we did, but they are just bawling. I said, 'Man, this is bigger than I ever imagined.'"

Castille, the eighth of nine kids, grew up in Phenix City, Alabama, in a home that he describes as dysfunctional. "My father was a workaholic, and my mother was an alcoholic. It was a tough life growing up."

He also describes himself as a "bad kid" who got expelled from junior high school for fighting. Then, the summer after a very rocky year, he attended a

Baptist revival and became a Christian. "My life changed from that point on," Castille said. "I had a dream of making life count for something."

In high school, one of his coaches reinforced this message by telling him he had the potential to become a great athlete and do something positive with his life. He kept playing and improving and dreaming.

"I used to watch Coach Bryant's TV show," he said. "Woodrow Lowe, who was seven or eight years older than me, came from my hometown. He was my hero. Coach Bryant would say, 'That's Woodrow Lowe from Phenix City.' That motivated me more than anything. I wanted him to call my name on that show."

A few years later, Coach Bryant did mention Castille's name while replaying game highlights on his show. He mentioned it a few times during Castille's freshman year, the national championship season of 1979, when Castille played back-up cornerback behind Don McNeal.

As the years went on, fans heard the name Jeremiah Castille more and more as he methodically went about setting the school record for career interceptions (sixteen). He was a familiar sight during memorable games such as Coach Bryant's 315th victory, which at the time made him the winningest coach in college football history. He played in two Cotton Bowls, one Sugar Bowl, and that unforgettable Liberty Bowl.

Castille went on to play in the NFL; four years with the Tampa Bay Buccaneers and two years with the Denver Broncos. There were some magical moments during those six years as well, including a trip to the Super Bowl with the Broncos and a classic play during the 1987 AFC Championship Game against the Cleveland Browns, when Castille stripped the ball from Browns' running back Earnest Byner in a play still known as "the Fumble."

"I enjoyed playing in the NFL," Castille said. "It was the opportunity to compete at the highest level.

"Being my size [five nine and 165 pounds], I was small for my position. When you get to that level and become successful, you feel a sense of accomplishment, especially when people tell you that you don't have the physical tools to do that."

Another satisfying aspect of playing in the NFL was the opportunity to do some good with the money he made. After he signed with the Bucs, he could afford to move his mother to a better, safer neighborhood and enroll her in a rehab program. She has been sober ever since.

After retiring from pro ball, he also made peace with his father, whom he had never been close to growing up. His dad had suffered a stroke, and Castille returned to Phenix City to help care for him until he passed away in 1994.

"When I moved back home and started feeding him and holding him, I was able to develop the kind of relationship I had desired," Castille said. "God tells you to honor your parents. It is not how you feel. It is doing what is right. I had to make the decision to take care of my dad and live off what we had saved or let my mom try to handle it by herself. The Lord said, 'I let you make some money so you can do this. You have an opportunity.'"

After his father's death, Castille got a job coaching football at a private high school in Columbus, Georgia. He was then hired as an assistant football coach and head track coach at Briarwood Christian Academy in Birmingham.

"If you're a coach, you can really have an influence in a young man or young lady's life," he said. "That's what happened to me in my athletic career. I had coaches who had invested in me. I'd been tutored by the greatest college coach. I found myself wanting to do the same thing."

While coaching at Briarwood, Castille also began the work he believes he was meant to do all his life: he founded Jeremiah Castille Ministries. This Birmingham-based organization reaches inner-city youth with the Gospel of Jesus Christ through sports, mentoring, and tutoring.

"We do football camps that we call 'character camps,'" Castille explained. "We're not just teaching football skills, but we emphasize character traits during our camps. The reward and joy of your work is when you see these athletes embrace different philosophies and when you give them a spiritual aspect to their life. When you're mentoring these kids, you come to see them as your own sons."

In 2002, Castille left his coaching job to become director of the Fellowship of Christian Athletes at the University of Alabama. After two years, he resigned that position but stayed on as the team chaplain for the Crimson

Tide. Since his two oldest sons, Tim (fullback, Class of 2006) and Simeon (defensive back, Class of 2008), were Alabama players, he had the opportunity to see them play and minister to them as well.

Photograph by Drew Crouse. Used by permission.

Team Castille—Simeon, Jeremiah, and Tim

"I coached my sons in high school—then to be their chaplain in college has been a great experience for me as a dad," Castille said. "Football has been a family experience for us."

According to Castille, he didn't push his sons to play football. He also says he didn't push them to attend the University of Alabama. But he admits to being mighty pleased and relieved when they did.

"Tim was recruited by Tennessee," he said. "Can you imagine? I was already down here as chaplain. What would I have done if he wanted to go somewhere else? I thought, *Man, how am I going to live in this state!* We'd have to move!"

But Tim did choose Alabama. Twenty-something years after he played for the Crimson Tide, Castille is once again on the sidelines of Bryant-Denny Stadium. He stood alongside Tim and Simeon, and when he looks up in the stands he sees his mother, his wife, Jean, his three daughters (Leah, Rachel, and Danielle), and his youngest son, Caleb.

"I've raised my six kids with a lot of Coach Bryant's philosophies," Castille said. "I repeat often what he used to say: 'God blessed you with an ability and a talent. He's going to hold you accountable for what you do with it.'"

People often ask Castille if Coach Bryant was a spiritual man.

"His mother wanted him to be a preacher," Castille said. "He said, 'Mom. I am a preacher. I just have a different congregation.' You cannot love people the way he loved people and not have a Christian faith. His love for people was powerful. That's why he impacted so many people. A woman told me she met him only one time, at a book signing in Mobile. There was a long, long line but when it came to be her turn, he made her feel as if she was the only person in the whole room."

Coach Bryant was also known to bring handicapped or terminally ill people out to the football field to meet his players.

"It would always make us think," Castille said, "what have I done today?"

RICHARD COLE

"Playing college ball was a dream of mine, and I was fortunate to be able to play it at the best place at the best time."

— RICHARD COLE

WHEN RICHARD COLE WAS GROWING UP IN CROSSVILLE, ALABAMA, IN the late fifties and early sixties, he and his family sometimes would visit the University of Alabama campus. He remembers once standing in front of Denny Chimes and putting his hands in some of the imprints left by past captains of great Crimson Tide teams. He never imagined that a few years later he would be sticking his own hand and foot into wet cement on the very same spot.

"I never had enough confidence to dream that someday my name might be there," Cole said. "I was thrilled when I got to do that."

Cole and his teammate Ray Perkins were the co-captains of the great 1966 team, the undefeated squad legendary for its success (11-0, along with arguably

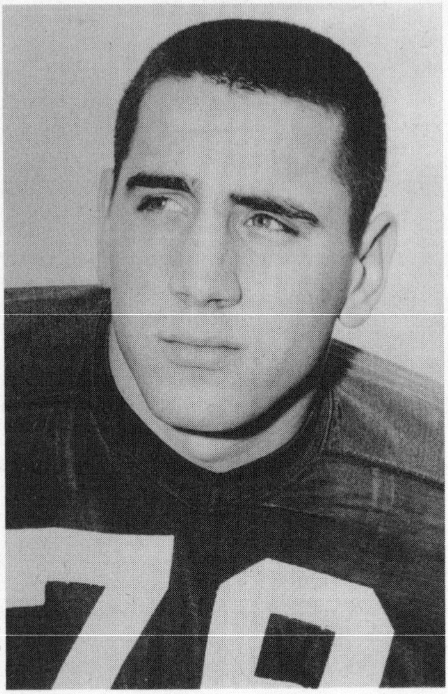

Photograph courtesy of Richard Cole

Richard Cole: a combination of heart and "want to"

the best defense in Alabama history) and for its heartbreak (pollsters named Notre Dame national champs despite their lesser record).

"That was probably my greatest honor, being captain of that great team," said Cole.

A great honor on top of great honors: Cole, a defensive tackle, was named all-American and departed Tuscaloosa with two national championship rings (from 1964 and 1965). He also left the University with something truly priceless: a work ethic that would serve him well for the rest of his life.

Cole went to high school in Crossville, Alabama. It was a small school in a very small town. He was, as he describes himself, "a pretty good player."

Growing up with two older brothers helped him hone his skills.

"We fussed and fought a good bit," Cole said. "You have to get pretty tough when you always get beat in fights. When it came time to deal with folks my own size, I could hold my own."

Cole mostly played football because he enjoyed the game. He thought he would probably join the army after high school, but then the light went on when his older brother signed a scholarship with Mississippi State.

"My brother was two years ahead of me, but he and I were about equal in ability," Cole remembered. "I thought if he got an SEC scholarship then I had a chance too. So I started applying myself to my studies a little bit more. After that, playing football in college became my dream. And my goal."

Prior to his freshman year at Alabama, in 1963, Cole's high school coach, who had played college ball, shared some insight. "He said in high school you might get one out of ten real hard licks from who you're playing against," Cole said. "In college, you can expect it nine out of ten."

When he got to Tuscaloosa, he found out this was about right. But he was determined to succeed.

"I always had the attitude that if anybody else can take it, so can I," Cole said.

According to co-captain Ray Perkins, Cole's attitude served him well: "Richard was one of those guys who didn't weigh a lot. He lacked in ability, like all of us. But he just got it done. He had the biggest heart and turned out to be a real good player. But it was mostly due to his heart and his 'want to.'"

The will to succeed also came in handy during the famous off-season gym classes Alabama players had to endure in the sixties.

"Those classes really were the toughest part of being a player," Cole said. "Fortunately they only lasted six to eight weeks, two or three classes per week. And they were only forty-five minutes long. But those forty-five minutes were so bad that we dreaded them from the time the bowl game was over until it came time for spring practice."

During the classes, the football team was split into three groups. Each spent fifteen minutes at one of three stations furiously doing push-ups and chin-ups, climbing ropes, walking overhead horizontal ladders, wrestling teammates, or performing running drills. Then they'd switch positions and do it again.

"I had several friends go into the army who said they never dealt with anything tougher than the gym class," Cole said. "Of course they had to deal with people shooting at them. We didn't have to worry about that. Sometimes we thought the coaches would kill us, but they never shot at us."

Kidding aside, Cole says he respects the sacrifices military people made and continue to make. Back in high school, Richard had considered a career in the military. But when he got his scholarship to Alabama, his life took a different path. Students were mostly exempt from the draft in the mid-sixties; although, as the war escalated, the rules fluctuated and at one point some students were listed as eligible despite their enrollment in school.

Early in his senior year, Richard, along with several of his teammates, went to Montgomery to take an army physical. He was led to believe he would receive a deferment. But then he got a scare.

"I was drafted in early December of 1966," he said. "When I opened up the draft notice, I think it was three pages long. I read all the fine print, and reality was starting to set in. Then I flipped to the last page and saw 'deferment.' If I had just looked at the back page to begin with, I would have saved myself thirty minutes of misery."

So, Cole finished school, and after graduation he accepted the head-coaching job at Albertville High School. One of the players he coached was future Alabama and NFL Hall of Famer John Hannah.

"What a way to start a coaching career, by coaching the best lineman ever!" Cole laughed. "I'd like to take credit for his success, but I can't. About 75 percent of it was natural talent. John was very much a hustler. He had goals and wanted to be the best. He had the tools to do it and the attitude to work at it."

Despite the satisfaction of turning out players such as Hannah, Cole quit coaching after three years.

"I enjoyed playing ball more than coaching it," Cole said. "I enjoyed the fundamental work in practice—the nuts and bolts of working up the game plan and everything. But I didn't like all the administrative stuff, especially while trying to teach school. I took it all too seriously and ended up developing an ulcer."

So Cole, newly married to his wife, Shannon, an Albertville native, went into teaching full time. He worked as a PE teacher for several years then returned to school at the University of Alabama at Birmingham to get his administrative degree.

His next stop? The principal's office. He's been there ever since.

As difficult as it might be to understand how becoming a principal would be less stressful than coaching high school football, Cole, who is the principal at Albertville Elementary, makes a solid case: "You don't have too many sideline coaches and Monday morning quarterbacks in education as you do on the football field," he said. "As a principal, you've got strict guidelines to go by, while in football, the best team doesn't always win. If you're out-muscled week in and week out, and you're playing schools with more and better athletes, then it's going to be hard to win."

According to Principal Cole, the responsibility of his job made him appreciate the enormous responsibility Coach Bryant shouldered every day. As a player, there wasn't the time or opportunity to empathize with your coach. Mainly, guys just tried to stay out of the coach's way.

Cole remembers such a moment from a game during his senior year. After Alabama scored a touchdown, the players on the extra-point team ran out onto the field. All but one.

"I wasn't paying attention, so I didn't go out on the field," he remembered. "We had to call time-out, and Coach Bryant hated wasting a time-out. They counted off who was missing and quickly realized it was me. I jumped up, and when I ran by I came within about two yards of Coach Bryant. That was one fierce look he had on his face."

Alabama kicked the extra point, and the players jogged off the field toward the bench. All but one.

"I ran over to the end zone and came up the sideline staying as close to the fence as I could get to make sure I didn't have to make eye contact with him," Cole said. "I never did miss being out there again when I was supposed to."

Men who played for Coach Bryant often talk about how Coach Bryant kept in touch and stayed on top of what was going on in their lives.

Cole experienced this firsthand when, in 1981, he found out he had cancer. After undergoing surgery to

Photograph courtesy of Richard Cole

Principal Cole

have a tumor removed, Cole was at home recovering when he got a call from Bryant.

"I was a little nervous just to talk to him," Cole said. "And he seemed a little ill at ease talking to me about that subject. I can see how that would be tough. It's hard to talk to somebody who might be facing death in a few months. I really appreciate the fact that he took the time to call me and address a tough issue that you'd like to just ignore and not think about. He wanted to be involved in our lives."

After a second surgery, Cole made a full recovery. Soon after, he took his family to visit Tuscaloosa. He wanted his two young sons, Nathan (then four years old) and Jason (then eight) to meet Coach Bryant.

"My wife wondered why I was so nervous around him," Cole said, chuckling. "But the boys weren't nervous at all."

Nathan poked around the coach's office and discovered a small refrigerator stocked with cans of Country Time lemonade.

"Coach Bryant asked Nathan if he wanted one. So he, Coach Bryant, and his brother sat there and had themselves some lemonade," Cole said.

Years later, Nathan, a pharmaceutical sales rep, and Jason, an industrial sales rep who played on Alabama's 1992 national championship team, now wish they had kept those cans.

Visiting the coach was a great memory for Cole. Other great memories from his teams' playing days were recently immortalized in Keith Dunnavant's book, *The Missing Ring.* It's a chronicle of the 1966 season, one that many people thought should have been a national-championship year for Alabama. Despite going undefeated and untied, the Crimson Tide, who were two-time repeating national champions from 1964 and 1965, finished third in the polls.

"It still hurts," Cole said. "You don't dwell on it, but it still hurts. If we had been granted the championship, it would have been three in a row. Having a three-time, back-to-back winner still hasn't happened. Glory like that isn't the reason you play ball, but if you've earned it, you'd like to get some of it."

Maybe the book made up for some of that. No one can take away the team's accomplishments. As Dunnavant said in his book, "No college team since the early sixties has guarded the end zone like the '66 Bama squad, which held every single opponent scoreless in both the second and third quarters. They matched the 1961 team's six shutouts and allowed just five touchdowns. In retrospect, they were the strongest defense in the two-platoon era (1964–present)."

"It's good to have your story told," Cole said.

PAUL CRANE

**"So much is timing and just being lucky.
I was in the right place at the right time."**

— PAUL CRANE

HOW LUCKY CAN ONE MAN GET? PAUL CRANE'S HIGH SCHOOL FOOTball team won a state championship. His college team won the national championship. Twice. Then, after he joined the pro ranks, his team went to the Super Bowl. And won.

Most Crimson Tide players tell stories of growing up dreaming of playing football for the University of Alabama. Crane, who grew up in Prichard, Alabama, where he starred on the Vigor High School football team, tells a different story.

"I had no loyalty toward any particular school," he said. "But I knew I wanted to stay in state. So that left me with Alabama and Auburn."

Crane says he visited Auburn first and was leaning toward signing with the Tigers, but that was before he made a trip to Tuscaloosa.

"They flew me up to Alabama, and I visited with the coaches," he said. "Then I met with Coach Bryant, and that sealed my fate."

Crane did right by number 54.

As luck would have it, at Crane's first practice his sophomore year, the equipment manager tossed him a jersey bearing the number 54.

That number previously belonged to Lee Roy Jordan, a two-time all-American and arguably Alabama's best-ever linebacker. Thinking it was a good omen, Crane threw on the jersey and ran out to the field. But immediately, he was stopped in his tracks by Coach Bryant's unmistakable growl.

"Coach Bryant yelled and wanted to know why I was wearing that jersey," Crane remembered. "He told me to take it off. I was embarrassed and headed back to the dressing room when he yelled again, 'No! Leave it on.'"

What Crane didn't know was that Coach Bryant had been considering retiring Jordan's number. Then he changed his mind. Maybe he knew what no one else knew at the time, that Crane would do right by number 54. Crane became an all-American center and linebacker in 1965, and he was named captain of his team. None of those honors came courtesy of luck.

Crane worked extremely hard at every grueling practice. He led by example and walked the walk. And he was part of a group of players who became the very definition of what you can become if you stick it out: national champions.

"We had such a great group of guys," Crane said. "They signed fifty-five guys when I was a freshman and we had thirteen walk-ons—sixty-eight players total. Of that group, when I was a senior, only nine were left. There was a lot of attrition but the guys who stayed, stayed and had success. Guys like Ray Perkins, Steve Sloan, Steve Bowman, Jackie Sherrill, and Jimmy Carroll. We had that core group that were such great people."

At the conclusion of his final season at Alabama, Crane played impressively in the Senior Bowl. Among the pro scouts at the game were those from the New York Jets, who then offered him a free agent contract.

Crane signed with the Jets and went to New York, where he played for the Jets from 1966 through 1973.

"I enjoyed playing pro ball immensely," said Crane. "I was like a kid in a candy shop. It was hard work, but we had success, and I played with a great team—Namath, Matt Snell, Emerson Boozer, and all those guys. It was just a great time in our lives. We were young and single, for part of the time anyway. And we had a little bit of money. Not like they do now. But we were in the big city.

"So much is timing and just being lucky. I was in the right place at the right time. I went to college with Namath and got to go to the Jets with him too. We had some great years."

A guy doesn't survive and thrive playing pro football by sheer luck. Crane was always considered small by football standards, but as his coaches said, "He played a lot bigger than he was." He credits his high school and college coaches' emphasis on fundamentals with preparing him for the bigs. Beyond that, it took major dedication to become the devastating blocker, nearly flawless snapper, and tremendous all-around athlete that he would become.

During his Jets career he experienced many memorable moments. He made a habit of blocking kicks: in 1968 he smothered three punts, and in 1969 he blocked a punt, grabbed the loose ball, and ran it in for a touchdown. Then of course there was Super Bowl III, the one where Joe Namath guaranteed that the Jets would beat the heavily favored Baltimore Colts. And they did.

"That game still stands out as one of football's greatest games, and to know that I was part of that is incredible," Crane said.

After retiring from the Jets in 1974, Crane returned to Tuscaloosa to join Coach Bryant's staff as linebackers coach. According to Barry Krauss, a

Crimson Tide linebacker from 1976 to 1978, Coach Crane was a favorite of all the players. "He was laid-back, a leader. We all listened to him," Krauss said.

Crane explained what it was like to go from being one of Coach Bryant's players to being one of his assistants.

"Being a coach was different from being a player," Crane said. "The relationship definitely changed. Although Coach Bryant still ruled!

"We'd have meetings in the morning and he would question us about certain players; how they were doing and so forth. What you found out is that you'd better be honest about it! If you weren't—if you said a certain player was doing great and he wasn't—Coach would say, 'I don't think he's doing worth a darn.' Then you're sitting there with egg on your face. You learned pretty quickly not to pad it—he wanted a real honest answer. He expected you to be there and work and do your job."

Crane absorbed a lot from Coach Bryant and his other coaches. But he ultimately had to find his own coaching style.

"I think I was kind of a quiet coach," said Crane. "It just depended on what was happening. I wouldn't get on somebody in front of everybody and bash him. I'd do something more individual."

One player who appreciated Coach Crane's individual attention was linebacker Woodrow Lowe, an outstanding player who, after injuries and some personal troubles (he was a newlywed whose wife was ill), found himself struggling during the 1974 season.

"Coach Crane told me never to quit no matter how hard it was 'raining,'" remembered Lowe. "He also made me realize that football wasn't the most important thing in the world and that life was going to continue and the sun was still going to shine."

Coach Bryant and Coach Crane were a lot alike in their philosophy of football and life. In Mike Bynum's book, *Bear Bryant's Boys of Autumn*, Crane summed it up: "I think, basically, Coach was a teacher or preacher at heart. A dozen times I've heard him say that the physical, the spiritual, and the mental are the three main areas of your life. He'd tell us that that's what football is all about, but we'd better carry those commitments over into life, long after we'd stopped playing football, or we'd be fall-on-your-face failures.

"'Relationships,' he'd growl. 'Relationships with people. Mutual appreciation and support. They win games. They get your life's work done.'"

Crane cherished his relationship with Coach Bryant. If he has a regret in his life, it was leaving Bryant's staff in 1978 to join ex-teammate Steve Sloan, who had been named head coach at Ole Miss.

"The worst mistake I made in some ways—I say some ways because I'm real happy with where I am now—was when I went to coach at Ole Miss," said Crane. "Coach Bryant tried to talk me out of going, but I'd made up my mind. If we had been successful at Ole Miss, I'd probably have ended up a head coach somewhere, but we weren't successful. He was right. The mistake I made was not listening to his advice." Like every less-than-successful experience, Crane learned from the losing seasons he spent at Ole Miss.

"Steve Sloan is one of the finest gentlemen you'd ever meet," he said. "But when we went over there, he decided the kids at Ole Miss had been worked real hard and that we didn't need to work them quite as hard. We had some wonderful young men, but we didn't have a whole lot of talent. I just don't think we were able to work the kids as hard as we should have. With Coach Bryant you never worried about that."

These days Crane lives in Mobile, Alabama, with his wife, Heike, who he

Photograph courtesy of Paul Crane

Paul, Heike, and Paul Crane Jr.

met in New York while playing for the Jets. (His son Paul, Jr., who works on tugboats, lives nearby.) After leaving Ole Miss in 1981, Crane got involved with the Catholic Youth Organization (CYO) in Mobile while finishing his master's degree in education and coaching at McGill Toolen High School.

Although he's no longer a full-time coach, Crane still has his hand in teaching and guiding young athletes as the executive director of the CYO for the archdiocese of Mobile.

Since 1984, Crane has been running the sports program, which includes basketball, football, volleyball, soccer, and golf, for kids from second to eighth grades from over a dozen schools.

"It's a pretty extensive program," Crane said. "We have 160 basketball teams. For me, this has been a wonderful thing."

When he is not busy training young officials or organizing the enormous CYO Spring Field Day, Crane takes time for a little personal competition on the golf course.

"I've got the bug," Crane said. "I enjoy getting together with friends at least once a week and playing, even though it's frustrating for these old football players. Football is a contact sport, so we think if we just swing harder we'll all be better. But it makes it worse. Golf is more disciplined in the sense that you have to relax and try to hit the ball.

"But you can't ever beat the course. If you shot par, tomorrow you'd want to shoot par. It's always competitive somehow."

Years ago, Crane hit the links with a guy who knew something about competition.

"Coach Bryant was very competitive," Crane said. "At the time he had a whole set of woods and would play with [pro golfer] Jerry Pate, who had to have better than par to win. And Coach Bryant liked to win. I don't imagine there were many times when he was happy about losing at anything."

On the golf course, at home, at work, Crane remembers Bryant often.

"I think about him almost every day in some way," he said. "I miss him. He was a great figure in my life."

SYLVESTER CROOM

"I wanted to be the best there's ever been at my position. That's what being around a man like Coach Bryant does to you."

— SYLVESTER CROOM

OF ALL THE THINGS SYLVESTER CROOM LEARNED AS A PLAYER AND assistant coach for Bear Bryant, there is one lesson he applies every day as head football coach at Mississippi State.

"Coach Bryant was highly, highly competitive," he said. "But people were more important to him than games. He and a guy like [longtime Grambling head coach] Eddie Robinson were cut from the same cloth. They knew that the long-term effect their decisions had on their players was more important than what happens today."

Croom, who was an assistant coach at Alabama from 1976 to 1986, remembers the meeting where Bryant outlined this priority.

"I remember something came up about a certain player," he said. "Coach

Bryant was sitting there, just listening. Everybody in the staff room said what they had to say. He paused for a while and said, 'Well, men. Remember this. When you're trying to decide what's best for your program or what's best for your player, do what's best for the player. Because what's best for the player is best for the program.'

"That has been the most valuable thing to me. When we're making decisions at Mississippi State, I try to think like a parent. I try to do what I would do for my own son to help him whether he was in football or out of football."

According to Croom, one of the best decisions he made personally was when he accepted a football scholarship at the University of Alabama. "Sly," as many of his friends call him, grew up in Tuscaloosa. Even though he attended high school right down the road from the university, he didn't seriously consider playing football for Coach Byrant. First of all, Alabama was not yet recruiting African Americans. In fact, the racial situation was tense. Croom remembers watching on TV the confrontation between George Wallace and the National Guard as a nine-year-old.

But living under the same roof as his father, Sylvester Croom Sr., Sly learned to be hopeful. His father was a prominent minister and civil rights leader who fought for positive change. (Reverend Croom would later serve as the team chaplain at Alabama, and in 2003 he was honored posthumously by the university as one of forty civil rights pioneers in the state.)

Photograph courtesy of Paul W. Bryant Museum/The University of Alabama

Croom basks in the sidelines glow.

While he was in high school, there was another reason young

Croom didn't have Alabama on his radar. He didn't think he was good enough to play for Coach Bryant.

But year by year, things began to slowly change. By Croom's junior year of 1970, he was a star player, rotating between fullback, tight end, and offensive guard on his Tuscaloosa High School football team. At the university down the road, the Crimson Tide had signed its first African American player, Wilbur Jackson, to a football scholarship.

Still, Croom figured he would most likely sign with Alabama A&M, his father's alma mater. But then, something started to gnaw at the young athlete.

"I played on losing teams, and I was tired of getting beat all the time," he said. "I knew if I went to Alabama, there wasn't any question whether or not we were going to win. The only question was whether or not I was good enough to play for them."

Then one day Coach Bryant called.

"In his deep, rumbly voice he said, 'This is Coach Bryant at Alabama,'" Croom remembered. "I don't think I said anything back. I just nodded. He said, 'Some of my players told me you are good enough to play at Alabama. Do you think you are?'"

Croom, who said he had goose bumps after the conversation, decided it was time to find out.

When Croom arrived on campus (a mere ten miles from his house), he had modest expectations.

"I had no idea about being an all-American," he said. "I had no idea about being a starter. I just wanted to sit on the bench on a winning team."

But at the end of his sophomore year of 1972, Croom began to feel differently.

"I looked around and realized my roommate is playing, my friends are playing. I said, *Wait a minute; I can play with these guys.* Then I got obsessed with not only playing, but I got caught up in the tradition. When they moved me to center, which was a big deal in the Alabama program, I thought about guys like Paul Crane and Lee Roy Jordan. I felt a responsibility to be as good as they were. I wanted to be the best there's ever been at my position. That's what being around a man like Coach Bryant does to you."

Photograph courtesy of Paul W. Bryant Museum/The University of Alabama

Croom and company give Bryant a victory ride.

Coach Jack Rutledge, Bryant's longtime assistant who worked with the offensive line, remembers the shift in Croom's confidence.

"We were going to play Kentucky," Rutledge said, "and they had a great nose guard. We told Croom if he couldn't block the nose guard, we weren't going to win the game. So we get out there and Croom comes off the field with his nose a little bit bloody. He had tears in his eyes. He said, 'We can't win, coach. I can't do it. He's going to be tough.'

"So I said, 'All you've got to do is go out there and hit him and hit him. Like we practiced. Like we talked about.' So then [Alabama] turned around and made a long run on a kick-off return and scored. Then Croom went back out the next series and came back with a big ol' smile on his face and said, 'I've got him in my hip pocket.' So that's the way he played the rest of his career. He just put them in his hip pocket!"

It was a long way from riding the bench to wearing a championship ring, but Croom made the journey. He played on three SEC championship teams, the national championship team of 1973, then in 1974 he received all-American honors, was voted senior captain, and earned the Jacobs Blocking Trophy.

"I wasn't a great player," he said. "But being under Coach Bryant's motivation and playing with the guys I played with, I went far beyond what I ever thought I was capable of."

After one season playing in the NFL for the New Orleans Saints, Croom returned to the University in 1976 to earn his master's degree in educational administration and to join Coach Bryant's staff as an assistant coach. As Croom points out, most of the coaches who worked for him over the years were former players.

"Most of us on his staff played for him," he said. "So, even though he's the boss now, you've still got that father figure thing going on. But now you're working for him. He's signing your paychecks. Quite often he would test you to see what coaching meant to you. You knew if you listened to him and if you could measure up to his expectations, you could be as good as any coach in the country."

Photograph courtesy of Mississippi State University

Croom: still on the sidelines

Croom was certainly on his way. He worked for Coach Bryant from 1976 until his retirement in 1982, then spent four more years at Alabama under Coach Ray Perkins. He coached some tremendous players during those years and stored up a stack of incredible memories.

"I worked with a lot of great players," said Croom. "Cornelius Bennett and Derrick Thomas were very special to me."

But team-wise, the 1979 national championship team really stands out.

"That team was as close as a group as I've ever seen," he said. "It was so much fun being around those guys. They were just great people. Don McNeal and all those guys. A lot of them came from small towns. And not a lot of them were highly recruited. Take Dwight Stephenson. I tell my coaches he was the third guy in a three-way package, and nobody ever even heard of him. Now he's the best center to ever play the game, and I don't remember who the other guys were!

"When we went on trips, these guys conducted themselves with character and class. I was just starting coaching, and I was broke, but they'd come over to the house and have hamburgers and hot dogs. It was truly family."

Fun, yes. But young Coach Croom got very serious on the field.

"Sylvester Croom was the most intense person I've ever been around," said Dwight Stephenson. "One day my freshman year I wasn't having a good day. He took me by the collar and shook me and woke me up! I needed it. I'm glad he did it.

"I really respect him. He was the first black center to ever play in the Southeastern Conference. He opened the door for guys like myself and Terry Jones. Sylvester Croom broke the mold."

And Coach Croom continues to break the mold, although he is consistently low-key about it. As a player in 1971, he was just one of a handful of black football players to follow Wilbur Jackson and John Mitchell as the first African Americans to suit up for the Crimson Tide. Then, when he became the first black center in the SEC, he just went about his business.

His coach wouldn't have it any other way.

"Coach Bryant didn't have black players or white players," Croom said. "He just had football players. The only thing he cared about was your effort; he didn't care about the color of your skin."

When Coach Croom left Alabama in 1986, he went on to a sixteen-year career as an assistant coach in the NFL. He was running backs coach for the Tampa Bay Bucs, the Indianapolis Colts, and the San Diego Chargers, and he then took a turn as offensive coordinator for the Detroit Lions. After that he coached the running backs for the Green Bay Packers before he returned to college football in 2004. When he took the reigns at Mississippi State, he became the first African American head football coach in the SEC. Once again, Croom was breaking down barriers.

"Intellectually, I understand that," he said. "But that was never my intent. Looking back, I'm just now starting to realize that as far as the guys I came up with at Alabama and some of the things that have happened to me, I have been very blessed. I've always known that. But it's always been about me doing the best that I could do with the opportunities that present themselves."

And for the foreseeable future, that's exactly what Coach Croom intends to do. He is optimistic about the potential of his team, which he says is in a position to compete on an even keel with other teams in their division.

"We feel like when we came here and started this adventure it was going to be a three-to-five-year period to be able to do that, and we're right on schedule."

According to Coach Croom, he has learned that building a college program takes time.

"Patience is the most important virtue you need as a head coach," he said. "In the pros, you pretty much have a finished product. It is what it is when you get it. But players develop at different paces in college. You have to be patient with them. You can try as you will, but you cannot speed up time."

For Croom and his wife, Jeri, one of the best aspects of living in Starkville, Mississippi, is its close proximity to Mobile, where their daughter, Jennifer, lives with her husband, Ira Bates, and the Crooms' granddaughter, Ryan.

"I'm loving being a grandfather," Croom said. "I get all the joys of being around a little one with none of the work."

But back on the field, there is still work to be done. Coach Croom says he intends to keep doing what he is doing because he is still enjoying it. Plus, there is still one thing he wants to accomplish.

"Coach Bryant told me once if I could be half the man my dad was, I'd be OK," he said. "I'm still trying to be that man."

JERRY DUNCAN

"Coach Bryant wouldn't let you be ordinary. That spilled into everything and affected us all in so many ways."

— JERRY DUNCAN

JERRY DUNCAN LOVED ALABAMA FOOTBALL SO MUCH THAT EVEN when his playing days were over he refused to leave the field. After graduation in 1966, he stayed there to attend graduate school and joined Coach Bryant's staff as an assistant coach. Even after he got his second sheepskin, he refused to leave. In 1971 he became Alabama's first sideline radio reporter. And he remained on the field in that role for twenty-four years.

"It was the best part-time job ever," Duncan said. "I loved being in the thick of things and being around Coach Bryant. I had no ambition to be a real broadcaster. I knew I wasn't going to be the next Keith Jackson."

Even though he was very dedicated and successful at this endeavor, Duncan's sideline gig was just that—a sideline. His "real job" for the last thirty-plus years

Photograph courtesy of Paul W. Bryant Museum/The University of Alabama

Duncan's team had plenty to smile about.

has been as a stockbroker, most recently for Smith Barney in Birmingham, where he lives with his wife, Karen, and their son Luke Bryant. (Named for guess who.) Duncan also has two grown children, Melissa and Evans, and both are University of Alabama graduates. He also has five grandchildren. Although he thinks of cutting back on work and even retiring to his North Carolina mountaintop farm, he hasn't done so yet.

It's too much a challenge for Duncan to slow down after spending so many years building a client list that reads like a "Who's Who" of Alabama football. Past and present clients include Gene Stallings, John Forney, and Steve Sloan, among others. He's been with many of his clients for years—in some cases decades—guiding them through the inevitable ups and downs of the market.

Nonfinancial types might have a difficult time imagining what it feels like to shoulder that kind of responsibility. It doesn't seem to phase Duncan.

"You just have to know your client," he said. "You need to know what their objectives are and how much risk they want to take. Investing is nothing more than giving a man a dollar and telling him what kind of return you are expecting."

When Duncan first came to Tuscaloosa in 1963, he knew what kind of return he wanted from his investment as a player.

"Some people are great players and might not have to practice hard," Duncan said. "But things didn't come so easy for me. When I finally got a chance to wear that red (starter's) jersey, I was greedy. I didn't want to give it up."

Duncan practiced hard. He even seemed to enjoy practicing, a trait that didn't go unnoticed. A few years later Coach Bryant created the "The Jerry Duncan I Love to Practice Award," still given to a deserving Alabama player every spring. (Some past recipients of the coveted prize include John Croyle, Van Tiffin, and Bobby Humphrey.)

"I think Coach Bryant made more of that than he needed to," Duncan said. "Sometimes I didn't like to practice, but I had to pretend to like it, because I wanted to show Coach Bryant how much I wanted to play."

Duncan grew up in Sparta, North Carolina, a town with one stoplight. He was a great high school halfback, rushing for more than seventeen hundred yards. Despite leading the state in rushing his senior year, he was relatively small for a college football player. Recruiters weren't exactly tripping over blocking dummies to get to him.

The turning point came when his high school coach met Coach Bryant at a coaching clinic. According to Keith Dunnavant, author of *The Missing Ring*, a 2006 book about the 1966 Crimson Tide team, the coach made a strong pitch about a "hard-driving guy who wasn't very fast or strong but who had something deep inside that made him play his guts out on every snap."

Bryant liked what he heard and immediately sent Coach Clem Gryska to Sparta with a scholarship in hand. Gryska made the offer at the local café over ham hock sandwiches (hence Gryska's nickname for Duncan: "Ham Hock"), even though no Alabama coaches had watched film on Duncan or ever seen him play in person.

Duncan felt a little bit like a gridiron chess piece his first two years. He was moved from halfback to fullback to guard, before he finally landed at offensive tackle. The problem was, there were two guys in front of him. He was third string.

At the beginning of his junior season, Duncan caught a break. Actually, he caught two breaks. The first-string player failed to make his time in the mile run. Then, the second-string guy sustained a knee injury. So Duncan was in. The small scrappy lineman held his own during the entire 1965 national-championship season.

In fact, he did more than hold his own. He basically defined his position. Or, more specifically, Jerry Duncan became synonymous with a certain play: the tackle-eligible play.

This innovative, somewhat controversial "trick" play took advantage of a little-known rule allowing a slight shift in the offensive formation, where the weak-side tackle can become an eligible receiver. Enter Duncan.

The Tide ran this play only a few times a year. But it always seemed to work. Especially in the exciting, come-from-behind 17-16 victory over Ole Miss in '65.

"On our winning drive, we had a third and fourteen, and lined up to run the play," remembered Duncan. "[Ole Miss head coach Johnny] Vaught noticed our formation, and I'll never forget him running up the sidelines yelling, 'Tackle eligible!' But no one heard him and we got the first down."

The play worked against Ole Miss more than once, and Coach Vaught,

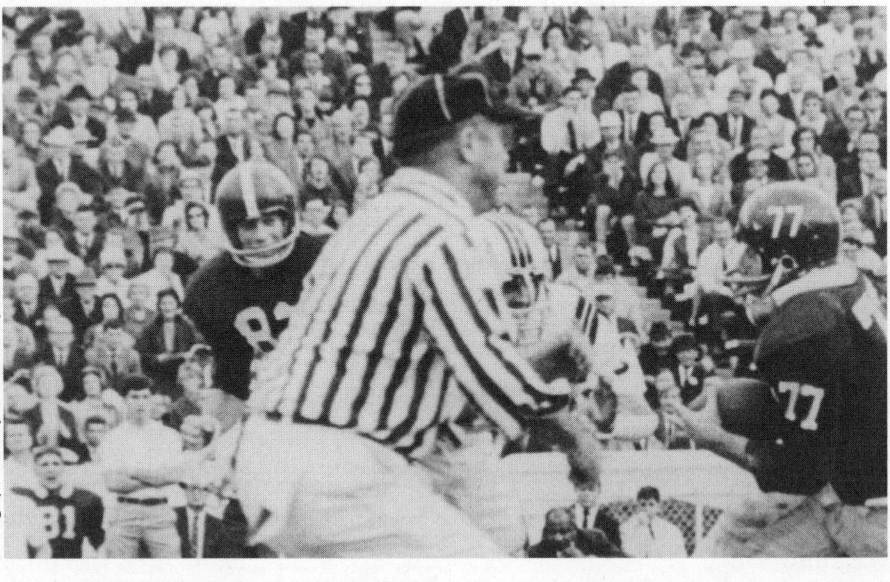

Photograph courtesy of Paul W. Bryant Museum/The University of Alabama

Duncan defined the tackle-eligible play.

who served on the SEC rules committee, helped get the play outlawed by the end of the sixties.

Duncan loved the play because he got a chance to do more than block. He got to catch and run with the ball. He also got a kick out of how much Coach Bryant enjoyed working the play.

"He had fun with it," Duncan said. "He'd climb down from his tower and demonstrate the blocking and faking himself."

If you had to pick a game that defines Jerry Duncan (and to a larger degree, most of the players of that decade), it would be the January 1, 1966, Orange Bowl against Nebraska.

The Cornhuskers were a really good team. A really good, really big team. They outweighed Bryant's "quick little boys" by thirty-five pounds per player. Duncan, at 185 pounds, lined up against 245-pound defensive tackle Walt Barnes.

Just prior to the game, Birmingham sportswriter Alf Van Hoose wrote an article predicting that Alabama's "David" would defeat Nebraska's "Goliath."

He singled out Duncan in particular: "all-American Barnes' number is 77. The man across from him will be Duncan, all-Alabama. His number is 62. The 77-62 duel should be interesting, like Jack Dempsey against Jess Willard."

Interesting, indeed. The Tide opened with the tackle-eligible play, and Duncan and Co. proceeded to run circles around the bewildered Goliaths all afternoon, winning the game 39-28.

The 1966 season was stellar, but when the polls were in, undefeated Alabama was named #3, after #1 Notre Dame and #2 Michigan State, which both had notched a tie.

Duncan remembers being very disappointed at the time. But looking back, he finds the event insignificant. He had a fantastic career and got a chance to block for Namath, Stabler, and Sloan. Plus, he had many Alabama football milestones in his future. Any negatives have been erased.

After he got his master's degree in education in 1969, Duncan thought of becoming a full-time coach. But that plan was derailed when it was discovered he had rheumatoid arthritis. He would eventually have six operations on his feet.

So, partially on Coach Bryant's advice, Duncan accepted a position in the brokerage business. Then, in 1971, folks at the radio network floated the idea of having a sideline reporter at the games. True to form, Coach Bryant was initially reluctant. But when John Forney approached him with the idea of making Duncan the guy, the Coach relented.

"He said, 'Well, if you're going to be down there, I guess it's all right. I don't want anybody there who doesn't know what's going on.'"

So, Duncan was back on the field, back in the middle of things. As part of the broadcast team, he sat in on Coach's meetings so he would know what to expect on Saturdays. But that still didn't guarantee that Duncan, who often found himself standing behind a cluster of six-foot-five linemen, was always in the know.

"The sideline is not the best position to see the game," Duncan said. "You're not seeing the whole picture like they do upstairs."

In the early seventies, technology wasn't what it is today, so sometimes Duncan would learn more about what was going on by listening to the radio.

But no question, he was in the thick of it. He was the one standing at the fifty yard line for the coin toss, hearing the crunching of bones and getting sweat flung on him. His experience as a tough, relentless player came in handy when he got knocked over more than once.

Just think of what he saw. He was there for the entire Bryant era, beginning with the introduction of the wishbone, when the players and others (including the broadcast crew) were privy to the new offense and had to keep it a secret. He was there for the 1979 Championship and Coach Bryant's 315th win. He stood by Coach Ray Perkins, Coach Bill Curry, and Coach Gene Stallings, who led his team to the '92 National Title. He worked with John Forney, Doug Layton, Paul Kennedy, and myself.

I loved working with him. Fans definitely knew where his loyalties stood.

"I worked for the University of Alabama," he said. "I wasn't about to go publicizing the other team."

He became famous for "Duncanisms," including the time the University of Tennessee band began marching toward him at Neyland Stadium.

"They don't like me and they know how I feel about them," Duncan quipped.

Who says a reporter has to be neutral?

There was another time Duncan made little attempt to hide his feelings. During the 1989 Penn State game, the Nittany Lions had lined up for what looked like a sure-fire field goal to win the game. Duncan called out, "Block it!" Then, Thomas Rayam did just that. Duncan jumped up and landed in my lap. He hugged me and gave me a kiss. You know you really haven't lived until you've been kissed by Jerry Duncan.

Photo courtesy of Jerry Duncan

2007 Alabama Sports Hall of Fame inductee, Jerry Duncan

Although this moment surely plays first in his imaginary highlight reel, Duncan picks the Van Tiffin field goal in 1985 as tops.

"That was probably my most exciting moment as a sideline reporter," he said.

His only regret? Leaving his life as a roving reporter before Snake Stabler came on board as the Crimson Tide Radio Network's color man in 1998.

"He and I played together, and I would love to have worked with him," Duncan said. "Then again, we probably would have gotten into too much trouble."

Even though he no longer prowls the field, microphone in hand, Duncan continues to contribute to his community, courtesy of his extensive charity work with the Monday Morning Quarterback Club, a civic group that raises money for Crippled Children's Charities.

Duncan also gives back to his favorite university. In the late eighties, inspired by Coach Bryant's generous scholarship fund for children of former Alabama football players, Duncan set up his own scholarship endowment fund.

"For some, it might have been their only chance for an education," Duncan said.

And, the university continues to give back to Duncan. In 1997, he was awarded the prestigious Paul W. Bryant Alumni-Athlete Award, which is given annually to Alabama athletes who have made great contributions to the university and community.

Also, in 2007 Duncan was inducted into the Alabama Sports Hall of Fame. What a fitting tribute to one of Coach Bryant's all-time favorite players. A guy who played better than his talents allowed. A guy who was successful in so many ways. A guy whose crimson runs through and through.

MIKE HALL

"Coach Bryant had a heart big as all the world."

— MIKE HALL

THERE'S A FAMOUS SCENE FROM THE HBO SHOW *THE SOPRANOS* IN which mob boss Tony Soprano, fresh from surgery after being shot in the stomach, picks out the biggest, strongest man in the room and beats him to a pulp. Tony wants to show everyone that he is still the boss. Classic alpha dog behavior.

Although Coach Bryant was never shot in the stomach (as far as we know), he often reminded his players who was in charge by getting somewhat physical.

Even when they outweighed him or could bench-press their own weight.

During one particular practice in 1966, freshman linebacker Mike Hall was a strong man having a weak practice. At one point, Coach Bryant stormed up to him, grabbed him by the facemask, spun him around, and

Big Mike Hall takes the plunge.

kicked him squarely in the butt. But over forty years later, Hall says he doesn't remember being singled out and he has no hard feelings.

"He did that to everybody," he laughed. "He wasn't any tougher on me than he was on anybody else. It was equal opportunity abuse!"

Hall bears no grudges, having nothing but kind words for the man known for doling out daily punishment.

"Coach Bryant had a heart as big as all the world," Hall said. "You didn't see it on the practice field or when you were playing, but he was just a big teddy bear. He taught us how to get by in life.

"He showed us that when things get tough—there are things that come up in your lifetime when you think you just can't go on—you have to reach back and pull up something that somebody gave you that gets you through it."

In other words, as tough as his practices were, Coach Bryant wanted to teach his players that, inevitably, they would face bigger challenges than climbing ropes, running tires, and pounding tackling dummies.

"He'd tell us all the time that at some point in our lives things were going to get really tough," Hall said. "He'd say, 'When your wife runs off with the drummer and you lose your job, by golly you've got to know how to get through it.' That's the reason he put us through those gym classes!"

Former Crimson Tide players shudder when they remember the infamous gym classes all football players were required to take in the sixties. Jack Rutledge, an offensive guard and linebacker on the 1959–61 teams and a longtime assistant coach to Bryant (1966–82), experienced the classes as both player and coach.

"You walked in that door [to the gymnasium] and you never stopped for the next hour," Rutledge said. "I don't care how good a shape you were in. That was an exhausting endurance contest, like Marine boot camp."

Hall excelled in gym class, especially during wrestling competitions, where he displayed his awesome strength and bested many of his teammates.

He also excelled on the football field. During his senior year of 1968, Hall was elected team captain and named all-American. (He was all-Southeastern Conference in both '67 and '68.) A highlight of 1968 was the annual Iron Bowl against rival Auburn, his last regular season game as a player for the Crimson Tide. Alabama won 24-16, and Hall was named AP National Lineman of the Week after leading his team in tackles and making two interceptions. For good measure, after switching over to tight end, he snagged a five-yard touchdown pass from quarterback Scott Hunter.

The 1966 season, Hall's sophomore year, was one of the Crimson Tide's most storied seasons. After two back-to-back National Championships in '64 and '65, many fans, and certainly the players and coaches, expected a three-peat at Alabama. They were well on their way to an undefeated year when Tennessee gave them a fright during a rainy, sloppy game in Knoxville.

At halftime, after several fumbles, the Tide was down 10-0. The players shuffled into the locker room expecting to be chewed out royally by Coach Bryant. Instead, Bryant surprised his players by doing just the opposite. "This is perfect," he told the team. "We got 'em right where we want 'em."

The players were stunned. But the reverse psychology tactic worked.

Hall played a major role in the turnaround by putting the smack-down on Tennessee wingback Charles Fulton, forcing a fumble. Alabama's Mike Ford recovered the ball, and the Tide went on to win 11-10.

Another highlight of the year for Hall was when he played on live TV for the first time, when the Tide took on LSU. Nearly his entire hometown of Tarrant, Alabama, gathered to watch, and they cheered when Hall blocked a punt and stopped LSU runners again and again. (Final: Alabama 21, LSU 0.)

The '66 team went undefeated that year and, despite soundly beating Nebraska in the Sugar Bowl, they were not voted national champions.

"What an awful feeling," said Hall. "We were just devastated."

The disappointment of that year faded soon enough. The incredible team was comforted by Coach Bryant's comment at the end of the season: "This is the greatest football team I've ever been associated with."

After graduation in 1969, Hall was drafted by the Super Bowl Champion New York Jets.

"I stayed with them for most of the exhibition season before I got cut," remembered Hall. "We played the college all-stars and the Giants, Vikings, Raiders, and Cardinals. It was a great experience. There were some real characters up there!"

Hall has some amazing memories of his football years. As an Alabama businessman, he frequently has the opportunity to rehash these good times with fans who remember Bear Bryant and his incredible teams. But to Hall, the best part of being a player at Alabama was not the honors or the cheers or even the wins. It was the playing.

"It was fun!" he said. "Whatever troubles and cares that you have when you walk in the dressing room you can leave them there, and you can strap on your shoulder pads and your chin strap and take out all the discontent you

Photograph courtesy of Mike Hall

Gwen, Sam, and Mike Hall

have on someone else. It's fun. I mean, it was then. I don't think I'm going to do it now! I'll stick to fishing."

Indeed, these are kinder and gentler times for Hall and his wife, Gwen, who live near Moundsville, Alabama. They moved there in 1999 due partly to its proximity to an inviting river.

"I'm a perch jerker," Hall explained. "I also fish for crappie and brim. Unfortunately, though, I have to work sometimes."

Hall and Gwen run All-American Signs, an advertising company. Gwen, a graphic artist, started the company many years ago. (Yes, the name was inspired by her husband's gridiron accomplishments.) Together, they create custom signage (safety signs for mines, and entrance and permit signs) and promotional products such as hats, caps, jackets, and bags.

Working in a two-person business is a switch for Hall. For twenty-five years he worked in sales for Birmingham's Southern Equipment Company, a job that involved a lot of entertaining and big-dollar volume sales. But as much as things change, some things remain the same.

"What I really love about what I'm doing is I still enjoy seeing people," he said. "Most of the customers we have are the folks I called on when I was in the tractor and equipment business. So I built a good relationship with them and I still have a good relationship with them. I enjoy getting out and seeing them, and I really enjoy when the weather gets to about seventy degrees for two or three days in a row and I can hook up the boat and go fishing."

When out on the river, Hall says, no one wants to hear old Alabama football stories. But customers always do.

"I don't have a problem talking about it," he said. "When I get into a situation that reminds me of something that went on back then or that reminds me of a moral-of-the-story kind of thing, I'll tell about that."

The most important life lesson he learned as a player for Coach Bryant was to never quit.

"No matter what," Hall said, "you have to get up and move forward."

The other lesson Hall took away from the University of Alabama was to always be punctual.

"When Coach Bryant called a meeting, or anyone called a meeting, he taught us to be five to ten minutes early, and if we were on time we were late," Hall said. "I've used that on a daily basis."

Hall has talked about Coach Bryant often to his son, Sam, a University of Alabama at Birmingham graduate student who is studying to be a physical therapist.

"At my age, I need a physical therapist in the family," Hall laughed. "But I'm in pretty good shape. I'm still at my playing weight, although for a while there I did catch the furniture disease."

The furniture disease?

"That's where your chest falls into your drawers."

For the last few years, Hall has had the chance to laugh, joke, and reminisce with his teammates at an annual reunion hosted by Steve Bowman (fullback, 1963–1965) at his hunting camp in Centerville, Alabama. And of course, there are Alabama home games.

"I confess, I don't go to the stadium much," Hall said. "When I was playing, we had a police escort in and a police escort out. So I'm spoiled. The stadium gets a little crowded. So I go up and visit the A-Club room, or I visit a friend who lives six blocks from the stadium and watch it on TV. We're close enough to hear the noise at the stadium, and we don't have to fight anyone for the restrooms or the refrigerators!"

Mike Hall is definitely a guy with no hard feelings.

JOHN HANNAH

"John Hannah is the finest lineman I've been around in over thirty years as a coach."

— PAUL W. "BEAR" BRYANT

AFTER ESTABLISHING HIMSELF AS THE OFFENSIVE LINEMAN IN COLLEGE football during his playing days at Alabama, John Hannah was selected by the New England Patriots in the first round of the 1973 NFL Draft. Soon after he arrived in Boston to embark on an incredible Hall of Fame pro career, reporters asked him how it was going to feel playing in front of fifty-five thousand fans on national TV.

"I told them I wasn't going to be too disappointed," Hannah remembered. "At Alabama we were playing in front of eighty or ninety thousand people!"

From an early age, it was John Hannah's goal to become a professional football player. He was partially inspired by his father, Herb, who played one year for the New York Giants in 1951. Herb was also an offensive lineman for the Crimson Tide from 1948 to 1950, followed by John's uncle, Bill Hannah, who played for Alabama from 1957 to 1959.

It's no wonder Hannah and his brothers, Charley and David (who would also go on to play for the Tide), grew up hearing all about Alabama football. They were fans of the team during the sixties era of Coach Bryant's "quick little boys"—lean, fast athletes who played both offense and defense.

Young Hannah was quick and strong, but he was definitely not little. In the first grade, his mom had to buy him husky jeans, and he was ruled too big to play Pee Wee football. But Hannah had an early passion for the game and played football with his brothers in the front yard every chance he got.

"John started out loving it as a little boy," Herb told a *Birmingham News* reporter. "He loved contact sports from day one. When he was two or three years old, we'd get out in the yard and run around. I'd get a stick like I was gonna hit him, and he'd run and look back laughing. As early as he could, John loved contact. He had a tremendous tolerance for pain. He didn't hurt and cry like a lot of kids."

He was tough. And big. And luckily for Hannah, things were changing in college and pro football. By the time he came of age, size would definitely matter.

Photograph courtesy of Paul W. Bryant Museum/The University of Alabama

John Hannah: the best of the big men

Hannah attended Baylor School in Chattanooga, Tennessee, for his first three years of high school. He excelled at football and track, and in 1967 he won the individual national prep championship in wrestling.

His coach, Luke Worsham, was Hannah's mentor and surrogate father while he attended school away from his Albertville, Alabama, home.

"I trace all my accomplishments back to him," Hannah said. "He decided to turn me into something."

His senior year, Hannah transferred to Albertville High School, where his head coach was former Alabama all-American Richard Cole.

"I felt very fortunate to have Hannah back at Albertville and on our team," said Cole. "Ability-wise, he was head and shoulders above everybody else. No one came close to him playing one-on-one."

Although other schools recruited Hannah, there never was much question in the Hannah household about where he would go to school. Alabama, of course.

"Dad says, 'Do you want to eat here or not?'" Hannah laughed. "I pretty much knew I was coming to Alabama."

Steve Sloan, the former Alabama quarterback-turned-assistant-coach, recruited Hannah for the Crimson Tide.

"He wasn't hard to recruit," Sloan said. "His family was Alabama to the core. I felt all along he was going to sign with us. He turned out to be an extraordinary player."

At six foot two and 275 pounds, Hannah was the biggest man on Alabama's 1969 freshman team. In fact, he was one of the largest players to ever to wear a 2XL crimson jersey. According to Alabama assistant coach Clem Gryska, "We felt the trend was going toward the big men. We started with John Hannah."

Coach Bryant, a strong believer in a solid defense, said on many occasions that the best athletes should play on defense. But the other coaches convinced him Hannah's talents could be best used on the offensive line. In that position, he could clear the way for star halfback Johnny Musso.

"One of my greatest memories is of lining up and seeing Big John over there," Musso said. "That was pretty nice. With that huge body, all he had to do was get out of the way, and I had a huge hole to go through! He was good at clearing the way."

Very good, as it turned out. After four years, sportswriters were calling Hannah the best lineman in college football. After his senior season of 1972, Coach Bryant told reporters: "John Hannah is the finest lineman I've been around in over thirty years as a coach. He has all the physical tools of greatness, plus has a burning desire to excel. I've seen him do some things on the

Photograph courtesy of Paul W. Bryant Museum/The University of Alabama

Alabama linemen made the switch to the wishbone. L to R: Hannah, Krapf, Faust, Rouzie, and assistant coach Pat Dye

football field I couldn't believe. Even as great as he is, he has never gone backwards. He is always working, even after practice, to improve."

Another reason for his gridiron greatness? Hannah liked to hit.

"I had a coach once tell me, the difference between a defensive lineman and an offensive lineman is the defensive lineman had to jump up and down and holler to get fired up to hit somebody," he said. "Offensive linemen are just naturally mean. They hit people because they enjoy it. They don't have to holler or do anything, they just hit people. Offensive linemen like to hit folks. That's all it is."

The big story during Hannah's Alabama years was the drastic switch to the wishbone offense, which Coach Bryant dramatically revealed at the season opener in 1971. Alabama beat USC 17-10 in the match-up, a game that Hannah called the most satisfying of his career.

As Alabama assistant coach (and current athletics director) Mal Moore told the *Birmingham News,* "We went to the wishbone his junior year, and he was devastating coming off the ball. Our first game in the wishbone was against Southern Cal, and he played head-on with a three-hundred-pounder. He destroyed him. No question, Hannah was the best one-on-one blocker I ever saw in college."

With Hannah making significant contributions on every offensive down, the Tide finished both the 1971 and 1972 seasons as SEC Champs.

By the time Hannah left Alabama, he was a two-time college football all-American, and he also managed to letter in wrestling and track and field. (He was the 1972 SEC champion in the indoor shot, the outdoor shot, and discus.)

Years later, Hannah was named to Alabama's Team of the Century, ESPN's All-Time College Football Team, the College Football Hall of Fame, and the Alabama Sports Hall of Fame.

The one thing he left Alabama without was his diploma.

"I never did enjoy college as far as schoolwork is concerned," Hannah told author Tommy Ford in his book *Bama Under Bear.* "I approached football different from the other guys. Football was my school. Other people were training to be a banker, doctor, lawyer, or whatever. I was going to college to learn to be a football player. I never got my diploma—maybe I should have. But I got my diploma in what I went after and that was football."

And football came after him. The New England Patriots drafted him fourth in the first round. Hannah had a phenomenal NFL career as well. He was a starter his rookie season and went on to play for the Patriots for twelve years. His team played in one Super Bowl, and he was named all-pro nine times. Another huge milestone: in 1981, *Sports Illustrated* put him on its cover and named him "The Best Offensive Lineman of All Time."

According to Hannah, he enjoyed the style of play in the NFL and obviously enjoyed plenty of success, but some aspects of playing for the Patriots were disappointing. For instance, the stadium and facilities in New England were less than stellar.

"Pro football was a step down [from college ball] as far as the trappings instead of a step up," Hannah said. "I was really disappointed in that. Because they didn't have the pride and the class that Coach Bryant had brought to the University of Alabama."

Another difference between college and the pros was the practices. According to Hannah, they were much tougher on Coach Bryant's field.

"He sent ten guys to the hospital my senior year with heat stroke and dehydration," Hannah said. "And a bunch of people quit. The next day we go in the locker room. He comes in and winds his watch and says, 'Boys, you learned a big lesson yesterday. The human body is an amazing thing. You will push it and push it and think you are going to die. But you will not die. The human body will always pass out before it dies.'"

Former Alabama players wax eloquent about the reasons for Coach Bryant's success. Was it his work ethic? His charisma? His passion? What did he have? Hannah puts it bluntly: "We were scared to death of him. He was a great man. I admire him and love him. But he was tough. Let's call a spade a spade."

In the book, *What It Means to Be Crimson Tide,* Hannah takes it a step further: "I never had a comfort level with Coach Bryant. Even after I was in pro ball, I wasn't one of those who was close to him. We had an arm's-length relationship because I was so scared of the man. I didn't talk to him much except when I needed his permission to do something. My relationship with him was mostly just looking up in the tower and knowing he was there."

Hannah explained that his comments weren't meant to be a criticism of Coach Bryant.

"I know it was special to play for him," Hannah said. "The biggest thing he gave me was the ability to see what I could do, which was more than I thought I could. He drove me to play harder, to practice harder than my opponent. I needed that experience. But I had to get out of that environment of fear to become the best athlete I could be."

Offensive linemen are the quintessential under-the-radar players. They do their grunt work, and no one notices them unless they miss their assignment and the quarterback gets sacked. But in this often thankless, rarely glamorous position, John Hannah got noticed.

In 1991, Hannah became the first New England Patriot to be inducted into the Pro Football Hall of Fame. He was presented by his father, Herb, and in his speech Hannah acknowledged his father's enormous influence on his life: "I thank my dad for one of the greatest lessons that a man can be taught: to never be satisfied with what you've done . . . and to press on to what lies ahead."

The ceremony was a great day for the Hannahs, a football family if ever there was one. Hannah's brothers both played for the Crimson Tide (Charley from 1974 to 1976, David from 1975 to 1979). Charley went on to pro ball and faced his brother as an opponent while playing for Oakland and Tampa Bay.

After retiring from the NFL in 1986, Hannah started the Hannah Group, an investment consulting firm in Boston. According to *Sports Illustrated*, when he sold the company to Advest Inc. in 1996, it was handling $3 billion in assets. "I wouldn't say that I've had the same kind of success in business as I had in football," Hannah said. "I'm no Peter Lynch. But I've done OK."

After selling his company, Hannah went to work for First Union Securities in Boston.

Then, in 2001, he volunteered as an assistant coach at his stepdaughter's school, Governor Drummer Academy in Byfield, Massachusetts.

Three years later, he signed on as head coach at Somerville (Massachusetts) High School.

"I came to the realization that the monetary rewards might not be as great as some of the satisfaction of doing something more important," Hannah was quoted as saying in the book *Legends of Alabama Football.* "When I talked to my wife, Elise, about it, she pointed out that when I worked in the financial services business, I had one look on my face, and when I coached football I had another, and it really seemed to float my boat to work with those kids."

Hannah's son, Seth, and daughter, Mary Beth, were grown by then and living on their own; so the timing was right to take a job defined by a nomadic existence and weekends and evenings away from home. No question, Hannah worked his players hard.

"I think the biggest thing is that it's easy to work hard when you have fun and you have a passion for the game," he said. "It's not very easy to work hard when you don't."

Things came full circle for Hannah when in 2005 he accepted a position as director of football development at Baylor School in Chattanooga, the same school he had attended his first three years of high school.

Recently, he moved back home to Alabama, a state always proud to claim him as one of its own.

DENNIS HOMAN

"I have more respect for Coach Bryant than any person I've ever known."

— DENNIS HOMAN

LIKE MANY FORMER ALABAMA FOOTBALL PLAYERS, DENNIS HOMAN has some wonderful mementos of his playing days on display in his Florence, Alabama, home. One of his prized possessions is a framed letter that Coach Bryant sent to all his former players after announcing his retirement in 1982. In the note, Bryant basically gave credit for his success to his players and challenged them to become even bigger winners in their post-football lives.

"That's a treasure," Homan said. "He gave all the praise and accolades to us. It's amazing."

Photos, magazine clippings, and other memorabilia fill up an entire room (the Homans call it the "red room") dedicated to all things Alabama. There is one thing missing, though.

"We used to visit Mrs. Bryant," remembered Homan. "Every time we'd

Photograph courtesy of Dennis Homan

Homan's name still litters Alabama's record books.

go over she was trying to give something away. Well, Coach Bryant had several of his hound's-tooth hats hanging on a hat rack. She said, 'Dennis, why don't you take one of these hats? Paul would love you to have one.' I said, 'Oh no, I couldn't.' Now I wish I had!"

Happily, this is one of this great Crimson Tide player's few regrets.

Dennis Homan grew up in Muscle Shoals, Alabama. That's where his hundred-year-old father still lives in the home Homan grew up in. In high school, he played football, baseball, basketball, and ran track. Baseball was his favorite sport, and he was even offered a contract with the Pittsburgh Pirates.

"Thank goodness someone talked me out of that," he said.

College football scouts recruited the talented receiver, who was considering Ole Miss when Coach Bryant called.

"It was like Uncle Sam called!" he said. "You didn't tell him no. I didn't even have to make a decision. I just said, 'Yes, sir!'"

When Coach Bryant came in person to Muscle Shoals to follow up on the call, it caused quite a stir.

"You would have thought the president of the United States was coming in," Homan said. "They lined the streets; people were buzzing. It made me feel like I made the right decision."

Right decision, indeed. By the end of his sophomore year of 1965, Homan and his teammates were wearing national championship rings (currently on display in the "red room"). In 1966, he played on one of the most storied

Crimson Tide squads of all time, which was denied the national championship despite its unblemished record. But his senior year was his season to shine.

The name, Dennis Homan, is still littered throughout Alabama's record books. He holds several receiving marks from 1967, including 54 receptions (sixth best of all time), 820 reception yards (third best), nine touchdown receptions (second best), and he's tied for first place for most touchdown catches in a game (three).

By the time his college playing days were done, Homan had been named all-SEC twice, all-American and Academic all-American once each, and was bound for a professional football career. But like almost every athlete who played for Coach Bryant, getting there was far from easy.

"A lot of what you did at Alabama wasn't a lot of fun, but you did it anyway," Homan said. "Although we didn't always agree with him at the time, looking back I realize that Coach Bryant was just trying to make us better."

For instance, when Homan asked permission to play baseball in the spring, Coach Bryant said no.

"If he felt like you didn't need to go through spring practice, he'd let you play other sports," said Homan. "I wanted to play baseball, but he made me and Ray Perkins go run track because he knew that was going to help us with quickness, agility, and speed. He was right."

Homan vividly remembers another time Coach Bryant turned down one of his requests.

"Back in those days, there weren't many married players," Homan said. "Coach Bryant didn't like married players, and he stayed on them on the practice field. But I was so much in love and wanted to marry this young girl my senior year. So, I finally got up the courage to go talk to him about it, which shows how crazy I was because you wanted to avoid him as much as you could.

"So I went in his office and sat on that infamous couch that sank to the floor. He said, 'What's on your mind?' I said, 'Coach, I came here to ask about getting married.' And oh man, it was a nightmare after that. He jumped up and threw stuff off his desk. He was ranting and raving and saying when he was a player, he got married before his senior year and broke his leg (in the Tennessee game in 1935). He told me I had one year to make all-American and the rest of my life to be married. The only thing I had in my mind after that was to get out of there!"

According to Homan, he walked out of Coach Bryant's office white as a sheet.

"If somebody offered me a hundred thousand dollars to go through that again, I don't believe I'd do it," he said. "I've never been so terrified in all my life."

Looking back, Homan said he realized the coach was right.

"He knew I didn't need any more responsibility. He was pushing me for all-American honors and knew I didn't need something else on my mind."

Following his senior year, after he had collected the above-mentioned honors, Homan did in fact marry Charlotte, the girl who had caused such a stir. Coach Bryant and his wife were guests at the wedding. Kenny "Snake" Stabler, Homan's college roommate, was the best man. As it turned out, Kenny was truly a good sport for accepting that honor since he had previously been interested in the future Mrs. Homan.

"That's true!" Homan laughed. "Of course, back then, Snake was after every

Photograph courtesy of Dennis Homan

Mickey Mantle, Dennis Homan, Ken Stabler, and Coach Bryant

girl he could find. I was too. But I remember seeing Charlotte for the first time coming down the Quad. She was on one side of the street and I was on the other. I started pursuing her, and little did I know my roommate was doing the same thing. I guess I had a little more speed than he had. I was a little quicker. Three months later, Charlotte and I were engaged."

Photograph courtesy of Dennis Homan

Homan played three years for America's team.

Many years later, Charlotte and Homan (who will soon celebrate their fortieth wedding anniversary) dropped by to visit Coach Bryant.

"He always loved to have his former players come by to see him," Homan said. "If you ever played four years for him, buddy, you got the red carpet treatment. We had our two kids with us. When we got ready to leave, he put his arm around Charlotte and said, 'You're not still mad at me are you?' She said, 'Coach, for what?' He said, 'For not letting you get married your senior year.' She said, 'No!' And they hugged."

The success Homan had on the field at Alabama led to a five-year NFL career. The Dallas Cowboys drafted him in the first round. He was ready when he arrived at his first NFL training camp.

"When I got to Dallas, it was a cakewalk as far as the physical part of it," Homan said. "Mentally, it was tougher because Dallas had a playbook as thick as the Sears Roebuck catalog! But physically I was in top shape. I was nothing but skin, lung, and bones when I played at Alabama. I could run all day long and not get tired. That was one thing Coach Bryant really emphasized. Being in shape and not being overweight."

Homan credits Dallas teammate and former Crimson Tide star Lee Roy Jordan with helping him adjust during his rookie year.

"Lee Roy really helped me when I got there," Homan said. "In college, you've got some really great players with really great skills. Then, in the pros, everybody's good. You have to start all over again."

Homan played for Tom Landry's Cowboys for three winning seasons, topping it off with a trip to Super Bowl V. (The Cowboys lost to the Colts.) In 1971, Homan played for another great coach and another fantastic team when he was traded to Kansas City and played for Hank Stram's Chiefs for two years.

After five years in the NFL, Homan retired and returned home to Alabama, where he got his broker's license and opened a real estate business with fellow ex-Crimson Tide player, Tommy Brooker. The business did well, but according to Homan, he couldn't stop thinking about football.

"That was a time in my life when I'd become a Christian," Homan recalled. "I started praying to the Lord, if there's any way you would allow me to play football, I would really appreciate it."

Two weeks later, the World Football League (WFL) opened for business and the Birmingham Americans offered Homan a contract.

Photograph courtesy of Dennis Homan

Charlotte and Dennis (front and center)

Although the league was short-lived and strapped financially (according to Homan there were many weeks the players didn't know whether or not they would be paid), Homan got to play football a few more years in front of an Alabama crowd.

"It was a great, great time," Homan said. "We won the championship (in 1974). I have a WFL championship ring, which is kind of like having an Edsel. There aren't too many of those floating around!"

When the WFL folded, Homan went to see Coach Bryant who said he would hire him if he wanted to coach.

"I was more of a family man at that time, so I decided I wanted to do something where I could be with my kids," Homan said. (His two children, Matt and Missy both later attended the University of Alabama. Matt is a computer engineer and Missy is an attorney.)

When a friend invited him to tag along on his sales calls for a pharmaceutical company, Homan knew he had found the ideal job.

"I went to work for Abbott Laboratories and stayed there for twenty-six years!" said Homan, who retired in 2002. "It wasn't like being behind a desk all the time. I was in a different town every day. It was like calling on your friends."

When he announced his retirement, many people warned Homan that he would be bored.

"I'm still waiting for that moment!" Homan said.

His days are filled with golf, grandchildren, speaking engagements, and fixing thing around the house. Plus, he continues to get mail from Alabama fans every week.

"That really shocks me," he said. "I still get letters and pictures that people ask me to sign. I'm amazed and honored."

Alabama fans don't forget, and they still want to hear war stories from those great seasons of the sixties. When asked to recount a memorable game, Homan often surprises people with his answer.

"Personally, the games I remember most are the three games we lost," he said. "In four years we only lost three games. Losing wasn't in the vocabulary at Alabama when I was there. Coach Bryant instilled that in us and made believers out of us. He made us the best we could be."

SCOTT HUNTER

"Coach Bryant knew what got you beat and he emphasized not making those mistakes. His theory was that if you kept your mistakes to a minimum, you always had a chance to win the football game."

— SCOTT HUNTER

WHEN IT COMES TO SHOOTOUTS, NASCAR FANS HAVE THEIRS—THE annual Budweiser Shootout race at Daytona. Old West history buffs have theirs—the gunfight at the O.K. Corral. And Alabama fans have theirs—Scott Hunter's famed Shootout with Archie Manning.

The Alabama version of proverbial gunplay took place on October 4, 1969, at Birmingham's Legion Field when the Crimson Tide faced off against Ole Miss in a nationally televised game.

The first half was lively but relatively run-of-the-mill. Then, late in the game, Ole Miss quarterback Archie Manning revved up his extraordinary passing arm and led his team from a 21-14 third quarter deficit to a 26-21 fourth quarter lead.

Things got tense around Alabama's bench. Scott Hunter recalls that things got so hectic on the sidelines that Coach Bryant stuck a cigarette in his mouth sometime during the third quarter and didn't take the time to light it until well into the fourth quarter.

At one point, Hunter was standing next to the boss discussing plans for the next offensive series when Manning fired a 25-yard pass for a first down.

As Hunter told it in *The Crimson Tide: An Illustrated History*: "Coach Bryant quickly forgot the plans and stormed down the sideline yelling at defensive coach Ken Donahue. 'Ken, what coverage are we in?' he roared. Archie's performance had paralyzed Donahue. He tried to mumble something. Coach Bryant fired him at that very moment. Assistant Coach Jimmy Sharpe was standing next to me talking strategy so I whispered to him, 'Coach Bryant just fired Coach Donahue.' Sharpe nonchalantly looked up at me and said, 'Don't worry about it; he's already fired him twice this half.'"

The teams continued trading touchdowns. Then, with Alabama down 32-27 and facing a fourth and long near the Ole Miss twenty, Hunter called time-out and ran to the sideline to consult with Coach Bryant.

"He turned to Coach Sharpe and asked him what he wanted to do," Hunter said. "Then Sharpe said, 'I don't know; I'll ask Steve.' So he called Coach Steve Sloan, who was up in the press box, but Sloan didn't answer."

Steve Sloan later confessed that he screened the call. "When I looked down on the field I saw Coach Bryant turn to Sharpe, then I saw

Photograph courtesy of Paul W. Bryant Museum/The University of Alabama

Coach Bryant called Scott Hunter "The best passer you ever met."

Sharpe look up at me," said Sloan. "So I pulled off my headphones! I said, 'Lord, what should we do?'"

Then the referee came over and said, "Time's up, Alabama captain."

According to Hunter, Coach Bryant told him, "Run the best thing you got."

The play that immediately came to mind was red right, 56 comeback. Hunter and wide receiver George Ranager had run this pattern so many times in practice, they could do it in their sleep. But no doubt about it, they were wide awake and on display in front of thousands of fans in a packed stadium, plus the tens of thousands of fans at home watching on TV.

According to Hunter, when he called the play in the huddle, he stared right into Ranager's eyes. Ranager didn't blink.

The Crimson Tide offense hit the line of scrimmage. The ball was snapped. Then, despite an Ole Miss blitz (Hunter credits Johnny Musso with a fantastic block), Hunter completed his picture perfect pass to Ranager who dove into the end zone for the touchdown. The Crimson Tide won the ball game/ shootout, 33-32.

It's incredible that a quarterback could pass for over four hundred yards, as Manning did, and end up with a loss. Hunter has empathy for that. But Hunter passed for a not-too-shabby three hundred yards and led his team to a win. He couldn't help but feel extremely happy about that.

According to Hunter, fans still ask him about that game. And he never gets tired of talking about it.

"I imagine Archie does, though," he smiled.

Today, Scott Hunter lives in Mobile with his wife, Debbie, who was an Alabama cheerleader in 1968 and '69. He is the proud father of three University of Alabama graduates, his two daughters, Mary Scott and Betsy, and his son, Jamie, who was a walk-on linebacker on the 1999 SEC Championship team. Hunter says he is in better shape than he was during his college playing days, courtesy of strength and cardiovascular training at the gym.

"Back then, I was always trying to get out of it," he said of his frequent workouts. "Now I'm trying to get in it!"

When he's not raising his heart rate on elliptical machines, Hunter gets his adrenaline rushes at Raymond James Financial Services, where he is an investment advisor. But he admits that although he is in charge of guarding and growing people's money—an enormous responsibility—he finds it a tame undertaking when compared with playing football in front of seventy-five thousand people.

Hunter grew up in Pritchard, Alabama, where he played quarterback at Vigor High School. Growing up, he followed Auburn more closely than Alabama, influenced by frequent visits with an aunt and uncle who owned an Auburn sporting goods store.

But when the Alabama scouts came to call on him in high school, he changed his mind. According to Hunter, they had two major selling points: Coach Bryant. And the winning.

Photograph courtesy of Paul W. Bryant Museum/The University of Alabama

At Alabama the expectations were high.

Some players might be intimidated by playing quarterback for a school whose recent graduates included Pat Trammell, Joe Namath, Kenny Stabler, and Steve Sloan. On the contrary, Hunter says it actually motivated him.

"I liked the idea of playing at a place like Alabama where the expectations were very high," he said. "I liked that. It didn't bother me in the least. I liked the challenge."

According to Steve Sloan, a great Crimson Tide quarterback who became one of Hunter's coaches at Alabama, Hunter was confident from the start.

"He was a confident guy," said Sloan. "He really believed in his ability to play quarterback. And it was challenging because we put in a more sophisticated passing game at the time and he picked it up real well."

Sloan says that some things—such as footwork—you can teach. But some things—such as the ability to throw a ball that is easy to catch—you can't.

"He had a natural ability to throw the ball," Sloan said. "He had a nice pass; one that was pretty easy to catch. A lot of people throw a harder ball but his was a soft ball when it arrived in your hands. And he was a very accurate passer. The receivers didn't drop many of his balls."

As impressive as Hunter's skills were on the field, especially in terms of his passing abilities, the Crimson Tide failed to win an SEC or national title during the three seasons he played for the varsity. Despite his contributions (he passed for 3,428 yards his last two seasons) and those of great players such as defensive end Robin Parkhouse and halfback Johnny Musso, Alabama struggled in 1969 and '70, finishing 6-5 and 6-5-1 respectively.

There are a number of reasons for this as Sloan explained: "That was one of the few times our defense wasn't that good. But the offense was good. We had to score a lot of points to win games."

Although he didn't leave the university with a championship ring, Hunter left behind school records in many categories. Most, such as his mark for season passing attempts (266 in 1969) and season passing completions (157 in 1969) have since been surpassed, but his records for single game passing attempts (55) and single game yards (484), both in 1969 against Auburn, still stand.

In 1970 Hunter was drafted into the NFL by Green Bay, where he played for three years. He started eight games for the Packers as a rookie and in 1972, took his team to the Central Division title.

In 1973, he was traded to the Buffalo Bills and stayed two years.

In 1975, he retired from pro football and returned to Alabama where he ran an appliance store and got involved in local politics.

"I had this crazy notion and decided to run for the Mobile County Commission," Hunter said. "I lost a tough race but it was a wonderful experience. I liked being out and about with people and listening to them. It helped me get my feet back on the ground. The NFL is kind of a la-la-land."

As it turns out, Hunter was not yet done with pro ball. After the election, he got a very interesting package in the mail from Pat Peppler, who was the Atlanta Falcons' general manager (and later head coach). Peppler was also the guy who drafted Hunter at Green Bay and wanted him to try-out for the Falcons.

His invitation? A football in a box. (Message: start throwing and come to camp.)

Hunter reported to camp and made the team, at first backing up quarterbacks Steve Bartkowski and Kim McQuilken. He had his best stretch in 1976 when as a starter, he led his team to three of their four victories.

In 1978, he was traded to Detroit and played his last year of pro football.

After that, he retired and returned to Mobile to put his finance degree to work. But, as it turned out he wasn't completely done with football. In 1982 he hit the airwaves as a radio broadcaster. He is still the host of the WNST weekly sports talk show, *Talkin' Football.*

Hunter's formula for on-air success?

"Mostly, I keep it between the lines," he said. "I don't talk about who is dancing with who. I talk about what the quarterback did last Saturday. Or what the coach did. What the other team did. Then I let the callers run the show. Establish a dialogue and go from there. It's a lot of fun."

Back in the late sixties, when Coach Bryant took his famous walks with the quarterbacks before the games, he also kept the discussion "between the lines."

"He said the same thing every time," Hunter recalled. "He would talk about the wind, crowd noise, and what to do in certain situations. Also, he would set up little signals in case he wanted us to do something or not do something. If he took his hat off, or put it on. That sort of thing."

And all this time we thought Coach Bryant was just being polite when he tipped his hat to a passerby. Turns out, winning was never far from his mind.

WILBUR JACKSON

"I just wanted to go to college, get an education, and play football. I didn't want to be Jackie Robinson."
— WILBUR JACKSON

IT'S DIFFICULT TO IMAGINE A TIME WHEN THERE WAS NO SUCH THING as satellite TV, DVDs, or pay-per-view; but in the 1960s, many homes across the country had access only to a maximum of three networks. In Ozark, Alabama, Wilbur Jackson's family could tune in only two. But on Sunday afternoons, that was plenty, because Jackson, a standout football player on his high school team, was only interested in watching two programs: *The Bear Bryant Show* and (full disclosure) *The Shug Jordan Show.*

Fast forward to 1973. Jackson was a star halfback and team captain for the Crimson Tide who loved to hang out in the athletic dorm lounge, relaxing and watching TV. At home in Ozark, his family still had access to only two TV stations. But luckily, one of them was ABC, which broadcast the Tennessee game

Photograph courtesy of Paul W. Bryant Museum/The University of Alabama

Wide receiver–turned running back Wilbur Jackson

where Jackson scored two touchdowns, one an eighty-yard sideline sprint. After he rushed for a total of 145 yards during that game, (Alabama won 42-21), ABC-TV named him outstanding offensive player of the game.

After he left the university, Jackson became a regular on *Monday Night Football* during his eight-year NFL career. His mother made sure to always watch him on the TV he bought her in 1974 with his signing bonus from the San Francisco 49ers.

Wilbur Jackson, one of four kids, grew up in a hard-working, down-to-earth family. His dad, Melvin Jackson, worked for the railroad for forty years. From his freshman though junior years, Jackson attended an all-black high school, D. A. Smith. When schools were integrated his senior year, he transferred to the formerly all-white John Carroll High School, where he was a three-sport star. Playing flanker his senior year, he caught forty-two passes, scored seventeen touchdowns, and was named all-state.

His on-field performance caught the attention of Crimson Tide scouts, including assistant coach Pat Dye, who once commented that Jackson could be as good or better than Terry Beasley, the star Auburn receiver of the era.

Although there weren't yet any African Americans playing for Alabama in 1969, people knew the time was coming. There had been a handful of black walk-ons (nonscholarship players who try out for the football team on their own) since the spring of 1967, although none made the team. Also, Alabama had a few black basketball players.

So, although it was definitely a historic moment, it wasn't too surprising when Jackson stood on the sidelines of the football field alongside eighty other high school prospects during a recruiting visit to Tuscaloosa.

According to *Bama and the Bear,* Jackson was impressed with Bryant the moment he saw him slowly making his way down the line, greeting each one of the recruits.

"We had lost to Eufaula the night before," Jackson remembered. "When he shook my hand he said, 'I'm sorry your team lost last night to Eufala.' That impressed me, that he knew about me and who we had played."

During another recruiting trip, Jackson had an even more memorable exchange with Coach Bryant while visiting the Bryants' home.

"He pulled me aside, took me into a separate room, and told me if I would come to Alabama, he'd make me the best wide receiver in the nation," Jackson said.

When he accepted Alabama's scholarship offer the following spring, in 1970, Jackson was thinking about Coach Bryant's promise. He wasn't thinking about becoming the first African American to sign with the Crimson Tide or breaking down barriers. Incredibly, he claims not to have even realized that he was the team's first signed black player.

According to John David Briley, author of *Career in Crisis,* a book documenting the 1971 season: "It's true. He didn't have the historical sense of it."

Jackson has said many times the toughest part of that year was leaving home and dealing with the problems of a typical college freshman. The second toughest part was playing football for one of the most demanding programs in the country.

"It was a tough experience on the field, but it was tough on everyone," Jackson said in *What It Means to Be Crimson Tide,* "I felt as though I was treated just like everyone else, and I also felt that is how it should have been."

Before the season started, Coach Bryant told Jackson that if he ever had any problems to come see him—and no one else—immediately, and he would take care of it. The coach was talking about racial problems.

According to Jackson, he never had to go to the coach. Like most freshman players, he hardly saw him.

"I didn't have that much day-to-day contact with him, but I always knew he was there," he said.

The only real trouble Jackson encountered his freshman season was playing on a not-quite-healed foot he fractured while playing baseball the previous spring. At practice, he was in the same boat as his white teammates, slugging it out every day.

According to freshman team coach Clem Gryska, Coach Bryant made sure his teams always played on an equal playing field. "He used to say, 'When you get on the field, I don't care if you're red, white, blue, or purple. You better perform.'"

Jackson was a quiet, unassuming guy—the kind of person you wouldn't expect to be a trailblazer. But according to Sylvester Croom, who along with several other African American players, followed him to the university in 1971, those qualities made him just the man for the job.

"Wilbur is a quiet person, but they couldn't have picked a better human being as a pioneer blazing the trail," Croom said. "People forget what it's like when you're going into that environment and you're the only minority player in uncharted waters. When you're first, it's tough. But he handled it with class and dignity. When I came there as a freshman with Mike Washington and Ralph Stokes the following year, we looked up to him. Still do! I have the greatest respect for the way he carried himself the entire time that we were there and ever since."

People couldn't help but notice how Wilbur Jackson carried himself on the football field as well. Despite Coach Bryant's promise to make him the best wide receiver in the country, Jackson was switched to running back during his sophomore year of 1971, which is when Alabama abandoned the pro-set, passing-style offense in favor of the wishbone.

Jackson was fast, so the running part wasn't a problem when he made the switch. But it was a challenge for this great athlete to learn an entire new skill set just when he was breaking in as a varsity player.

"He had speed, but he had to learn how to run the ball and block," John David Briley said. "In the wishbone, it was really important for those running backs to block. It was crucial. If they didn't block, they weren't on the field."

Photograph courtesy of Paul W. Bryant Museum/The University of Alabama

When Jackson's time came, he was ready.

Jackson definitely learned to block. According to assistant coach Jack Rutledge, he did it very well.

"He always did exactly what he was supposed to do," he said. "Wilbur turned out to be a lot greater even than we thought he was."

Although Jackson didn't play much during his sophomore year of 1971 (senior and all-American Johnny Musso played in front of him), several times he got the opportunity to show what he could do. One memorable display came during the Miami game when he subbed for Musso, who was sidelined with an injured foot. Jackson racked up 90 yards on 13 carries, including a spectacular 67-yard touchdown run in the first quarter.

According to Jackson, Musso had encouraged him from the beginning.

"Johnny would often come by my room during the season," Jackson said in the book *Career in Crisis.* "He would always tell me to hang in there and my time would come. When I was a sophomore, (we) went to Southern Cal and played on a Friday night. I had no idea whether or not I would get to play. As it turned out, I did not get to play.

"The next day we stayed over, and Johnny visited with me and told me not to get down on myself. He told me that my day would come and for me to keep my head up. That meant a lot to me."

Musso turned out to be right on the money. Jackson's "day" would come. And it lasted a full two seasons.

"Wilbur was probably one of the greatest running backs ever to play at Alabama because of what he accomplished in two years there," Sylvester Croom said. "To be moved from wide receiver to halfback in the wishbone and to accomplish what he did is remarkable."

By the end of the 1974 season, Jackson was the Alabama career leader in yards per rush, 7.2 yards per carry, with 1,529 yards on 212 rushes. He also joined three others in setting an NCAA record when he became one of four backs to rush for more than 100 yards in the same game.

According to Richard Todd, Tide quarterback from 1973 to 1975, if Bryant hadn't rotated his players so much during those years, Jackson's numbers would have been even gaudier.

"If Coach Bryant had played Wilbur Jackson the whole game, he would have rushed for more yards than anyone, ever! And he'd probably still hold that record," said Todd.

Jackson, who was elected team captain in the national championship season of 1973, left the university with all SEC honors and went on to play nine years in the NFL. He was drafted by the San Francisco Forty-niners in the first round and played there from 1974 to 1979. From 1980 to 1982, he played for the Washington Redskins, capping off his pro career with a Super Bowl ring from his team's victory against the Dolphins in January 1983.

After he retired from pro football, Jackson moved back to Ozark, where he and his wife Martha raised their daughter, a recent University of Alabama graduate, and built a successful commercial janitorial company.

College football and sports in general have come a long way since Jackson broke the color barrier at the University of Alabama in 1970. Within three years of Jackson's arrival in Tuscaloosa, one-third of the Crimson Tide's starters were African Americans. In the years that followed there have been dozens of outstanding African American stars, such as Ozzie Newsome, Cornelius Bennett, and Walter Lewis.

While the rest of the world embraces positive change, such as when two black head coaches (Tony Dungy and Lovie Smith) faced off in the 2007 Super Bowl, Wilbur Jackson downplays his role.

"I'm not sure I fully understood how big a thing it was," he told author Keith Dunnavant. "I just wanted to go to college, get an education, and play football. I didn't want to be Jackie Robinson."

LEE ROY JORDAN

"If they stay in bounds,
ol' Lee Roy will get them."
— PAUL W. "BEAR" BRYANT

IT USUALLY HAPPENS OFF-THE-CUFF. SOMEBODY SAYS SOMETHING about you, most often without giving it any thought, and the thing the guy said sticks with you for life. Especially if the guy was Paul W. Bryant.

"He had a way of saying things about people," Lee Roy Jordan said. "Then folks would remember those people because of what he said about them!"

The comment people remember most about Jordan followed a Crimson Tide match-up against Georgia Tech.

Jordan, who played both center and linebacker from 1960 to 1962, back in the days when players played on both sides of the ball, was playing center when a Georgia Tech player intercepted a Bama pass. Instantly, Jordan went from center to defender and chased down the runner, who dropped the ball near the sidelines.

That Sunday, on *The Bear Bryant Show*, Coach Bryant rolled the tape and said, "If they stay in bounds, ol' Lee Roy will get them."

"It was a tremendous compliment," Jordan said. "When he said things like this, it motivated us to do what he just said we were going to do! I didn't want to disappoint him."

And he didn't.

Jordan was one of the most outstanding players ever to wear the crimson jersey. He is on every Alabama fan's "greatest" list. Among his many honors, including the fact that he wears a 1961 National Championship ring, he was a two-time all-American and a captain of the '62 squad. He was named Player of the Decade for the sixties and was named to Alabama's Team of the Century. He also was picked for ESPN's all-time college football team, and in 1983 he was inducted into the College Football Hall of Fame. In 1987, he received the NCAA Silver Anniversary Award. And these are just some of the nods to his college success. We haven't even touched on his fourteen-year NFL career.

Jordan, a first-round draft choice taken by the Dallas Cowboys in 1963, once visited Coach Bryant during the off-season. The two men, no longer coach and player but by that time colleagues and friends, laughed about Coach Bryant's famous "Lee Roy will get 'em" quote.

Photograph courtesy of Paul W. Bryant Museum/The University of Alabama

Lee Roy Jordan—one of the best ever

Jordan remembered telling Bryant, "Coach, I may not always get 'em, but I'm still chasing them!"

These days, if he chases anyone, it's likely one of his seven grandchildren. Jordan and his wife of forty-three years, Biddie, have three sons, three daughters-in-law, six granddaughters, and (finally!) one grandson.

"I tried not to act excited about

Photograph courtesy of Paul W. Bryant Museum/The University of Alabama

Jordan and Coach Bryant: "He didn't have to make a big speach," Jordan said.

it when he was born last year, but I'm afraid I might have been overly obnoxious about it," Jordan said.

Jordan, who weighs almost exactly what he did as a player more than forty years ago, was slowed slightly by knee replacement surgery on both knees in 2006, but is back up and running. Well, walking—and sometimes jogging—anyway.

"My wife asked me why I was jogging," Jordan laughed. "I said I want to know how fast I can run. If I see a mugger, I want to know if I can run from him or if I'll have to stay and fight."

The Jordans live in Dallas, where Jordan runs a successful lumber business. They spend family vacations at their home in Point Clear, Alabama, or at their hunting lodge near Tuscaloosa. (Quail hunting is Jordan's passion.) He and his family visit the university often (two sons are Alabama grads), and Jordan plans to attend every game in the upcoming 2007 season.

"Alabama has the most loyal fans," he said. "I think we've gotten some unjust publicity the last few years that we are tough fans for a coach to please. We're not. We just have high expectations because we've had a lot of coaches do well and win SEC and national championships. We expect our teams to do well. It's our tradition."

A good part of that tradition, under Bear Bryant's watch anyway, began with Jordan's teams. The seniors on the 1961 National Championship squad were made up of Bryant's first season of recruits at Alabama. Along with the seniors, the sophomores and juniors, including Jordan, were the first players to come of age under the Bryant system, which featured huge doses of conditioning and preparation in practice and equally large helpings of confidence and perseverance on game day.

From 1960 to 1962, Jordan's teams not only won, but often they kept opponents off the scoreboard. In 1961, opponents of the Crimson Tide scored a total of three touchdowns for the season.

Jordan remembered: "We took every point as a personal insult."

Jordan was the very definition of an early sixties Bryant player—lean, quick, tough, and determined. He was also very receptive to his coach's methods and message.

"Coach Bryant never let us get flat," Jordan said. "His philosophy was that you're no better than the day after the game. You have to prove it each week."

Jordan remembers the highly effective way Bryant had of explaining, encouraging, and convincing players to do what he wanted them to do.

"He had a way of leaning on you and putting his arm around your shoulder that made you feel so good," Jordan said. "You'd hope it was something good he was about to say, and most of the time it was. He'd say, 'Man, I need you to do this to help the team.' I'd walk away from him and say, 'I'm going to do that. And I'm going to do it well.'

"It was like a gentle nudge. A word or two. He didn't have to make a big speech. He just had to kind of suggest that you needed to do something better or do something this way and you'd think, *I'm going to get that done!*"

Jordan always seemed to get it done. And there were no gentle nudges in his blocking and tackling technique. Assistant coach Clem Gryska explained, "When he hit, it even sounded different. Some players hit you. He hit through you." In Coach Bryant's second-most-famous quote about Jordan, he called him "one of the finest football players the world has ever seen."

In his autobiography Bryant continued: "I can remember nothing bad about Jordan: first on the field, full speed every play, no way to get him to take it easy. I can't ever recall him missing a practice. Or being hurt for that matter."

Jordan's work ethic was solidly in place when he came to the university in 1959. He grew up in tiny Excel, Alabama (pop. 250), a town with just one school for grades 1–12. The Jordans were farmers and grew everything they ate (except salt and pepper). Life was tough on the farm, although Jordan has nothing but kind words for his parents, Walter and Cleo Jordan.

"I had a great family," he said. "My mom and dad were tremendous Christians. My mom made the world's best pecan pie. (Note: Jordan's mom often sent pie back to school with him. It was so good it often became the target of thieves. Some thirty years later, Jordan's suitemate Mal Moore confessed to once swiping his pie.)

"My dad was the kind of man who would hug you before he'd shake your hand. And he knew how to say, 'I love you.' They both had a great work ethic, and I guarantee you understood it and knew it well when you left home."

The Jordans had six kids, and as the youngest of the four boys, Jordan got early football training.

"As early as I could hold up a pair of shoulder pads, the coach started letting me dress out with the big boys," Jordan said. "So I started playing early in my life. I would go out and at least fill in a practice spot when we didn't have enough players. Here! You stand back here."

Jordan soon went from tackling dummy to making tackles for the Excel High School Panthers. He excelled at Excel, and, although Auburn coaches passed on him, Alabama coaches took notice. None of his older brothers and sisters went to college, but Jordan was on the way.

Before long, he was hustling, blocking, and tackling his way to fame as a Crimson Tide player. His best, or at least his most memorable, game as a college player might have been his last one. In the 1963 Orange Bowl he amazingly made 31 tackles in Alabama's 17-0 win. As team captain, he was escorted by the Secret Service to meet his counterpart from Oklahoma and President John F. Kennedy for the coin toss. He still has the coin. And his award for game MVP.

Football was far from over for Jordan. He was drafted by the Cowboys and played middle linebacker for fourteen years. During those years, he was named all-pro twice, played in five Pro Bowls, and played on teams that won five conference championships and eight division titles. As a Dallas Cowboy, Jordan set a team record when he finished his career with 1,236 career tackles and 154 consecutive starts.

He also played in three Super Bowls, most memorably Super Bowl VI when the Cowboys beat the Miami Dolphins, 24-3.

People always ask Jordan what the differences were between his two famous, incredibly successful coaches—Coach Bear Bryant and Coach Tom Landry.

"There were extreme differences, but there were some similarities," Jordan said. "Both of them were good organizers. Both loved to recruit the type of people that would win for you and play for you every day and that they could motivate. Coach Landry was not near the motivator or the guy who could excite you about playing the game. He felt like you were a professional and you were paid to play the game and everybody should play at the level he worked at. Coach Landry was a brilliant guy.

"But Coach Bryant was the one I remember most. I had fourteen years of Coach Landry, and it was terrific and we had some great seasons. I had four years with Coach Bryant. And that four years overshadows that fourteen."

After he retired from football, Jordan considered coaching—either for Bryant or for Landry—but ultimately decided to go a different route.

"I wanted to try to find a business I could run where I could be the boss; the person responsible for everything," Jordan said.

Photograph courtesy of Lee Roy Jordan

His own boss: Dallas-based businessman Lee Roy Jordan

He considered an auto dealership but when he found lumber companies for sale in Austin and Dallas, he felt like it was a better fit. For the first twenty years of operation, the Lee Roy Jordan Redwood Lumber Company specialized in California redwood and western red cedar. It has since evolved into a full-line lumber company, selling products to custom home builders.

Although he recently sold Southern Valve Service, a Mobile-based business, he and his son still have other business interests in Alabama. Among other things, the Jordans are distributors for Rainbow Play Systems, a South Dakota company that makes play equipment (slides and swings) for kids.

According to Jordan, being an ex-football star can give you an edge in business.

"It helps you get in the door, but it doesn't keep the customer," Jordan said. "Your quality of product has to be there. And you still have to do the service part. When you get into the customer-satisfaction business, you survive only by working at it and being good at it."

In business and in life, Jordan still remembers one of Coach Bryant's simplest lessons. Never quit.

"That stuck with me in business," Jordan said. "I had a few times I could have taken bankruptcy real easy because it was tough. I mean, it was hard. But somewhere, there was something down deep that said, 'No, that's not the way I am going. That's not the way I was taught.'"

E. J. JUNIOR

"I'm just a humble coach who has the opportunity to teach you."

— PAUL W. "BEAR" BRYANT

E. J. JUNIOR HAS CALLED A LOT OF PLACES HOME. HE WAS BORN IN Salisbury, North Carolina, and grew up in Nashville. Then he spent four years in Tuscaloosa from 1977 to 1980, where he was an all-American football player for the Crimson Tide. Then came St. Louis, Phoenix, Miami, Tampa Bay, and Seattle during his thirteen-year professional football career, and later, Minneapolis and Jacksonville, where he worked as an assistant coach.

Of all the places he has lived, Junior never thought Dusseldorf, Germany, would be on the list.

In 2005 Junior accepted a position as linebackers coach with the Rhein Fire of NFL Europe, which consists of five teams in Germany and one in Amsterdam. The league is made up mostly of American players looking to improve their skills in the off-season, although according to Junior, about 20 percent are athletes from Europe, Japan, and Mexico.

Photograph courtesy of Paul W. Bryant Museum/The University of Alabama

Murray Legg and E. J. Junior with plenty to smile about

"The teams are made up of players who didn't get a lot of playing time or who play on special teams, like your third-team quarterback or back-up linebackers," Junior said. "Or sometimes guys on scout teams or practice squads come here to get tested. And the coaches are guys who have coached in the league or aspire to coach."

Junior feels grateful for his time overseas.

"It was like a paid vacation," Junior said. "I picked up a little bit of German. It's a beautiful language. I learned things about the people and the culture. For instance, you don't see a lot of fat Germans. Gas is expensive, so people walk, skate, ride the train, or ride their bikes. They smoke like chimneys, and they like their beer. But you don't see a lot of drunks. They are perfectionists. We can learn a lot from them."

In Dusseldorf, they are crazy for the American brand of football.

"It's second only to soccer," Junior said. "Their team is like the Dallas Cowboys of Europe. They're very used to winning."

And winning is something Junior knows something about.

In high school, he excelled on and off the playing field at Nashville's

Maplewood High School. He was named to five prep all-American teams and earned all-South, all-state, and Most Valuable Player in his conference. He was also honored as the top scholar-athlete in his division, which made his Ph.D. father and school principal mother very proud.

Then, despite never claiming to be an Alabama football fan (in fact, he said he hated Alabama because they always beat his Tennessee teams), the winning tradition as well as the campus and academic offerings at the Capstone won him over.

During his four years as a Crimson Tide player, his teams went 44-4, won three SEC titles ('77, '78, and '79) and were twice crowned national champions (in '78 and '79).

As a freshman, Junior immediately found himself on Coach Bryant's radar.

In the book, *What It Means to Be Crimson Tide*, Junior tells about a particularly memorable practice. Every player lived in fear of Coach Bryant descending from his coach's tower because, unless there was a visiting dignitary or someone was injured, it meant the boss was about to read someone the riot act.

That day there was no limo in the parking lot (and hence, no dignitary). No one was hurt. And the coach was walking straight for Junior.

"I was a freshman, practicing with the second-team defense. And I knew I was about to be chewed out," Junior said. "Coach Bryant looked at me and said, 'E. J., go over there and put on a white jersey and get in there with the first defense.' I was shocked. I guess I just stood there, because he said, 'Did you hear me?'"

Junior snapped into action, answered, "Yes, sir!" and hustled over to the equipment manager to trade in his sweaty, second-team shirt for a clean, first-team jersey. But he was right about someone getting chewed out. The ex-first team guy got an earful from the coach.

Years later, Junior found out that Coach Bryant had called Junior's mother and invited her to drive down from Nashville and watch practice that day. She was there—just out of sight—to see a great moment at the beginning of a great college career.

Junior and other players often talk about how much Coach Bryant tried to include parents in his grand plan for his players.

"When he came to my house when I was being recruited," Junior said, "he told me and my parents that I would get a quality education and that I would work my tail off. My parents liked the sound of that."

Both things, by the way, turned out to be true.

In his 2006 memoir, *Ain't Nothin' But a Winner,* Junior's teammate Barry Krauss talks about how every player was eventually tested in practice by Coach Bryant to see if he would quit. (The famous "gut check.")

Junior's test came in the spring of his sophomore year during a controlled scrimmage. He was just coming off an injury, so the coaches started him slowly, putting him in at strong safety, then eventually moving him back to defensive end.

"We kept going and going," Junior said. "I couldn't hold my arms up, I was so tired. We got to ninety plays, then a hundred. On about play 110, I made it into the backfield and hit someone hard, but I didn't have the energy to wrap my arms around him and complete the tackle."

Coach Bryant yelled down from the tower, "Hey, there's someone trying to be another E. J. Junior."

"Coach," responded defensive coordinator Ken Donahue, "that *is* E. J."

"Hell, Coach," Bryant answered, "I thought I took him out on play seventy-five! Get out of there, E. J."

"You never know how much you can do until you get pushed," Junior told his teammate-turned-author. "We all got pushed."

Junior's teams pushed hard—all the way to the national title in '78 and '79.

During the 1978 season, which culminated with the thrilling Goal Line Stand against Penn State in the Sugar Bowl, the team's momentum gained steam during their second game. After a good start, the Tide unexpectedly fell behind Missouri at halftime, 20-17.

After a strongly worded dressing down in the locker room by Coach Bryant, Alabama rebounded in the second half. They held the Tigers on their first drive, then Junior blocked the punt. Rickey Gilliland picked it up and went into the end zone on a thirty-five-yard run. Alabama won, 38-20, and E. J. Junior got the reputation as a "big-play guy."

In a 1980 *Bama Magazine* interview, Sylvester Croom, then Junior's position coach, said this: "Junior has made a lot of big plays over the years that you didn't realize until later; plays that turned the game around or kept momentum on our side or broke the momentum of the other side. Coach Bryant is always telling the team that a few big plays will win a close game and that any player can make the difference.

"The thing is, you never know when that play will come so you have to be going all out on every down. That's the way E. J. plays."

The big plays and the fantastic 1979 season (he and his defensive colleagues Don McNeal, Byron Braggs, etc. gave up just five points a game that season) got him noticed. It was Coach Croom who told him at the start of his senior season that if he kept doing what he was doing, he could be a first-round draft choice the following year.

Junior was shocked. But he began to believe it might be possible when the awards started rolling in (SEC Defensive Player of the Year, a finalist for the Lombardi Trophy, all-American honors, etc.).

But as Junior told it, Coach Bryant had a way of keeping accolades like this from going to a player's head. "You're supposed to be an all-American?" the coach said. "I haven't seen him play yet."

Junior was in fact selected in the first round of the NFL Draft. He was the fifth player chosen (just behind linebacker Lawrence Taylor) and went on to play for the St. Louis (and later, the Phoenix) Cardinals for eight years. He played for the Miami Dolphins from 1989 to 1992 and ended his career with the Seattle Seahawks in 1993.

There were many great times in his NFL career, including two trips to the Pro Bowl and a chance to work with Coach Gene Stallings in St. Louis. But Junior also experienced some serious lows, mostly resulting from the fact that for several years, he was regularly using drugs.

"I could have destroyed everything, but God gave me a second chance," Junior said.

Junior took that second chance and ran with it. After completing drug-and-alcohol therapy, he served for several years on the NFL's Drugs Advisory Committee and worked during the off-season as a counselor at Hyland

Photograph courtesy of E. J. Junior

Coach Junior leads his young charges.

Medical Center (a rehabilitation clinic for alcohol and chemical abuse) in St. Louis and as outpatient director at Care Unit in Coral Springs, Florida.

After retiring from pro football (and returning to Alabama in 1995 to complete his degree), he kept up his good works by serving as a mentor in the Dade County Public School System. Then, in 2003, he became the executive director for Overtime Youth Center, NBA star Alonzo Mourning's community outreach program.

As much as he enjoyed these roles, Ester James Junior hungered for a stronger spiritual life.

"I kept hearing God say, 'If you love me, feed my sheep,'" Junior said. "Then, I got it. He was calling me to feed them the word. I thought, 'God, you can't be asking me to be a preacher! There's no way! I'm the biggest devil in the world. I've been an adulterer, a liar; I've been on drugs. You can't want me.' But God said, 'I want you just the way you are.'"

So Junior became an ordained minister and took a position as an associate pastor for a small ministry, the International Prayer Village.

As much as he loved the ministry, he missed coaching. So he threw his résumé back in the ring and in spring 2006 joined the coaching staff of Southwest Baptist University in Bolivar, Missouri. Incredibly, Junior and SBU's head coach, Jack Peavey had lined up against each other as pro players.

"When he called, I said, 'I remember you!'" Junior said. "Number 71! The Hall of Fame Game in 1986!"

Junior says his position as coach and sometime minister is the perfect combination.

"Coaching creates a platform to draw men to you," he said. "We're trying to put out a good product on the football field with good young men who are spiritually based, who are going to compete and be men of character."

Granted, the SBU team has a ways to go.

"We're in the MIAA," Junior said. "It's a very competitive conference. We're like the little Vanderbilt. The mighty mouse who can!"

The SBU players are responding positively to some new concepts being introduced to their program. Concepts that in fact, go back a long way.

"A lot of the workouts are very similar to what we had at Alabama," Junior said. "We're trying to create a work ethic and a tradition of excellence. There was never a sense of tradition passed down. We're trying to create that continuity."

As an ex-player, Junior naturally brings his own experience to the field. And he approaches things differently than his coaches did.

"I tell my players I'm trying to make you all coaches on the field," he said. "Make you see what I see. Things that were not taught to me as a player, I'm trying to teach these guys now."

And off the field?

"I'm coaching football techniques and life skills, because that's what Coach Bryant, Coach Croom, Ken Donahue, and all those Alabama coaches taught," he said. "Sometimes it goes in one ear and out the other, and you don't see it until you're older. That's why there's such reverence for Coach Bryant. He was a father figure and a philosopher. He would take the simplest little things and teach you with them."

Of course, Junior does his share of teaching at home. He and his wife Yolanda met in college, fell out of touch, then reconnected at Byron Bragg's New Year's party in 1992 and married in 1993. They have three young children (ages five to thirteen) at home and five older kids between them. The family is selling their Florida home and moving to Missouri—for now.

Junior has aspirations to coach in the NFL. But no matter what opportunity comes his way, he'll always remember what Coach Bryant said to him, "Don't you all make me more than I am. I'm just a humble coach who has the opportunity to teach you."

BARRY KRAUSS

"When you're in a lot of trouble, cry!"
— BARRY KRAUSS

EVERY FOOTBALL PLAYER DREAMS OF MAKING THE BIG PLAY. THAT'S why he spends countless hours preparing and practicing—because he wants to be prepared to perform when the moment arrives when it really counts.

As every Bama fan knows, Barry Krauss made such a play—the famous Goal Line Stand against Penn State in the 1979 Sugar Bowl. All Alabama fans (and Penn State fans, as well) remember where they were when it happened. And even if Krauss' memory of the actual event is a little foggy—after all, he was knocked cold—the play was frozen in time on the cover of *Sports Illustrated*, so he can refer back to it anytime.

Talk about a Kodak moment.

The 1978 Crimson Tide ended the season with just one loss (to USC, 24-14). They were SEC champions and ranked second in the nation. They were set to face Joe Paterno's top-ranked Penn State Nittany Lions in the Sugar Bowl.

Photograph courtesy of Paul W. Bryant Museum/The University of Alabama

Barry Krauss with Dick Nolan and Jeff Rutledge

"It was our dream to play the number-one ranked team in the country," said Krauss, who along with the other seniors on the team were determined to top off their career with a national championship ring.

The game was close-fought, but as the clock ran down, Bama was up 14-7. Then, the Nittany Lions recovered an Alabama fumble and began a nail-biting drive toward the Alabama goal.

Enter the Bama "D." Don McNeal made an incredible play, forcing Penn State receiver Scott Fitzkee out of bounds just shy of a touchdown. Then on third and one quarterback Chuck Fusina handed off to Matt Suhey, who was subdued by David Hannah and Rich Wingo after Krauss stopped Suhey's blocker.

Finally, on fourth and inches, in the huddle the players held hands.

"It was everything we'd wanted and prayed about," Krauss said. "I mean, you want it on the line. With Coach Bryant, this was the way it was supposed to happen."

Everyone was thinking the same thought. But safety Murray Legg was the

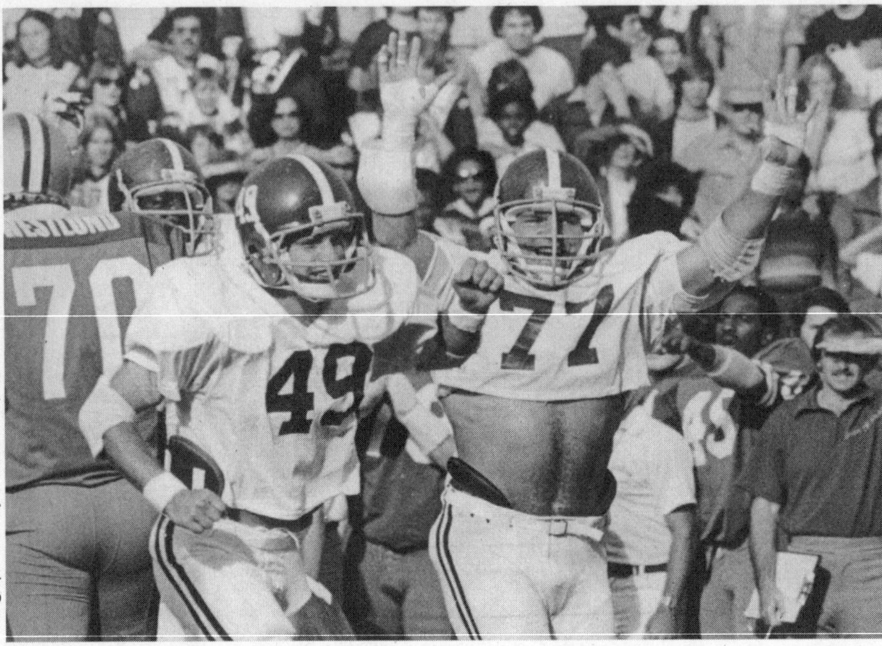

Photograph courtesy of Paul W. Bryant Museum/The University of Alabama

Post gut check celebration

first to say it out loud. "Gut check time!" He said it over and over. Everyone who has ever played for Coach Bryant heard the phrase many times.

This is it! Krauss thought.

The ball was spotted inches from the goal line. Then the snap. Penn State's Fusina handed the ball to Mike Guman, who went right up the middle. Right into Barry Krauss.

"Basically, he just cut back into me, and I hit him," Krauss said. "I was kind of holding him, then the next thing you know Murray Legg kind of pushed us over. I didn't know if we'd stopped them or not."

Krauss was dazed—he actually broke a chip off his helmet—and was temporarily paralyzed on one side. But then, his best friend Marty Lyons delivered the news.

"We finally did it," Marty said as he pulled Krauss to his feet. "We won the national championship."

That play, named one of ESPN's ten greatest in college football history, is of course burned into Bama fans' collective memory. It's been documented countless times in photos and artwork. Krauss, ever the Renaissance Man, even made his own painting of *The Goal Line Stand* and still sells the prints.

It's been nearly thirty years, but fans never seem to get tired of this story. In his 2006 book, *Ain't Nothin' But a Winner*, Krauss recounts how barely a day goes by when a fan doesn't approach him and say, "I remember it like it was yesterday. I was making onion dip."

No question, Krauss, who was named MVP of that Sugar Bowl by the way, was an incredible player.

He grew up in a pink house in Pompano Beach, Florida. As a young boy, the rambunctious and competitive Krauss played football on his front lawn and in the street. He also played on the beach, where he and his friends, who happened to be Alabama fans, came up with an innovative version of "the wishbone vs. the wave." The barefoot players would run the option down the sand with the fullback diving into the wave and the halfback attempting to leap over it.

Krauss credits his dad and big brother Bob with teaching him to play football. He also loved baseball, playing catcher because he liked the contact.

But focusing on the pigskin paid off for him. Krauss was recruited by several big schools including Georgia, Florida State, and Miami. But he was most intrigued by Alabama and their famous coach.

When Krauss made a recruiting visit to Miami, the Hurricanes were beaten soundly by the Crimson Tide. So Krauss leaned toward going to the Capstone. He loved Tuscaloosa. Then, a few weeks later, when Coach Bryant, who was in cahoots with his family, surprised him by showing up in his living room (scholarship in hand), the deal was done.

His freshman year was tough, as it was for most players. Krauss tells about grueling days spent wearing a zoot suit, a Michelin Man-like contraption that players wear to partly absorb the shock of being repeatedly pounded by runners.

"Basically, I was soaking wet all the time," Krauss said. "I was meat."

During his first year, the team still didn't get water breaks, so Krauss and others would sometimes feign injury and get ice from the trainer so they could suck some water out of the towels. Later on, water breaks became allowed, but players would line up holy communion-style and hit one knee while trainers brought water to them.

At the start of his sophomore season, Krauss wasn't playing much. He was frustrated and decided to blow off some steam late one night.

"In four years I played at Alabama, Coach Bryant checked curfew one night," Krauss remembered. "Guess which night I was out?"

Krauss was a wreck. He'd heard the stories of Joe Namath and Stabler being kicked off the team for similar infractions. And, as he puts it, they were stars and good-looking guys, "not butt-ugly linebackers."

Krauss summoned all his courage and went to the coach's office at 5:30 the next morning.

"Coach Bryant shuffled in, and I asked if I could speak to him," Krauss said.

His request was met with a look of disgust. Nonetheless, Krauss took a seat on the infamous sunken couch that made players feel as lowly as possible. Krauss felt low enough already. So he elected to stand.

"Coach Bryant, I just want to say I am sorry for missing curfew. I just feel like I wanted an opportunity to play for you but you're not giving it to me."

Photograph courtesy of Paul W. Bryant Museum/The University of Alabama

Nothing but smiles for the national champions

Bryant refused to look at Krauss, who continued apologizing. Nothing. Then, he took it up a notch. He started to cry. Still nothing.

"We talk about athletes taking it to another level," Krauss said. "I took crying to another level. I said, 'I'm so sorry! If you take me off scholarship and kick me out of the dorm, my mom is going to kill me!'"

Finally, the coach mumbled, "Son, you better straighten up." Krauss bolted out of the office.

"I learned when you're in a lot of trouble . . . cry!" Krauss said.

On a more serious note, Krauss was incredibly relieved and grateful for his second chance.

"What I took away from that episode was simple," Krauss said. "Coach Bryant saw something in me that no one else saw—not my coaches, my friends, my family, not anyone."

So Krauss rededicated himself. Not surprisingly, there were still a few "boys will be boys" incidents over the years (see Krauss' book for the streaking incident and the frequent ordering of items such as Ginsu knives delivered C.O.D. to an unsuspecting Marty Lyons).

On the field, things turned around for Krauss. The 1976 Notre Dame game, a pressure-cooker matchup where the Crimson Tide sought to avenge two lost national championships, was a major turning point even though the Fighting Irish eventually won the game, 21-18. Krauss didn't start the game, but when a linebacker missed an open-field tackle in the first half, he heard Coach Bryant growl, "Krauss! Get in there!"

During halftime, Krauss heard the coach say the line he'll never forget: "I want the same starting lineup, except I want Krauss in there because he wants to hit somebody."

Barry continued to "hit somebody" in every game for the next three years.

In 1976, he was named MVP of the Liberty Bowl after playing possibly the best game of his college career. He was named all-SEC and all-American in 1977–78. And then there was that play—the last play of the last game of his college career.

The Goal Line Stand opened a lot of doors for Krauss and other players on that national championship team. Krauss was drafted in the first round by the Baltimore Colts, the NFL Draft's sixth pick overall. He signed an amazing $1 million, six-year deal with a $300,000 signing bonus.

"I was living a dream," Krauss said.

The dream turned into somewhat of a nightmare though, during Krauss' rookie year when he realized the Colts had huge morale problems. There were frequent fights and racial tension, and many of the veterans didn't want Krauss replacing Ed Simonini, who wasn't ready to retire. Krauss said he felt ostracized and isolated. But he saw it through (Hadn't Coach Bryant taught him to never quit?), and he soon became a starter.

Like many ex-Bama players who later turned pro, Krauss faced an entirely new phenomenon: losing.

The Colts went 2-14 in 1981 and (ouch!) 0-8-1 in the strike shortened 1982 season. Eventually, things improved for the team and for Krauss personally. In 1984 the owners moved the Colts to Indianapolis; and although the move left fans in Baltimore bitter (the team literally left in the middle of the night), it was a positive move for Krauss, who was named MVP that year.

"I loved playing in Indianapolis," he said in his book. "I fell in love with the Hoosier Dome, and the people were great."

Then, in 1986, Krauss faced one of the toughest challenges of his life after he badly twisted his knee in a game against the New York Jets. After three surgeries to repair a torn ACL, he suffered a major infection and at one point, his doctors feared they would have to amputate his leg. After months of painful rehab (gut check time), Krauss returned to his team stronger than ever and was even honored with the Ed Block Courage Award for his comeback.

Nineteen eighty-eight was his last season with the Colts.

The Cleveland Browns invited Krauss to camp the next year, although he would end up being cut from the team. Krauss returned to Indianapolis depressed and wondering what to do with the rest of his life.

He tells a story about standing in his driveway unloading the moving truck when his wife, Darcy, called him to the phone.

"I don't want to talk to anybody," he said.

"You might want to take this one," Darcy said. "It's Don Shula."

Krauss suspected one of his friends was playing a mean joke. He had dreamed of playing for Shula since he was a kid playing on the beach in Florida. But it was Don—*the* Don—on the horn inviting him to give it a try with the Dolphins, and Krauss hightailed it to Miami and played for the Dolphins for three years.

"Playing for Coach Shula was like playing for Coach Bryant," Krauss said. "You always wanted to prove your worth."

After twelve years in the NFL, Krauss returned to Indianapolis, where he still lives with Darcy and their two daughters, Charlsie (fourteen) and Savannah (twelve), and their son Karsten (eight).

Krauss' oldest daughter Ashley, who graduated from the University of Alabama in 2005, attended school under the scholarship fund Coach Bryant set up for children of his players.

"Talk about class!" Krauss said. "I've never heard of any coach who put money away to take care of the former players' children."

Post-football has been a whirlwind for Krauss. He has taken up the mic and done radio and TV broadcasts for the Colts, the Arena Football League's Indiana Firebirds, and several high school teams. He was also the coach and owner of the NAFL Indiana Tornados minor league football team.

As if that wasn't enough, Krauss also makes frequent appearances giving motivational speeches to corporations. Guess what those guys in suits always want to hear about first?

"It was fourth down with inches to go."

WOODROW LOWE

"That's like getting a fifty-dollar gold piece for fifty cents."

— PAUL W. "BEAR" BRYANT

WOODROW LOWE MAY NOT KNOW IT, BUT HE WAS A HECK OF A recruiter for the Crimson Tide. And he actually did it on the playing field.

Simply by being the best player he could be.

Barry Krauss says he made his decision to sign with the University of Alabama because he was inspired by Lowe.

"When I finally made my recruiting trip to Alabama and I looked at Woodrow Lowe's helmet in his locker, it was over. I wanted to be here. Lowe was one of my heroes. Man, you talk about a hard-hitting football player."

In the book, *Game of My Life,* Jeremiah Castille claims a similar inspiration: "What attracted me to Alabama was Woodrow Lowe. I would watch Coach Bryant's show on Sundays and I would hear him say, 'That's Woodrow Lowe from Phenix City on the tackle.' I wanted him to be calling my name on that show for making a tackle or a big play. For what Woodrow had accomplished in high school and college, he was a great role model to me."

That's a lot of inspiration coming from a guy who was called "small" his entire football career.

Despite being a standout and the captain of his Central High School team, Lowe was not widely recruited, mostly due to his relatively small size. But Alabama assistant coach Pat Dye came to watch him play and told him if he worked toward getting bigger and stronger, there was a possibility he could play in college. So Lowe worked out with weights his senior year, gained twenty pounds of muscle, and packed his bags for Tuscaloosa.

Since he grew up in Phenix City, just down the road from Auburn University, people often ask Lowe why he didn't go to school there.

His answer? A flat tire.

According to *What It Means to Be Crimson Tide:* "Auburn had invited me to a game," Lowe said, "and I was going over with a buddy. But we had a flat tire, didn't have a spare, and had to hitchhike back to Phenix City to get help. I never made it to the Auburn game, and I never even met the Auburn coach who was supposed to be recruiting me."

Auburn's loss was definitely Alabama's gain. Lowe excelled on the field immediately. In the past, freshmen could not play for the varsity, but the rule had just been changed. So Lowe, a hard-hitting linebacker, was a varsity player from the start.

"He never played like a freshman," Coach Dye said. "He was a football player the first day he took to the field. He was a man—

Photograph courtesy of Paul W. Bryant Museum/The University of Alabama

Alabama's gain: Woodrow Lowe

mentally and physically. A lot of players may be tough mentally and not tough physically."

Lowe was such a tough player that some of the coaches started calling him "Lee Roy." At first, Lowe didn't know what they meant by that, but then someone explained that they were comparing him to none other than Crimson Tide great Lee Roy Jordan.

Lowe went to the library to look up information about the legendary Jordan, who was still playing for the Dallas Cowboys at the time. As he read about Lee Roy's accomplishments, a slow smile crept across his face.

The compliments kept coming. During the LSU game his freshman year, Coach Bryant sent Lowe in the game to turn up the heat on Tigers' quarterback Bert Jones. After he made a particularly stunning interception, Lowe jogged back to the sideline and got a pat on the back and a "Good job," from Bryant.

"Coach Dye came up to me," Lowe said in *Game of My Life*. "He had a big smile on his face, and he winked at me. That's when I knew I was doing what they wanted me to do."

Things only got better for Lowe, who was named team captain during his all-American sophomore year of 1973. He finished the year with 86 tackles and 48 assists. He and his defensive teammates gave up only eight points per game, and the Crimson Tide finished 11-0 and brought the national championship home to Tuscaloosa.

In the spring of 1974, Lowe approached Coach Bryant to ask the coach for permission to get married.

Coach Bryant told Lowe to think about it and come back and see him in a couple of weeks. He did. That time Bryant gave him his blessing, and Lowe and Linda Jean Wilson were married before the start of the 1974 season.

The Lowes' daughter, Briana (who along with her sister, Adrienne, and brother, Woodrow Jr., is a graduate of the University of Alabama), once asked her mother what would have happened if Coach Bryant had said no. "She said we would have had a different daddy!" Briana laughed.

Lowe faced major challenges his junior year. He was plagued by injuries and struggled financially when his new wife got sick. A deeply religious man, he began to wonder if playing football was the best way to honor his faith. He pondered quitting the team, but his coaches convinced him to stay.

Lowe credits Coach Paul Crane (an all-American player for Alabama from 1963 to 1965) with helping him stay the course.

"He helped me realize that football wasn't the most important thing in the world and that life was going to continue and the sun was still going to shine," Lowe said.

The Reverend Sylvester Croom, a Tuscaloosa Baptist minister and father of the great Alabama player of the same name, also helped convince Lowe not to quit football.

"I told him he could be an athlete and still preach," Croom said. "It would be an opportunity for him to be on national TV and testify for God because a lot of kids would look up to him."

In 1975, the Alabama defense was the best in the nation, giving up just six points per game. They finished the season 11-1 and as SEC champs.

Lowe's final game as a Crimson Tide player was perhaps his most memorable. He led the team with thirteen tackles against Penn State and was named most valuable defensive player in the 13-6 Alabama victory. But what he remembers most is the rocky pregame start.

Everyone who ever played for (or worked for or was acquainted with) Coach Bryant knows that he did not tolerate tardiness.

If you were five minutes early to a meeting with Coach Bryant, according to him, you were fifteen minutes late.

So, the day of the Sugar Bowl, the Alabama team was in New Orleans, excited to be on their way to the brand new Superdome. Lowe was standing in line at the hotel, waiting to pay for his incidentals. The line was moving slowly but the Alabama team bus was not—to his horror, he saw the bus rolling out of the parking lot without him.

"I knew the bill wasn't very much," he said in *What It Means to Be Crimson Tide,* "but I had a twenty-dollar bill in my hand and just gave it to the cashier with my key and took off running. Some of the players and coaches saw me and I could see they were laughing. I thought I would be in trouble, but I knew I would be in more trouble if I was late getting to the stadium. I just kept running.

"I was wearing my crimson blazer and a tie and felt like O. J. Simpson running through the airport in that television commercial that was popular at the time. Except I was running through the streets of New Orleans trying to catch the team bus. The bus would stop for a light, but just as I thought I might get to it, the light would change, and off it would go again."

Luckily for Lowe, the hotel wasn't that far from the Superdome and running a mile—even in a coat and tie—was not a challenge for a three-time all-American linebacker. He met the bus in the parking lot and casually blended in with the team, even if he was a bit sweaty and out of breath

After his superb college career, the NFL beckoned. Teams were impressed by Lowe's abilities, but as had been the case four years earlier, some were concerned about his relatively small size.

When the San Diego Chargers drafted Lowe in the fifth round in 1976, Coach Bryant told reporters, "That's like getting a fifty-dollar gold piece for fifty cents."

Without a doubt, the Chargers made an excellent bargain. Lowe played his entire twelve-year career in San Diego. He played and started more games for the Chargers (164 out of a possible 180) than any defensive player in club history. His Chargers teams won the AFC West Championships in 1979, '80 and '81. In 1981, he earned all-AFC honors and was a Pro Bowl pick. In 2000, he was named to the Chargers Fortieth Anniversary All-Time Team.

As a player, he is best described as the strong, silent type.

In 1984, a *San Diego Union* story described him as "a ten-watt bulb in a sea of klieg lights." The same story also said, "Woodrow Lowe just plays. Better yet, he burns."

Lowe always preferred to let his playing speak for itself. As Chuck Weber, who was linebackers coach for the Chargers at the time said, "Woody's a guy who doesn't make noise with his mouth, but with his pads."

He was an incredibly self-motivated person who learned from Coach Bryant that success belongs to the person who wants it the most—a lesson that, as a coach, he strives to pass on to his own players.

After he retired from the NFL, Lowe found his niche teaching young players. He coached for two years at Russell County High in Seale, Alabama, then moved to his alma mater, Central High in Phenix City. His team won the state title in 1992.

Next, he spent six seasons as a defensive assistant in the National Football League, first for the Kansas City Chiefs (1995–98) then with the Oakland Raiders (1999–00). In 2001, he returned home to Alabama to join the coaching staff at the University of Alabama at Birmingham, where he played many roles, including special teams coordinator and tight ends coach.

Once again, Lowe is close to home. In 2005, he accepted a position as head coach and athletic director at Smiths Station High School in Smith, Alabama.

Lowe's youngest son, Benjamin, plans to follow his older siblings and his Uncle Eddie (who played linebacker for the Crimson Tide from 1980 to 1982) to the University of Alabama in 2009.

Benjamin will hit campus in a very different era from the ground-breaking years of the early seventies, when his dad came to Tuscaloosa as one of only six black players in his freshman class.

College students today would benefit from the advice Coach Bryant gave Woodrow Lowe on his first day of school in 1972. "He told me to just do my best and be a good person," Lowe remembered. "He said if I did that, everything would be OK, and he was right. Some of the times I had there [at Alabama] where hard, but Coach Bryant set an example for me and pulled me through."

MARTY LYONS

"A winner in the game of life is a person who gives of themselves so others can grow."

— PAUL W. "BEAR" BRYANT

IN THE HISTORY OF ALABAMA FOOTBALL, THERE ARE A COUPLE OF really famous three-word phrases. One of them? "You'd better pass." The other? "Goal line stand." And the first is forever linked with the last.

On New Year's Day in 1979, number-one ranked Penn State and number-two ranked Alabama played in a Sugar Bowl game that would decide the national championship.

As seventy-eight thousand fans watched the thrilling game wind down, Alabama was ahead 14-7. Then the Nittany Lions drove all the way down the field to inside the Alabama ten yard line. Three more plays followed and Penn State was inches from scoring.

During a timeout, Penn State quarterback Chuck Fusina and Alabama defensive tackle Marty Lyons were standing near the ball when Fusina asked, "Marty, what do you think we ought to do?"

Lyons' answer? "You'd better pass."

Lyons swears he wasn't trash-talking. In fact, he and Fusina had met and become friendly a few weeks earlier when both were introduced as all-Americans on *The Bob Hope Show.*

He was sincere. And like the rest of the Tide players, he was confident.

Fusina didn't listen to Lyons. He called a run up the middle that was stopped cold by Alabama defenders, including Barry Krauss, Lyons' best friend. When the play was over, a stunned Krauss lay under the pile of bodies not knowing the outcome of the play.

"I picked Barry up off the ground," Lyons said. "First I wanted to make sure he was okay. Then I said, 'You know what? We finally did it! We won the National Championship.'"

Lyons grew up in Saint Petersburg, Florida, the fifth of seven kids. He was all-state in football, basketball, and baseball at Catholic High School. Even though the New York Mets expressed interest in Lyons, who struck out twenty-three players at the state baseball semifinals when he was a senior, football won the day. He had the opportunity to attend several colleges. Alabama was his first choice, because of the tradition and because of Coach Bryant, but the feeling wasn't completely mutual. The staff and team didn't exactly hit Lyons with the hard sell.

Photograph courtesy of Paul W. Bryant Museum/The University of Alabama

Marty Lyons: No excuses

"Alabama was my worst recruiting trip," Lyons laughed. "Dewey Mitchell and Rich Wingo were freshmen then, and they were supposed to pick me up. They never showed up! So I went to bed after the game. I never went out or saw the town. The next day I went over to meet Coach Bryant. He was completely different than coaches at other schools who told me if you come here you can start. Coach Bryant said, 'Son, we'd like to have you come play here. If you're good enough to play, the opportunity will be here.' Cut and dry!"

Nonetheless, Lyons was sold. He knew Alabama won games, so when he got there he figured Coach Bryant would insist that football always came first. He was stunned to learn that was not the case.

"All the coaches would stand up in front of you and tell you there were four things they wanted us to accomplish while we were there," Lyons said. "'1) Be proud of your family. 2) Be proud of your religion. 3) Get an education, and (if we have time), 4) Win some football games.'

"That was the biggest thing Coach Bryant did for us—teach us to prioritize our lives."

During his sophomore year, Lyons got another lesson in setting priorities. He went in to talk to Coach Bryant about playing baseball during the spring.

"That was part of my pitch to him when I signed," Lyons said. "I was a good baseball player in high school and wanted to play in college. He said, 'Yes. You have my permission. But if I can give you a little bit of advice, before you try to be good at two sports, try to be good at one and make sure it's the one you're on scholarship for.' That was the end of my baseball."

Lyons made football his one and only sport and excelled as a nonflashy, hard-working, solid, fundamental defensive ballplayer. He finished his college career with a long list of honors, such as being named all-SEC ('77 and '78) and all-American ('78), as well being named as his team's defensive captain. After a fantastic performance in the Senior Bowl, he was named "Most Valuable Defensive Lineman for the South." Perhaps the most thrilling honor of all was when his team won the national championship and Coach Bryant told a reporter, "Marty was our best player. We couldn't have won without him."

Years later, Lyons was named to Alabama's Team of the Century and the Team of the Decade for the seventies, and he was inducted into the Alabama Sports Hall of Fame. In 1979, he was drafted in the first round by the New York Jets, where he played his entire twelve-year NFL career.

Before his rookie year (and several years to follow), Lyons was surprised

Photograph by Ronald C. Modra. Used by permission.

A Jet all the way

and pleased to receive a telegram from Coach Bryant saying, "Show your class, stay healthy, best of luck in your upcoming season."

Lyons' pro career was off to a roaring start. In the early eighties, he became part of the famed "New York Sack Exchange," a group of Jets defensive lineman including himself, Abdul Salaam, Mark Gastineau, and Joe Klecko, who became famous for putting opposing quarterbacks on their backs.

During their heyday, the Sack Exchange was featured in *Sports Illustrated.* As part of the photo shoot for the story, the players posed on the floor of the New York Stock Exchange and later dined at The Palm in Manhattan, where each player ordered several steaks and an entire lobster (or two). When the bill for $992 arrived, the players noted that if they had been a little more diligent, they could have put the bill over a thousand. Lyons volunteered to order a bottle of wine "to go" in order to put it over the top.

On a more serious note, Lyons became well-known while playing in the NFL as an incredibly charitable guy. He gave generously of his time and money to many causes, including the New York Leukemia Society, Special Olympics, and the NY Alcohol and Drug Abuse Program. Then, in 1982, Lyons experienced a series of events that completely changed his life.

"My son Rocky was born on March 4, then my dad died on March 8,"

Lyons remembered. "Then on March 10, a little boy named Keith who I was mentoring through the Big Brother program died of leukemia."

Hurting from the loss of his father and his young friend Keith, but grateful for the birth of his healthy son, Lyons became inspired to start a program for terminally ill children, the Marty Lyons Foundation. Part of the inspiration for the project came from his ex-college coach.

"After I got drafted by the Jets, I went back to see Coach Bryant," Lyons said. "I told him, 'Coach, I really want to thank you for the education and the opportunity that you gave me.'

"He said, 'Ya know, Marty. You're very fortunate. You're going to be able to play a game you love and build financial security for your family. The one thing I tried to do for all my players is prepare them for the game of life. Remember this—a winner in the game of life is a person who gives of themselves so others can grow.'"

Lyons says that at the time, the advice went in one ear and out the other. But that week in the spring of '82, it hit home. So, funded by money from Lyons' speaking engagements, his foundation opened its doors and began granting wishes, including trips to Disney World, a pool filled entirely with spring water, and special renovations so a child could be cared for at home. As of their twenty-fifth anniversary in 2007, the organization was operating in ten states with an annual budget of nearly $1 million, and it has served more than four thousand kids and their families.

"The thing that is so inspiring to me is that these kids never complain," Lyons said. "Probably 60 to 65 percent of the children we work with will probably not live to see the age of eighteen. And they never ask, 'Why me?'"

Lyons has been recognized for his charitable efforts many times. In 1984, he won the NFL's prestigious Man of the Year Award, now named after Walter Payton. The New York Jets Outstanding Community Service Award has been renamed the Marty Lyons Award. And Lyons, who retired from pro football in 1989, continues to work with the foundation every day.

"One thing you have to realize is, you never know what you might say or do to change someone's life," Lyons said. "And you don't have to be a football player to change someone's life."

After he hung up his helmet, Lyons went back to school to earn his securities licenses. He worked for Paine Webber from 1994 to 1999. He also got involved in television and radio broadcasting for the Jets. Although he did television for ten years, he has settled into radio as the Jets' color man. He does a great job in a very competitive market. Part of the reason for his success? As a lineman, he had to know everybody's assignments on the field, so that gives him some excellent insight into the game. Plus, he's just good at it.

"I've been fortunate that when I got into broadcasting I learned from some of the better people in New York," Lyons said. "One of the guys I got very close to was Al Trautwig who did a lot of work for NBC. The best advice he gave me regarding radio was to pretend like you're talking to a blind man. You have to paint the picture."

According to Lyons, it's easier and more enjoyable to paint the picture when the team is winning.

"If they're playing well, it's easy to do," he said. "If they're 4-12, it's a little tougher."

After leaving Paine Webber in 1999, Lyons became director of marketing and sales for Landtek, a New York-based construction company that designs and builds athletic fields. The biggest growth area for the company has been the field turf product.

"It's probably the number-one synthetic grass in the world," Lyons said. "It's especially popular up here in the northeast where you can't keep and maintain grass."

Lyons and his wife Christine also frequent many athletic fields near their Smithtown (Long Island), home in a nonofficial capacity. His sons Jesse and Luke play soccer and lacrosse, and his daughter Megan, a gymnast, also runs cross-country.

"I love to watch the kids compete," Lyons said. "I try to be one of those silent observers. I'm not a screamer."

And after the game?

"If they win or lose, hopefully they played their best and had fun," he said. "And if they could have played a little better, I just want them to be honest and hold themselves accountable. No excuses."

Photography courtesy of Marty Lyons

Parties aplenty for Marty's kids and volunteers

Although he also put in time on the playing fields of Long Island, Lyons' oldest son Rocky is now a medical student at University of Alabama Birmingham.

"I'm extremely proud of everything he has accomplished," said Lyons. "I think he has a great future because he has planned out everything."

Sounds like someone who has his priorities straight.

To this day, Lyons strives to live by the four-part credo (family, faith, education, football) that Coach Bryant taught, only these days he substitutes "career" for football.

"We can all make more money," said Lyons. "We can't make more time. So the time we have for our families and friends is precious time. Use it wisely."

Lyons is grateful for the time he spent with Coach Bryant, who started out as his teacher and became his friend.

"I've never been sadder than the day I learned of Coach Bryant's death," remembered Lyons. "I cried like a baby. No one made more of an impact on me except for my own father."

GAYLON McCOLLOUGH

"Coach Bryant taught us a way of life."
— DR. GAYLON MCCOLLOUGH

BACK WHEN THE RENOWNED PLASTIC SURGEON AND FORMER CRIMSON Tide Academic all-American Gaylon McCollough was a high school senior, in 1961, he faced a choice. As a star center and linebacker from Enterprise High's state championship football team, he was being recruited by several great schools, including Georgia Tech and Alabama.

At first, Georgia Tech had the edge because it had an architectural program, and Alabama did not. But then Coach Bryant came to Enterprise for a visit and promised McCollough if he came to Alabama, he would leave with a national championship ring.

"That was some kind of experience for an eighteen-year-old boy," he said.

So, considering the fact that Alabama had an excellent pre-med curriculum, and McCollough's second choice was to study medicine, he went for Plan B. And sometimes, Plan B turns out to be a very good thing.

During his second year of medical school at the University of Alabama School of Medicine in Birmingham, McCollough found a way for his love for architecture and medicine to coexist.

"A plastic surgeon came to our class to give a lecture, and he showed us a number of before and after photographs of faces," he said. "It was like turning on a light in a dark room. I realized at that moment that the field of plastic surgery was architectural medicine. It gave me an opportunity to merge a career path that I had chosen with one that I had turned away from."

It all made sense to McCollough, who as a little boy used to draw faces of famous people he'd seen in the encyclopedia. He finished medical school in 1969, then got busy with his residency training in general surgery and otolaryngology (head and neck surgery).

One of the jobs he had while working his way through med school was medical director for a group of nursing homes.

"During that time, I saw the physical components of aging," McCollough said. "I saw the psychological components. I saw the social and the financial aspects of the aging process. I said to myself, *If I'm ever in a position to do anything about this, I want to do it.*"

In 1974, he opened The McCollough Plastic Surgery Clinic in Birmingham, which grew and expanded over the years. Dr. McCollough's reputation as a teacher also grew, as he taught seminars around the world and wrote three major textbooks on facial and nasal plastic surgery. (He has also written three nonmedical books to date, including a book about his playing days, *On the Shoulders of Giants.* Another book, *Let Us Make Men,* is due out in 2007.)

Over the years, he continued to add to his impressive résumé as president of the American Association of Cosmetic Surgeons (1980), the American Academy of Facial Plastic and Reconstructive Surgery, Inc. (1986), and the American Board of Facial Plastic and Reconstructive Surgery (1989). Then in the late nineties, McCollough sold his clinic and briefly attempted semi-retirement.

"I went to a two-and-a-half-day work week," he said. "I played a lot of golf, saw a lot of movies, read a lot of books, and took a lot of trips. Then after about six months, I realized the happiest days of the week were the days I went to work."

So McCollough and his wife, Susan (a former Miss Alabama who he met and married while still in college), decided to relocate to Gulf Shores. (Their son Sted and daughter Chanee and their families also live in the area.) Then, they built a new clinic that turned out to be much more than they initially intended.

Photograph courtesy of Dr. Gaylon McCollough

Gaylon McCollough in his pre-doctoring days

The result is the thirty-two-thousand-square-foot McCollough Institute, a personal enhancement center located in Craft Farms Coastal Golf Resort. The institute houses the new McCollough Plastic Surgery Clinic as well as a medical spa. Also, McCollough has been able to realize his early dream by incorporating many other age-management services into his business, including wellness, disease prevention, fitness, and nutritional programs.

"I'm trying to establish a model for a private healthcare system," McCollough said. "That's our future. I believe we're going to see a small private healthcare system built up that will be focused primarily upon prevention of disease and early detection of disease and wellness programs rather than focus so much on the illness and disease processes."

Like many athletes who played for Bear Bryant, McCollough learned many things from his coach that he carried with him long after his playing days.

"Hardly a day goes by that I don't reflect back on something Coach Bryant said during certain incidents or situations," he said. "I have patterned my organization very much after the way he patterned his organization; the athletic department. I use a lot of the same principles he used. And although I'm doing

Doctor Gaylon McCollough

Photograph courtesy of Dr. Gaylon McCollough

a different thing, I have a staff like he had a staff. The difference is our product is turning out happy patients, and his product was turning out winning football teams."

McCollough was a valuable lineman on several of Coach Bryant's most memorable winning teams, including the national championship team of 1964. Playing center, he was primarily responsible for snapping the ball to Joe Namath and Steve Sloan. When he talks about either of these great quarterbacks, he chooses a common adjective: smart.

"Steve was smart," McCollough said. "He knew the right plays to call. He knew when to switch to another play. He could get the job done. The team had a lot of confidence in Steve. He is one of the finest human beings you will ever meet. He is a very, very nice man but a tough competitor."

And Joe?

"When he came on campus, within a week or so he was running the Alabama offense as effectively as some of the quarterbacks that had been there a lot longer. You have to be smart to learn that much in a short period of time."

McCollough was part of one of the most famous games—and plays—in Alabama history. The 1965 Orange Bowl, which capped off the stellar 1964 national championship season, ultimately resulted in the Crimson Tide's only loss that year, when Texas squeaked by Alabama, winning the game 21-17.

Alabama was down 21-7 at the half, but Namath came off the bench and led the Tide back to within four points of Texas as the clock wound down.

Then, with seconds remaining, it was fourth down and inches to go. Namath called a sneak and dove over the line.

As McCollough remembered: "Joe was lying right on top of me. I was in the end zone and Joe was in the end zone, too. We all jumped up and down and started celebrating."

One official called touchdown. Another one said no. They conferred and called the game for Texas.

Namath said (and has said many times since), "I'll go to my grave knowing I scored."

McCollough was standing near the coach when another player walked by and mumbled, "We scored."

He saw Coach Bryant shake his head and tell the player, "If he'd walked into the end zone with a football, then there'd be no question about it, would there?"

The message was not lost on McCollough. "I think the lesson was, that if you want to accomplish something in life, don't do just enough to get by. The world's referees might rule against you."

As football fans everywhere know, Joe got over the loss. After that game he went on to become the highest paid and one of the most memorable pro football players in history.

When he graduated, McCollough was drafted by the Dallas Cowboys. This was a dream come true, to play for America's Team. But he was conflicted because he was also anxious to begin medical school. "It was one of the most difficult decisions I've ever had to make," McCollough remembered. "Frankly, I needed the money. The bonus money alone would have financed my entire education."

Like many other players who came before and after him, he sought out Coach Bryant for advice.

"Coach Bryant said, 'If you could do without football, you'll have a good career. You'll have your health. You'll have all your limbs. If you could do without it, put it aside and go on and get your medical degree.'"

So, he did.

"I thought a lot of days that I wish that I had at least gone out there and tried it," McCollough said. "I walked away from it, and though I regretted it for a while, later on I saw some of my teammates [who had gone on to pro ball] were looking for something to retire to and some of them had to play longer than they wanted to. And my career was taking off in the medical field, so I realized then I had made the right decision."

One man who was glad McCollough had gone straight into medicine was Coach Bryant.

"The last ten years of his life we became very close," said McCollough. "He had a lot of health problems late in life and confided in me a great deal."

McCollough even frequently served as Coach Bryant's medical liaison, getting him in the back door to see his doctors so he could have some privacy from the press. Then, incredibly, McCollough actually became his doctor when he performed a face-lift on the most famous of coaches.

"I would never have told anyone about it, but he told everybody!" said McCollough. "I was so honored that Coach Bryant would entrust his life and his face in my hands. It was the biggest compliment I ever received from a person that I thought was bigger than life. To ask me to do something for him of that magnitude was just humbling."

Something that might surprise people about Coach Bryant, who was known to be a "my way or the highway" kind of guy: "He was a model patient," McCollough said. "He really was! I never had anybody I ever took care of who was more compliant with instructions and doing things right by the book. He was very motivated. He wanted to hurry up and get back to his routine."

And his routine, of course, was all about football. But in 1982, he decided to retire. When he confided in McCollough regarding his decision, he tried to talk him out of it.

"I told him to at least stay on as athletic director," said McCollough. "Take some heat off the new guy."

McCollough also suggested Coach Bryant teach a class, a leadership seminar, at the University of Alabama, in which he would bring in leaders from other fields to help him inspire new classes of students.

"At first he said, 'What in the world do I have to teach?'" remembered McCollough. "But then he warmed to the idea."

Sadly, Coach Bryant passed away before he could explore the idea further or watch another generation of players come through the Capstone or see all the wonderful things his former players would accomplish after football.

"He was the toughest man I'd ever known," said McCollough. "When he died, I felt like I lost my best friend."

DON MCNEAL

"Dreams do come true."
— DON MCNEAL

DON MCNEAL IS SITTING BEHIND HIS DESK IN THE EXECUTIVE offices of the New Testament Baptist Church in Miami, Florida, where he is a pastor and youth minister. He is surrounded by football memorabilia (a poster commemorating Coach Bryant's 315th win, Superbowl swag) from his days as a defensive back for the Crimson Tide and Miami Dolphins. He seems peaceful and extremely content as he gestures to the photos of great moments on the football field and happy times with friends and family.

"Dreams do come true," he says with a smile. "They absolutely do."

McNeal is living proof.

Tide fans probably remember him best for his tremendous play that preceded the famous Goal Line Stand during the Sugar Bowl of 1979. In fact, were it not for Don McNeal, there would be no Goal Line Stand.

Alabama was leading Penn State, 14-7, in the fourth quarter when the

Photograph by Ronald C. Modra. Used by permission.

Reverend Don in his Miami office

Tide fumbled. Bama fans held their collective breath as the Nittany Lions drove toward the goal line. On second down, McNeal was covering his man in the end zone when out of the corner of his eye, he saw Penn State quarterback Chuck Fusina throw the ball. McNeal reacted, ran toward the receiver, and knocked him out of bounds.

Barry Krauss, who had the starring role in the play that slammed the game home said in his book, "The play by Don McNeal was the best play by a defensive back I have ever seen."

McNeal picks up the story: "I remember my roommate Curtis McGriff came and picked me up, saying, 'Mac! That was a great play, man!' But I was just playing football. Doing what comes natural. We were prepared. Coach Bryant and [defensive] Coach Oliver made sure of that."

On the next two plays the Tide held the Nittany Lions on third and goal and then fourth and inches to clinch the victory and the 1978 National Championship. In 1979, McNeal's senior year, the Tide again took the national title.

According to McNeal, the 1979 Crimson Tide was such a fantastic team that they made winning look easy. There weren't as many dramatic plays that year because there simply wasn't the need for them.

As much as McNeal appreciates the memories of playing for two national championship teams, it was being voted captain of the team his senior year that means the most to him.

"I cherish that more than anything else because my teammates elected me," he said. "Even though I wasn't exactly a vocal guy, my teammates told me I was a leader. It was a great feeling to get that honor."

McNeal's fellow players could spot a winner. But for McNeal, the opportunity to put his hands and feet in the cement (alongside all the captains of past Crimson Tide teams) in front of Denny Chimes was a hard-fought prize.

Don McNeal grew up on a five-acre farm in Atmore, Alabama. He was the ninth of eleven children: six girls and five boys. When he was six years old, his mother died suddenly of a brain hemorrhage.

Photograph courtesy of Paul W. Bryant Museum/The University of Alabama

McNeal made interceptions look easy.

As devastating as that was, it could have been more so had his father, Henry McNeal, split up the family and sent his children away. But he didn't.

"My father kept us all together," McNeal said. "I don't know how he did it."

McNeal says his father was extremely strict. In fact, when McNeal was young he thought his father was "the meanest person in the world." He also says he came to understand why his father was such a tough disciplinarian.

"He wanted us to stay in line," McNeal said. "Today, my brothers and sisters and I are all happy, in the church, living for God, and trying to do the right thing. Because of him."

McNeal's father, who passed away in 1985, never remarried. McNeal asked him about this once. "He said he didn't know how the next lady would treat his kids," McNeal remembered. "That says a lot about him. Every time I talk about this, I realize he's my role model."

Even though he was a natural athlete, McNeal didn't play football until his junior year. That's when a high school coach encouraged him to try out for the team. His father wasn't too keen on the idea, but he finally relented when McNeal promised to do his chores after practice and that he would even skip practices if he was needed to help on the farm.

After navigating an awkward start (at his first practice, McNeal put his thigh pads in backwards and his helmet slid around on his head, causing his ears to bleed. Who knew a guy needed ear pads?), McNeal quickly got the hang of the game. He was an instant gridiron success and was eventually named MVP after contributing to Escambia County High School's 3A championship in 1974.

After that, his dad was more open-minded about this football thing when he realized his youngest son could get a college scholarship. Almost all the SEC schools recruited McNeal. But he was an Alabama kid, so there was always one coach who had the edge. His senior year, McNeal got the call.

"I remember it like it was yesterday," McNeal said. "We didn't have a phone, but our neighbor did. So, he comes running, 'Don McNeal! You have a telephone call from Coach Bear Bryant!'"

The deal was done. McNeal played four years at Alabama, finishing his college career as an all-American and all-SEC cornerback who played on two national championship teams and three SEC title teams.

The spring of his senior year, the Miami Dolphins came calling. (This time, McNeal had a phone.) He became the first-ever defensive back to be drafted by the Dolphins in the first round.

McNeal went on to play nine years, his entire pro career, for Coach Don Shula in Miami. He played in two Super Bowls (1983 and 1985) and was twice named Dolphins Player of the Year. Coach Shula, who much like Coach Bryant, finds his name forever attached to the word "winningest," made a strong impression on McNeal.

"He told me to put my best foot forward and always be prepared," McNeal said. "He said to always know your opponent. We knew our opponents better than we knew ourselves. That way we could anticipate what they're going to do. That carries over in life too."

As in life, sometimes even when you know your opponent inside and out, you might still make a mistake. Unfortunately for McNeal, his famous "miss" came when he let a bulldozing John Riggins (who had some fifty pounds on him) escape his grasp and run into the end zone for the Redskins' winning touchdown against the Dolphins in Super Bowl XVII.

It's a moment McNeal will never forget: "I had to face it. That night a reporter asked me, 'What's Coach Shula going to do to you? You let Miami down.' But Coach Shula told me that people miss plays. My play was just magnified. He said, 'Don't worry about it. We'll come back next year.'"

That's what counts. How we deal with disappointments.

"I tell young people that it never comes down to one play," McNeal said. "I tell them, you're going to make a bad grade in school. Sometimes you're going to fail. What are you going to do? You can't cry over it. If you do, it will dominate you. You've got to find a way to be better for it."

It's easy to behave well when you're on top. But when life is a struggle, that's your chance to show your class.

"Coach Bryant always talked about class," McNeal said. "When bad things happen to you, don't get all flustered. Show your class about it."

Like most Crimson Tide players who played for Paul Bryant, McNeal still felt slightly in awe of him, having a deep respect for his college coach. Even though as team captain he got to spend a little more quality time with his coach than did many of his teammates, he never got over this feeling even when he was a successful NFL player.

Bryant's players put him on a pedestal, figuratively speaking. On the practice field, he literally stood above his players—on his coach's tower, a very imposing structure where only a handful of players ever set foot.

During the NFL players' strike in 1982, McNeal went to Tuscaloosa to visit. He was watching practice one afternoon when Coach Bryant spotted him and hollered down from his tower: "Don McNeal! Come on up here!"

McNeal's first thought was, "Is he talking to me?"

So McNeal scaled the thirty-three steps of the famous tower and watched practice with the coach. Then, to his shock, Coach Bryant invited him to dinner.

"I still can't believe it!" said McNeal. "He sent his driver for me. We ate dinner in his house. I don't know what we ate. Chicken, I think. Mrs. Bryant was there, and he showed me his room. I pinched myself. Did I really do this?"

McNeal's memory is clear, however, about some of things they discussed including the fact that Coach Bryant was instrumental in getting Coach Shula to take a look at him when he was getting ready to graduate.

"He told him I should be high on his radar," McNeal said. "I really appreciated his help with that."

These days it is Don McNeal, or Pastor McNeal, or Reverend Don, who is helping people. He actually has two jobs: one as youth minister at New Testament Baptist Church and another as a motivational speaker for Sports World, an organization committed to keeping at-risk kids across the country on the right path.

Almost every week, McNeal hits the road for Sports World, often joined by other NFL players such as Rich Garza, Lee Rouson, and Herman Weaver, among others. The players speak to small groups of kids or assemblies of up to three thousand students at public schools, churches, and even juvenile detention centers. McNeal's message often surrounds a single theme.

"I talk to them about choices," he said. "I tell them about some of the choices I made and the people who helped me make those choices, like Coach Bear Bryant. I could gravitate to people who make negative choices, but I dare not to. Life is about the right choices. Kids who have made mistakes can recover, although they have to suffer the consequences first. We talk about drugs and alcohol. And sex because of the AIDS situation. I ask them, 'What are you going to do?' You still have to make a choice every day."

McNeal and his wife Rhonda, who works side-by-side with him as New Testament's Special Events Coordinator, have done their best to impart these lessons to their daughter, Jessica, who is studying design and business at the University of Alabama.

"She could have gone anyplace else, but my money's going to Alabama," said her proud dad, who encourages her to pass by Denny Chimes from time to time and dust off his name.

Technically, Jessica and her father are both students, since McNeal is working part-time toward his master's degree in counseling at Trinity College in South Florida.

"It's not easy," he said. "But it's something I really want to do."

Recently, McNeal was presented with perhaps the most difficult test of his life when he was diagnosed with M.S.

"I've given it to God," McNeal said. "I feel great. I don't anticipate anything negative happening to me. I want to be an example. I have M.S. for someone else because God knows I can handle anything that comes my way. It's for me to be a role model for someone who has it and may be having a bad time in life. Don't feel sorry for me. Because I don't."

Don McNeal. The very definition of class.

JOHN MITCHELL

"I don't have any black players.
I don't have any white players.
I only have football players."

—PAUL W. "BEAR" BRYANT

IN JANUARY 1971, COACH BRYANT AND SOUTHERN CAL'S COACH John McKay got together for a drink after playing in the Bob Hope Desert Classic golf tournament in California.

Even though the two men were rivals, they were very good friends. McKay, whose team had badly beaten Alabama the year before, couldn't resist tweaking his colleague by telling him USC was on the verge of signing a big linebacker who had gone to junior college in Arizona but hailed from Bryant's home state. Then McKay made the mistake of saying the player's name: John Mitchell.

Bryant politely excused himself to make a phone call to assistant coach Clem Gryska. His mission? Find Mitchell immediately.

Photograph courtesy of Paul W. Bryant Museum/The University of Alabama

Mitchell was big and fast: a lethal combo.

According to Mitchell, he got a call from a local alumnus, Judge Ferrill McRae, who found him by calling all the "John Mitchells" in the Mobile phone book. (Lucky for McRae, John Mitchell Jr., and his father, John Mitchell Sr., shared the same name.)

The recruiters were dispatched and offered him a scholarship without even seeing him play.

"I guess they thought if Southern Cal was offering me a scholarship, I was qualified to go to Alabama," Mitchell said.

So, despite being excited about playing at USC, and despite the many, many offers on the table from other schools, Mitchell signed with Alabama. It had always been his first choice. But as an African American growing up in Alabama in the sixties, he never dared to dream of actually playing there.

"It was the highlight of my life listening to the Alabama games on the radio and watching them on TV," he said. "They had so much success with Coach Bryant winning those national championships. That's where I felt any high school guy in the state of Alabama would want to go, if he was worth his weight in salt. Whether they were African American or whatever. If they had the opportunity, they would like to go there."

Until 1970, when Alabama awarded its first football scholarship to a black player named Wilbur Jackson, the opportunity did not exist. But the barrier had finally been broken, and Coach Bryant wasn't about to let any more talented black athletes from his home state slip away.

Actually, 1971 was the second time John Mitchell was offered a scholarship to the University of Alabama. During his senior year of high school, he and four of his classmates from Williamson High School won a state science fair. After taking their project—a hovering flying saucer—to the national competition in South Carolina, they were each offered academic scholarships from several schools, including the University of Alabama. But Mitchell wanted to play football, and since Alabama was not yet recruiting black athletes in 1969, he declined the offer.

After two years at Eastern Arizona Junior College, Mitchell had a second chance. As happy as that made him, he couldn't help but feel some trepidation going to a school that just a few years before had to be desegregated under court order. He watched on TV when George Wallace stood in the doorway attempting to keep black students out.

But he was a kid. He was hopeful. And he wanted to play for Bear Bryant.

So, Bobby Jackson, a former Crimson Tide player, drove Mitchell and his parents to Tuscaloosa for a meeting with the coach. Mitchell remembers the conversation word for word.

"He looked me squarely in the face and said, 'If you come here, you're probably going to have some problems. But the one thing that I ask is that you bring the problem to me before you go to the press.'"

Then Mitchell's mother lightened the mood.

"In the middle of the conversation she asked him, 'What's your name again?' My mama never knew anything about football. His name meant nothing to her, and there had been a lot of coaches in and out of our house. So he laughed and said, 'I'm Coach Paul Bear Bryant, ma'am.' That kind of broke the ice!"

Bryant's assurances meant a lot to the Mitchells. Mitchell kept his word and never went to the press with any problems. He didn't go to Coach Bryant either. Mostly, because according to Mitchell, none came up.

Mitchell and his roommate, Bobby Stanford, a white player from Albany, Georgia, set a precedent when they became the first black-white roommates at Alabama.

"We were really good friends," Mitchell said. "We still are. He was in my wedding. He's been up to see me in Pittsburgh. Back at school his parents would come to visit. If they brought him something, they would bring me something too. When his mom kissed him good-bye, she'd kiss me too!"

Mitchell, who was elected co-captain by his teammates in 1972, obviously made a lot of other friends on the team.

"Athletics opened a lot of doors for people to see who you really are and what you could be," he said. "When you interact with others, it changes attitudes. I had never gone to a school with any whites because the high school I went to was all African American. And there were a lot of white kids who had never interacted with African Americans because their school was all white. So it was breaking ground for both me and them. But I figured if those guys could help Alabama win some ball games, they could be a friend of mine, and I hope they felt the same way about me."

Since Wilbur Jackson was a freshman and not yet eligible to play varsity, Mitchell became the first African American to play for the Crimson Tide. The milestone was enormous, but as Mitchell remembers it, he wasn't thinking about making history. He was thinking about making his family proud.

"My family never had a chance to see me play when I was in Arizona," he said. "But my mom never missed a game in my two years at Alabama. When you get to walk out of the dressing room and see your mother and father, your sisters and brother, that was the greatest feeling. No matter how I played, I knew they loved me no matter what."

As it turned out, the Mitchells had plenty to cheer from the start. Mitchell's first game (ironically, against USC) was a huge victory for the Crimson Tide, when they unveiled their new, top-secret wishbone offense and avenged the previous season's loss, 17-10.

"I can still remember when we recovered a fumble late in the game to clinch the victory," he said. "That was about as happy as I've ever been."

According to Mitchell, some of his best memories as a player were created the following season, in the 1972 match-up against Tennessee.

The Vols were leading 10-0 at the half. It was a subdued locker room when Coach Bryant entered. Instead of hollering, as many players expected him to do, he simply said, "Get those frowns off. You're Alabama. They have to beat you."

The Crimson Tide came back in the second half to tie the game with just a minute or so to go. Then, Mike Dubose knocked the ball loose and Mitchell recovered the fumble. Terry Davis scored and Alabama won it, 17-10.

Photograph courtesy of Paul W. Bryant Museum/The University of Alabama

Mitchell made a successful switch from player to coach.

The Crimson Tide finished the 1972 season as SEC champs. Mitchell, a two-time all-SEC player, was named all-American. He was then drafted into the NFL by the San Francisco 49ers, only to be released on the final cut. He returned home to Mobile, planning to return to the university to enroll in graduate school. But first, he needed a part-time job to help pay for it. He called Coach Bryant.

"He said he wouldn't talk to me over the phone, so I drove up to Tuscaloosa on a Wednesday morning," Mitchell remembered. "I get there and he's sitting behind his desk. He's got his glasses on his nose and never looks up. He says, 'I'm going to offer you a full-time position on my staff. Are you going to take it?' What am I going to say? No? I didn't even have time to think about it. I said, 'Coach, I'll take it.' He said, 'All right then. Get to work.'"

Mitchell explained to his new boss that he had to go home first. He hadn't even brought a change of clothes with him. Coach Bryant replied, "You're working now. You'll go home this weekend."

So Mitchell was a full-time assistant coach. And his first week, he wore the same clothes to practice every day.

"Coach Bryant gave me a room in the athletic dorm," he said. "Every night I would wash my shirt and pants and hang them up in the dorm room and let them dry. I'd put them on again the next day, all wrinkled, and go to work."

During Mitchell's first season as defensive line coach, the Crimson Tide won the national title.

"I look at that 1973 national championship ring every day," Mitchell said.

He worked for Coach Bryant for four years before joining Coach Lou Holtz's staff in 1977 at Arkansas, where he spent six years coaching the

Photograph by Michael Fabus, Pittsburgh Steelers team photographer. Used by permission.

Mitchell tells his pros: "I'd rather die than quit."

defensive line. In 1983, Mitchell went to the pros as defensive line coach for the USFL's Birmingham Stallions. In 1986, he returned to coaching college players at Temple.

In 1987, Mitchell began a four-year run as linebackers coach at LSU. In 1990, he made history (again) when he was named LSU's defensive coordinator, the first African American to hold such a position in the SEC.

From 1991 to 1993, he coached the defensive line for the Cleveland Browns.

Then, in 1994, he joined the staff of the Pittsburgh Steelers, where he has been defensive line coach ever since.

"The fans in Pittsburgh are pretty similar to Alabama fans," he said. "They're crazy! They follow the team everywhere. When we play on the road, we'll sometimes have just as many fans as the home team."

Since Mitchell has been with the Steelers, the team has twice made it to the top. They played in Super Bowl XXX in 1996, where Dallas won, 27-17, and in Super Bowl XL in 2006, where the Steelers beat Seattle, 21-10.

"One of the worst defeats of your career is when you lose the Super Bowl," he said. "But when you win, it's the most incredible feeling you will ever have. When the last second ticks off the clock and they put 'World Champion' on that ring, you will never forget it."

Over the years, Steelers players have heard a lot about John Mitchell's college coach.

"They probably know more about Coach Bryant than I do because I've told them almost every story about him and about all the things he taught me," said Mitchell. "When I went to Alabama, I was a little nineteen-year-old kid that didn't know anything. Coach Bryant made me grow up to accept responsibility. He told me once when I was struggling and thinking about quitting, 'If you quit this time, you won't even think about it the second time.' That has stayed with me to this day, and I never think about quitting anything. I'd rather die than quit, and I tell the players I coach the same thing.

"He showed me how to compete. He showed me what hard work is. He showed me what dedication means. I want my players to be dedicated. They've got to be disciplined. There are some things they can't do because they're professional football players. They've got to work hard at their craft. I stress that every day."

John Mitchell plans to continue working hard and hopes to return to one more Super Bowl, before retiring to Birmingham with his wife, Joyce, in five or six years. He says he will have no problem shifting from the demanding life of a coach to the kinder, gentler days of an ex-coach and player.

"There are so many things I want to do," he said. "I like to jog. I'm a big-time reader. I'm a wine collector. And I collect European and African American art."

Much like other ex–Crimson Tide players, Mitchell also collects memories.

One of his fondest came a year or two before Coach Bryant passed away.

After Arkansas played in the Cotton Bowl, Mitchell drove down to Tuscaloosa to see him.

"We were in his office and he says, 'It's time to go to practice. Come walk out there on the field with me.' We walk out on the practice field and I said, 'Coach, I know you have a lot of things to do, so I'm going back.' Then he said, 'Come on, walk up here on the tower with me.'"

As ex-players know well, only a handful of people were ever invited up to Coach Bryant's practice tower.

"I had to turn away from him because tears were falling down my eyes," Mitchell said. "I said, *Hey, this is the highlight of my life.* I was truly one of Bear's Boys when he invited me to go up there."

MAL MOORE

"We have a great name, the Crimson Tide, and a great tradition, which comes from great success. This kind of tradition is something you can't buy; you have to earn it."

— MAL MOORE

Normally one doesn't see the word "bling" and the name "Mal Moore" in the same sentence. But the guy does have a fantastic collection of jewelry. In fact, if he is still athletics director when Alabama wins its next national title, Mal may have to start wearing national championship rings on his thumbs.

Mal Moore's seven championship rings were awarded as a player (1961), as an assistant for Coach Bryant ('64, '65, '73, '78, and '79), and as an assistant for Coach Gene Stallings (1992). Although he has made coaching stops at Montana State, Notre Dame, and Phoenix (for the NFL's Cardinals), he has spent most of his life playing, coaching, and overseeing football at the University of Alabama. In Moore's role as athletics director, people refer to him as a link to the past and a bridge to the future. And that suits him just fine.

"We have a great name, the Crimson Tide, and a great tradition, which comes from great success," said Mal. "This kind of tradition is something you can't buy; you have to earn it."

Photograph courtesy of Paul W. Bryant Museum/The University of Alabama

Mal Moore began his Alabama career as quarterback.

Dozier, Alabama, native Mal Moore began contributing to the Alabama tradition as a player in 1958, Coach Bryant's first year as head coach at the university. He played quarterback. As a freshman, he had the crucial job of helping prepare the varsity defense for games. He and the other freshmen were especially important to their team that year since the roster was a little thin—many players had quit after being subjected to Coach Bryant's extremely tough brand of practice.

Mal was redshirted in 1960, then played backup to Pat Trammell on the 1961 national championship team. The following season, Mal found himself competing for a starting spot with none other than Joe Willie Namath.

"My claim to fame is when Joe beat me out when I was a senior and he was a sophomore," Mal said. "But I tell people he really had to strain to do it. I brought the best out in him."

After completing his undergraduate degree in sociology, Mal spent a year as an assistant coach at Montana State. He then returned to Alabama to earn a master's degree in secondary education and began his coaching career as a graduate assistant for Coach Bryant. In 1965, he was named defensive backs coach. From the start, players could see he was dedicated and knew his football.

"Mal is a great guy with a great mind," said Dennis Homan, who played for the Crimson Tide from 1965 to 1967. "As a coach, he was very intelligent. He knew what Coach Bryant was trying to do. [Bryant] laid out his plan and his coaches did what he wanted them to do."

In 1971, Mal was named quarterbacks coach. During his first year in this role, which he retained for over a decade, the Crimson Tide switched to a completely new style of offense that was being successfully employed by powerhouses such as Oklahoma and Texas: the wishbone.

Named for the shape in which the backs line up, the wishbone is a formation designed for running and passing on a roll. Basically, it's a triple-option ground offense, where the quarterback looks to both his fullback and his trailing halfback. As Bryant's longtime assistant coach Clem Gryska explained, "The wishbone is a very disciplined offense. Everyone has to know what everyone else is doing. It's about execution."

The summer before the 1971 season, in complete secrecy, Coach Bryant had enlisted his friend, University of Texas head coach Darrell Royal, to teach him the system. Then, again in complete secrecy, Coach Bryant shared what he had learned with his assistants who had only a few weeks to learn it themselves and teach it to the players.

In *Career in Crisis,* Mal tells the story of Coach Bryant breaking the news that the Crimson Tide was going to "sink or swim with the wishbone."

"He told us that we were going to open the season in the Coliseum in Los Angeles against Southern California and we're going to end it at Legion Field in Birmingham against Auburn. We were not going back to our old offense three or four games into the season like others have tried. He gave us no way out. We had no playbooks. We had nobody who had played it and had no one who had been involved in it. There was no resistance to it. He made his decision and we knew what we had to do."

It has often been said that Coach Bryant didn't coach the players. He coached the coaches. It is also well known that one of the keys to Coach Bryant's success was that he hired good people and let them do their jobs.

For a great example of this, imagine Mal and Coach Jimmy Sharpe spending hours breaking down films and cramming to learn the wishbone. When the Crimson Tide unveiled their new offense during the season opener, it was a smash. And today, no one is ever surprised to see the word "wishbone" and the name "Mal Moore" in the same sentence.

Although the wishbone was never considered a passing offense, Alabama's

Photograph courtesy of Paul W. Bryant Museum/The University of Alabama

Mal Moore, the player, shows off his moves.

1970s teams were considered extremely innovative among wishbone teams for exploiting the pass. But, as Mal remembered it in *What Made Him a Winner*, Alabama was taking a lot of heat one particular season for being too conservative on offense. Then the team headed to Jackson to play Ole Miss.

"We took the opening kickoff, ran three plays, and punted," he said. "The Ole Miss offense was on the field, and our offense was at the blackboard looking at the pictures and getting ready to go back onto the field.

"It was a bright, sunny, hot afternoon, about 1:40 PM, and Coach Bryant had his hat pulled down close over his eyes to keep the sun out. He looked out from under his hat and cut his eyes at me and said, 'Now, Mal, I want you to throw one before it gets dark.'

"On the next series, we threw a pass to Bart Krout for about a 50-yard touchdown. I wanted to lean over and ask if that's what he had in mind, but I didn't."

Certainly the Crimson Tide marked its share of successful passes during the wishbone era. But more often than not, it was about blocking and running.

"Coach Bryant would needle me about throwing," Mal remembered. "We didn't throw the ball a lot when we would run the wishbone. He liked misdirection stuff. He thought the wishbone was too much of a flow offense; it was easy for the left-side linebacker. He'd say, 'Mal, we are making an all-American out of every linebacker we play. We need more counter options, misdirection reverses.'

"So, we were playing the University of Houston when the split-back veer was at its height. We would score, they would score. We couldn't ever quite get away from them. They punted in the fourth quarter, dead on just about our eight-yard line. I am trying to get it off the goal line because we can still lose the game. I call a play. Coach Bryant says, 'Gosh, Mal, the backside linebacker made the play; run a reverse.' I'm thinking run a reverse down here; it's either a big play or a big loss, no in-between. We call another play and pop it out ten or fifteen yards, first down. He said, 'The backside linebacker is killing you. Run the reverse.'

"I call another play with another big gain with a fullback. We are out about midfield. It's first and ten. He grabs my arm. I could tell when he meant what he said. We locked eyes. He said, 'Run the reverse.' So I went left, thirty-six, low, wide reverse. We ride that fullback deal back to the wide receiver. Houston's big ol' end was 'give out'; he didn't pursue. You know, he sees it and comes up the field. We lose about fifteen yards. They hit the ground right in front of Coach and me. We were both backing up. Coach Bryant looked at me and said, 'Damn it, I meant the other way!'"

Mal coached a lot of great quarterbacks, including Gary Rutledge, who played on the 1973 national championship team.

"Mal was no-nonsense," Gary said. "He was business-like and tough. He wanted the quarterbacks to be perfect and running the wishbone—it's a very, very intricate offense. You go down the line and pitch it or keep it. We learned by doing it over and over in practice. Mal is a good coach and taught us extremely well. He was the smartest coach I ever played for. By game day, we were prepared."

Richard Todd, who shared quarterbacking duties with Rutledge, said many people don't realize that players spent much more time with their position coaches than they ever did with Coach Bryant.

"Mal was the one I was with all the time," Todd said. "Coach Bryant surrounded himself with great people. The majority of the time, other coaches were running things. Coach Bryant was more like the CEO who managed his company from his tower."

Even though they were a step up the football totem pole from the players, coaches were not immune to the intimidating presence of the boss.

"You tried not to look up in the tower," Mal said. "If a good play happened, you wanted to look to make sure he was watching. But you wouldn't turn your head, you just cut your eyes."

Out of the corner of his eye, Mal caught Coach Bryant dispensing many approving looks over the years. In 1975, he was named offensive coordinator, a post he held until Coach Bryant retired in 1982.

In 1983, Mal accepted a position as offensive coordinator at Notre Dame. After two years there, he moved to the NFL, where he coached receivers for the Phoenix Cardinals. In 1990, when Gene Stallings was named Alabama's new head coach, he brought Mal back as assistant head coach and quarterbacks coach. (See national championship ring No. 7.)

In 1994, Mal moved into administration as associate athletic director for external affairs. Then, in 1999, he was named athletics director, the job that he calls the high point of his career. Just after accepting this position, Mal gave a nod to his famous head coach: "Coach Bryant was successful, in great part, because he had a plan. I have firm concepts and ideas that I am ready to implement for this department."

There have been many ups and downs for the Alabama football program during Mal's reign. But confronting the inevitable challenges of a major university athletic department pales in comparison to the enormous personal struggle the Moore family has endured.

Photograph courtesy of The University of Alabama

Longtime A.D. Mal Moore

In 2001, Mal's wife Charlotte, who suffers from Alzheimer's disease, was moved to an assisted living facility when the challenges of caring for her at home proved too great.

Mal, who has one daughter, Heather, who lives with her husband and two children in Scottsdale, Arizona, tries to focus on the blessings in life.

"We should all be thankful for every day of our lives and for the opportunities that we have," he said.

No one can deny the major contributions Mal has made to the

university. The most significant of these is the Crimson Tradition Fund, a five-year, $150 million facilities and endowment initiative.

"Mal's legacy is going to be all the money he's raised for the university," Richard Todd said. "They've really upgraded all the facilities. It's just incredible. The expansion of the football stadium, the coliseum, plus a million-dollar complex for the men's and women's golf teams. It might be the best one in the country."

As athletics director, Mal has not just put his energy into the revenue-producing football and basketball programs, he also has been a champion of other sports as well. Baseball is on the upswing. Every year the women's softball team goes to the championships. The gymnastics team is always in the NCAA and has won a handful of national titles. In 2006, Alabama added crew to its roster of sports.

Recently, the university saw fit to honor Mal for his good work by re-naming the football building the Mal M. Moore Athletic Facility. After all his contributions to the Crimson Tide tradition over the years, no doubt about it. He has earned it.

JOHNNY MUSSO

"I think I stumbled into a business I was well-suited for."

— JOHNNY MUSSO

SEVERAL YEARS BEFORE SYLVESTER STALLONE FIRST UTTERED THE words, "Yo! Adrian!" Bama fans had their own "Italian Stallion"—hard-charging halfback Johnny Musso. These days, the former Crimson Tide star-turned Chicago Bear-turned commodities broker is so low key and matter of fact about his accomplishments on and off the field that he might be ready for a new nickname. The King of Understatement? Mild-Mannered Musso? Or maybe we'll just stick with the original.

Growing up in Birmingham in the early sixties, Johnny Musso was a fan of the awesome early Bear Bryant Alabama teams. His heroes were players such as Lee Roy Jordan, Pat Trammell, Kenny Stabler, Steve Sloan, and Ray Perkins. When he was eleven years old, he and an older cousin set out to watch Bama play Auburn at Legion Field.

Musso chalks up another great gain.

Since they had no tickets, they decided to scale a fence. The cousin got caught. Young Musso slipped in and even managed a glimpse of the growly coach and his impressive players as they filed off their team bus. Bama won big, and Musso couldn't help dreaming of someday playing football for Bear Bryant at the University of Alabama.

Soon after his first Bear-sighting, Musso started playing YMCA football, and as he puts it, "I was pretty good at it." He went on to become a star on Birmingham's Banks High School football team. When recruiters started hovering, even though fellow-local hero and friend Pat Sullivan signed with Auburn, Musso stuck with his original plan. He was Bama bound.

Musso didn't take long to prove his worth on the Bama playing field. As a sophomore, he led the Tide in scoring (90 points) and rushing (516 yards), was second in receiving (26 catches for 321 yards), and completed the only pass he threw (for 32 yards).

His junior year was even better. In fact, it was fantastic. After piling up 1,137 yards on 226 carries, Musso became the first Alabama player to rush for more than one thousand yards in a single season. (He held the record until Bobby Humphrey, and, later, Shaun Alexander came along and topped the mark.)

Perhaps the biggest thrill for Musso came after the season, when Coach Bryant told reporters: "Johnny is the finest running back I've ever coached. He is better than John David Crow."

(One can only imagine how Crow, a Heisman Trophy winner under Coach Bryant at Texas A&M and at the time the Bama backs coach—Musso's coach—felt about the comment!)

Coach Bryant continued: "Johnny is a great football player, and the thing that doesn't show up in his statistics is the way he blocks. He simply wipes people out."

For all the accolades, the one less-than-impressive stat during the seasons of 1969 and 1970 were the win-loss records for the Crimson Tide. The team went just 6-5 in '69 and 6-5-1 in '70. With the exception of his first year as Bama's head coach, Bryant's Alabama teams had never lost like that.

But according to Musso, there was a simple explanation.

As he told author Keith Dunnavant in his book *Coach*, "We were just outmanned in a lot of our games. There were a lot of teams who had been taking it on the chin from Alabama for a long time, and they ran it up on us when they got a chance."

Everyone, including Coach Bryant, knew that Alabama had to make some changes. At the end of the 1970 season, fans were griping about the losses. Then, word got out that Bryant was in talks to become the new Miami Dolphins head coach. But he declined the pro offer and rededicated himself to bringing Bama back.

Now that the coach was committed, he needed a plan. After watching Oklahoma run the wishbone, a triple-ground offense, very effectively against his team during the 1970 New Year's Eve Bluebonnet Bowl, Coach Bryant became inspired. He liked the wishbone. It was a disciplined offense more about execution than finesse. Very Bear Bryant. So during the plane ride back to Alabama from Houston, Bryant got out his felt-tipped pen and yellow legal pad and worked out the proverbial *X*s and *O*s.

Photograph courtesy of Paul W. Bryant Museum/The University of Alabama

Words of wisdom from the Bear

Then, during the summer before the 1971 season, Coach Bryant went back to school. He visited his friend Darrell Royal, head coach at the University of Texas, who graciously agreed to teach him the wishbone.

Just before the start of fall practice, Bryant let his players in on his plans.

According to author John David Briley, whose book *Career in Crisis* documents the 1971 season, Bryant stood at the chalkboard and presented the wishbone to his team. He then called on Johnny Musso to repeat what he just said. In the book, Coach Bill Oliver explained why: "He knew Johnny was smart, and it would leave a strong impression on the players."

Lucky for Musso, he did in fact repeat the coach's speech almost to the letter.

The players, coaches, and staff were all sworn to secrecy regarding their new battle plan. Alabama would unveil its new offense at the game opener against USC, who had soundly beaten them (42-21) the previous year, and not a moment before.

"It was fun because we kept it stealth," said Musso, who along with his team had to revert to their old offense when the media came to watch practice to keep their game plan under wraps.

The Crimson Tide practiced under a literal shroud of secrecy—a huge curtain—except for the last practice the night before heading out to LA to face USC. There was a pep rally going on next to the practice field, and at the last moment Coach Bryant told his assistants to lift the curtains and let the students in.

"They could see that we were doing something new," said Musso. "They were excited and had the same hope we did."

From the very first play of the USC game—a triple-option right where quarterback Terry Davis chose the final option, a pitch to Musso who ran for seven yards—the wishbone worked. Musso scored on the first drive. He finished the day with sixteen rushes for eighty-five yards, two touchdowns, and the game ball, which he gave to Coach Bryant. (Who coincidentally was marking his 200th win, a 17-10 victory over the Trojans.)

The victory set the tone for a fantastic SEC championship season where The Tide finished 11-1. Musso, a team captain, finished his senior year with an incredible list of stats, gaining 1,088 yards in 1971 on 126 carries, scoring one hundred points and catching five passes for eighty yards.

He rounded out his college career as a two-time all-American, two-time all-SEC, and tied with his childhood friend and Auburn star Pat Sullivan for SEC Player of the Year. He came in fourth in balloting for the Heisman Trophy. (Sullivan won.) Years later, Musso would be named to the Alabama Team of the Century and the College Football Hall of Fame (2000).

Musso's 1971 honors extended to the classroom as well. Majoring in finance, he was named both Academic all-American and National Scholar Athlete.

After college, Musso was drafted by the Chicago Bears, although he instead signed with the British Columbia Lions of the Canadian Football League (CFL). After three seasons, he returned to Alabama and played for the World Football League's (WFL) Birmingham Vulcans.

When the WFL folded, Musso signed with the Chicago Bears and played from 1975 to 1977, rushing for 365 yards and six touchdowns. In 1978, knee injuries forced him onto injured reserve before he ultimately retired from football.

Musso was fully prepared for his next stage of life. While playing football in Chicago, he stayed in town during the off-season and put his financial smarts to work, trading commodity futures at the Board of Trade. Swapping the pigskin for pork bellies seemed to be a natural transition. So, post-football, he bought a seat on the board and traded for the next thirteen years.

"Commodities is one of those things that are directly related to the competitive arena," said Musso. "There's a lot of self-discipline required. A lot of emotional ups and downs like those that athletes go through. You need to have the ability to concentrate on what's important in the middle of a lot of emotion and noise. It's very much like a free-throw shooter trying to concentrate on the rim when there's movement and noise behind the goal. Or the wide receiver trying to hear an audible in the middle of a crowd."

Musso, who became a Bama fan favorite by sheer grit—he was always the player clawing, scraping, and scratching for one more yard—said football was "child's play" compared to the intensity of the commodities game. He also says it's tougher to be a trader because you're on your own and don't have your teammates on which to rely. But looking back, he is exceptionally glad he played for Coach Bryant, an experience he credits with preparing him emotionally for the challenges of the trading pit.

"My relationship with Coach Bryant was extremely positive," Musso said. "But he was not a warm and fuzzy guy with his players. He worked you hard and pushed you hard. He kept a good deal of distance. His motivating style was more an intimidating presence. It took players being away from him and growing up and getting into adulthood for them to truly appreciate him."

Musso grew to appreciate Coach Bryant more and more as the years went by. During the seventies and early eighties, he visited his former coach in Tuscaloosa when he and his wife Tanner made trips down south to see Musso's parents in Birmingham and her parents in Columbus, Mississippi.

"We'd bring the kids through his office, and he'd throw one of those tiny little Alabama footballs he had in his desk around with them," he said. "I cherish that time because I got a chance to sit down and just talk to him. To pick his brain and find out what he was thinking when he did this or that."

Photograph courtesy of Johnny Musso

Johnny Musso, his mother, Josie Musso, and friend, Masaya Hibino (2003)

As we all know, Coach Bryant left this world way too early when he died in 1983.

"He passed away before I got to that age in life when I think I would have been able to talk to him person-to-person rather than looking up at him with my mouth half-open," Musso said. "I would have liked that."

Today, Musso says he is trying to figure out what he's going to do when he grows up. He is still a trader, although not full-time. He is transitioning into being an investor and focusing on private equity. He is involved with several charitable organizations, mostly those focusing on disadvantaged kids such as Kids Across America, a sports camping ministry for inner-city youth, and Cornerstone Schools in Birmingham.

He and Tanner live in Chicago, where they've made their home for thirty years and raised five children—four boys and a girl. Their youngest, daughter Tyler, was set to graduate from the University of Alabama in 2007 and hopes to be a jewelry designer. Having her graduate from the Capstone feels "unbelievably good," according to her proud pop, who claims none of her friends know who her father is but that some of their parents might.

The Mussos escape the Chicago winter by heading to Naples, Florida, for a good part of the year. They spend summers in Michigan. Musso plays golf a lot these days. He also fishes from time to time, although he claims he doesn't catch much. Mostly, he counts his blessings.

"We feel blessed beyond our ability to verbalize it," he said.

JOE NAMATH

"Joe Namath is the greatest athlete I have ever coached."

— PAUL W. "BEAR" BRYANT

A FEW YEARS AGO, JOE NAMATH WAS HANGING OUT WITH HIS DAUGHTERS, Jessica and Olivia at home in Tequesta, Florida, when Jessica, a high school senior bound for the University of Alabama the following year, made an innocent comment.

"Daddy," she said, "I'll be the first one in our family to finish college."

This wasn't a challenge to her dad, who attended the University of Alabama in the sixties but never finished his degree. (A few things such as the New York Jets and Super Bowl III got in the way.)

But Namath, a competitive guy if ever there was one, couldn't help but take his daughter's statement as a challenge. He looked at her and answered, "Want to bet?"

So that's why some incredibly surprised eighteen-year-olds saw a very famous sixty-something guy standing in line to register for classes at the university the following fall. Since then, mostly by way of private classes and the Internet, Namath has been working on his degree, which he is quick to point out, is neither in basket-weaving or journalism. (It's in humanities.)

He makes this distinction because of an old, well-circulated story. When he was playing for the Jets, a reporter tried to rile him by asking if he majored in basket-weaving at Alabama. Namath famously answered: "Yeah, that was pretty tough. So I dropped it and went into journalism."

Namath laughs about it today. "I don't know if that was the right way to start out with the writers," he told author Kirk McNair in *What It Means to Be Crimson Tide.*

Finishing school was something Bryant always emphasized to all of his players, from the stars to the scrubs. This was a very appealing selling point to many player's parents, including Joe Namath's mother, Rose, who made her son promise he would get a college degree.

Namath grew up in Beaver Falls, Pennsylvania, a mill town about thirty miles northwest of Pittsburgh. His father, John, was a steelworker who encouraged his boys to play sports. (Namath was the youngest of five, with three brothers and a sister.) His father also instilled incredible confidence in young Namath, teaching him to believe he was the best.

Sadly, before Namath started seventh grade, his parents split up and went through a prolonged and bitter divorce. Namath lived with his mother until he graduated from high school.

Nicknamed "the Hungarian Howitzer," Namath was a star athlete at Beaver Falls High School. He had an incredible arm and was one of the top high school quarter-

The one and only Joe Willie

backs in the country. But he also dunked basketballs and hit his share of home runs too.

He was offered several professional baseball contracts (the Cubs reportedly offered him a $50,000 bonus); but, heavily influenced by his mother and older brother Frank, Namath opted for college. He certainly had plenty of choices. By several accounts, he had more than fifty schools recruiting him to play football.

Namath decided to attend the University of Maryland, but when he failed to meet their required minimum score on the college boards, he was up for grabs. Maryland's head coach didn't want Namath playing for a school on his team's schedule, so he tipped off Coach Bryant that the talented Pennsylvanian was available.

Coach Bryant dispatched assistant coach Howard Schnellenberger to Beaver Falls to bring Namath to Tuscaloosa. Schnellenberger had several things going for him. For one, he played football with Namath's brother Frank at the University of Kentucky. Coach Bryant had actually recruited Frank for the Wildcats when he was head coach there, so Frank knew he would be a good influence on his rebellious brother. Also, Namath's mother liked Schnellenberger. He knew the deal was sealed when, after a week in Beaver Falls, Namath's mom came into the room with a small suitcase and said, "Take him, coach."

Schnellenberger breathed a sigh of relief when he finally delivered his charge to Tuscaloosa. Still, he couldn't help worrying about Namath's appearance.

"He looked like a street hustler," Schnellenberger remembered, "with a checkered sport coat and his pocket watch and chain."

Coach Bryant's longtime secretary Linda Knowles remembers the day Namath came to town. "I thought he looked like a hoodlum! Compared to the guys with butch haircuts, he really did! He had long hair, blue jeans, z-ring zipper boots, and a men's undershirt with the sleeves rolled up. I thought, *My goodness. We are scraping the bottom of the barrel.*"

True to form, Coach Bryant overlooked Namath's questionable fashion sense and got right to business. Much to the astonishment of his players and coaches, he immediately invited his young recruit to join him on his coach's tower.

Only a few honored guests such as Governor George Wallace and University President Frank Rose had ever been asked up to the tower. Namath was the first player to ascend. At the time, he didn't understand the significance.

Photograph courtesy of Paul W. Bryant Museum/The University of Alabama

Namath: head and shoulders above the onslaught

He also had a hard time understanding the low southern drawl of his coach.

"I didn't understand a word he said, except for one word, 'stud,' and I didn't know what a stud was," Namath said.

Despite the culture shock experienced by a Pennsylvania kid in the deep South, Namath acclimated quickly and soon got a lesson in what was expected of him.

"The freshmen were scrimmaging one night," Namath said, "and I ran out to my left on an option play. As I started to pitch out, some big lineman hit me, and the ball fell loose. I didn't scramble for the ball. Hell, the guy who made the tackle was holding on to me for dear life. It seemed he didn't want to get up either.

"Coach Bryant came out and said, 'Goldarn it, Namath, it's not your job to pitch the ball out and lay down there on the ground and not do anything.' He kept grumbling, and I started to walk away toward the huddle, half listening to him and not looking at him. Suddenly, he grabbed hold of my face mask and yanked it around, nearly lifting me off my feet.

"'Namath!' he shouted. 'When I'm talking to you, boy, you say, "Yes sir," and look me in the eye. I don't like no sideways looks.' He scared me half to death. From that day on, if Coach Bryant just said, 'Joe,' even if I was fifty or sixty yards away, I'd run like hell to him, stop a yard away, come to attention and say, 'Yes, sir, Coach.'"

Beginning with his sophomore year of 1962, Namath contributed mightily to the 10-1 Crimson Tide, setting school records for completions (76) and passing yards (1,192) and tying Harry Gilmer's single-season record for touchdown passes (13). Then, during Namath's junior year, with only two games left to play (the regular season game against Miami and the Sugar Bowl against Ole Miss), the unthinkable happened. After word got back to Coach Bryant that Namath had been seen drinking off campus, which was a violation of training rules, Bryant had a big decision to make.

He called his assistants together to discuss the situation. The majority said Namath should be punished but not suspended. The sole dissenter? Assistant Coach Gene Stallings.

"It was straightforward to me," Stallings said. "I felt like he had violated a rule. Namath was a great player and a great person. I thought in order for Coach Bryant to get the most out of him the following year, he had to get his attention."

So Namath was suspended for the final two games, which Alabama won even without their starting quarterback. After the suspension, Namath could have quit the team. He could have transferred to another school or accepted an offer to play in the Canadian Football League. But to his credit, he stuck it out.

According to Namath's biography, *Namath,* Mrs. Bryant came to Namath's rescue by cooking him meals and letting him stay in the Bryant's basement without the Coach's knowledge. "She hid me out," said Namath, who needed a place to stay since he had been kicked out of the dorm. "I was hurt. She knew that and responded by protecting me, helping in a motherly way."

The lesson in tough love worked. Namath has said many times over the years that he deserved the suspension.

"In the long run, it made a very positive impact on me," Namath said in *Legends of Alabama Football.* "Rules are rules, and they're not made to be broken. I have two daughters, and I'm trying to teach them that too. Like it or not, we need to understand that and to understand that life's not always fair. Coach Bryant did the right thing, and I had to accept it and move on."

Namath returned to the team his senior year and led the Crimson Tide to a national championship. Following the Orange Bowl game of 1965, Namath signed what up until then was the most lucrative deal in pro football history, a three-year, $427,000 contract with the New York Jets.

Was Namath worth the huge (for its era) asking price? Here's a three-word answer: "I guarantee it."

Midway through his rookie season, Namath became the starting quarterback. In 1967, his third season, he had 4,007 passing yards and threw 26 touchdown passes. The next year, he led his team to the AFL's Eastern Division title. Next stop? Super Bowl III on January 12, 1969.

Much has been made of Namath's famous quote guaranteeing his underdog team's win. But what player who believed in himself would do less? Even when his team's opponent was favored by as much as three touchdowns. Three days before the big game, at a Miami Touchdown Club dinner, Namath answered a heckler by saying, 'We're going to win. I guarantee it.'"

He then proceeded to back up his boast by completing 17 of 28 passes for 206 yards in the victory over the stunned Don Shula–coached Baltimore Colts.

Namath, who was named MVP of Super Bowl III, went on to gather many more victories and honors during his next eight seasons with the Jets. Despite being battered by injuries, he became one of the best NFL players in history. Beyond that, he became a cultural icon who became just as famous for his good looks, affection for women, and the New York nightlife as he did for his tremendous passing arm.

Namath further solidified his status as a household name by wearing a fur coat on the sidelines and putting on pantyhose and shaving off his mustache for commercials. He also dabbled in acting over the years, making guest appearances on many TV shows and starring in dozens of stage and screen roles.

Namath finished his pro career in 1977 playing for the Los Angeles Rams. In 1985 he was elected to the Pro Football Hall of Fame. In his Hall of Fame acceptance speech, he acknowledged his Alabama roots when his eyes welled with tears and he said, "Coach Bryant, Mrs. Bryant, wherever you are, we miss you."

Even before he was a man on a sheepskin mission, Namath visited the university often over the years to participate in special events and fund-raisers and to see old friends. According to Linda Knowles, he would drop by often in the seventies and early eighties to visit Coach Bryant and share tales of his latest acting projects.

"Joe is just wonderful," she said. "He's so honest and humble."

Although Namath became a close friend and contemporary of Coach Bryant's after he left to play in the pros, evidently, Namath could never quite shake the feeling of awe and respect he felt around the guy that some people—not him or any other players—called "Bear."

Dennis Homan, a Crimson Tide receiver from 1965 to 1967, said that a group of ex-Alabama players who were playing in the pros used to meet every summer in Tuscaloosa for workouts. Imagine Dennis Homan, Joe Namath, Ken Stabler, Lee Roy Jordan, and Paul Crane on one field preparing for their respective camps.

One afternoon, Dennis and Namath took a break to go fishing.

"I asked him, Namath, what's your feeling now when you go by and see Coach Bryant?" Dennis remembered. "When I go in there, I still feel like he's my coach. I get this knot in my stomach. Namath said, 'I feel exactly the same way.'"

His reverence for Coach Bryant never changed. And he constantly falls back on things he learned from him, whether he's dealing with injuries, as he did his entire career, going through a divorce, as he did in 2000, or successfully battling alcoholism, as he has done since 2003.

"I remember Coach Bryant telling us when we were freshmen that we'd probably remember the bad times more than the good, the bad games and the losses more than the good games and the wins, and he was right," Namath said in *Legends of Alabama Football.* "Sure, I remember the good things, but you really learn from the tough times. We're survivors. You can wallow in the pain and the bad memories or you can reflect on them and say, "OK, let's deal with that."

Broadway Joe. The Beaver Falls Bomber. Movie star. Sex symbol. Hall of Famer. Restaurateur. Dad. Alabama graduate. Of all the great things he was and still may be, he'll always be just "Joe Willie" to Alabama fans.

BILLY NEIGHBORS

"Playing at Alabama was the thrill of my life."
— BILLY NEIGHBORS

BILLY NEIGHBORS WON'T QUIT. THAT'S ONE REASON HE WAS SUCH A great football player. It's also one of the reasons he's been a successful stockbroker for more than forty years. He loves his work. And even though he passed the official retirement age of sixty-five a year or two ago, he has absolutely no plans to quit.

"They're going to have to carry me out of here," Neighbors said. "I don't believe in retiring. Everybody I know who retires dies."

"Big Billy," as his grandchildren call him, grew up in Taylorville, Alabama, listening to his dad talk about the great Crimson Tide Rose Bowl teams of the thirties and forties. None other than star halfback Harry Gilmer lived nextdoor and even bought nine-year-old Billy his first set of weights. It was inevitable that Neighbors would become an Alabama football fan. Then, while working as a concession stand worker at Denny Stadium during high school, Neighbors experienced the thrill of watching the team play live. The deal was done.

Actually, the deal was not officially done until a few years later, when Neighbors and his brother Sid met Coach Hank Crisp at a Northport fruit stand to sign scholarship agreements. The funny thing was, standing among the bushel baskets of Granny Smith apples, they didn't even know who their head coach would be.

Everyone knew J. B. "Ears" Whitworth was gone and a replacement was due, but the announcement hadn't yet been made.

Later that spring, Coach Paul W. "Bear" Bryant was named head coach.

"I didn't know a thing about him," Neighbors said.

Looking back, that might have been a good thing.

In the fall of 1958, Neighbors and the other freshmen reported for their first team meeting. Coach Bryant laid down the law. He also set the bar incredibly high.

"He told us if we did what he told us to do, we would win a national championship before we were through," Neighbors said. "We thought he was crazy."

As Alabama fans know well, the madman had a plan. And Neighbors' team did indeed win the national championship in 1961. But at first, it was a very slow grind.

Practices were grueling to say the least. Many of the veteran players, who had grown accustomed to a less-than-demanding regimen during the Tide's last several losing seasons, quit the team.

As Coach Bryant said in his autobiography, "The team I inherited in 1958 was a fat, raggedy bunch. The best players, the ones with ability quit us . . ."

Many of the new players quit, too. Half the freshmen were gone by the end of the first season. By Neighbors' senior year, only eight players from his class remained on the squad.

Young people might roll their eyes at stories about how tough it was in the old days: *We walked ten miles to football practice every day in the snow.* (In Tuscaloosa?) But think about it. In the early sixties, players played both ways. Starters like Neighbors, who was a tackle on both offense and defense, played for fifty-eight minutes straight every game. Every down.

Photograph courtesy of Paul W. Bryant Museum/The University of Alabama

Billy Neighbors: a daunting sight

"We had to be in great, great, shape," Neighbors said. "Coach Bryant didn't like for you to be too big. He would give you a weight to have every year. If you didn't make that weight, he wouldn't give you a uniform. As a matter of fact, he kicked my brother off [the team] for being two pounds overweight."

Neighbors worked hard to meet Coach Bryant's expectations. When the coach gave him a goal weight of 225 his senior year, Neighbors came in at a lean, mean 218. He wasn't taking any chances. Throughout his college career, he did his best to stay off Coach Bryant's radar.

"Pat Trammell was the only one who wasn't afraid of Coach Bryant," Neighbors said. "The rest of us were scared to death of him. When I saw him coming, I went the other way! I would hide!"

Isn't it hard for a 225- or even a 250-pound man (the coach let up on the weight thing after Neighbors proved himself) to hide?

"You can always find a place if you really want to," Neighbors laughed.

On the field, it was Alabama's opponents who wanted to hide from Neighbors. He was a tremendously effective and fearsome player on both sides of the ball.

"He could run full bore and hit you at the same level as his stance," said former teammate Lee Roy Jordan. "Most big guys can't do that, stay that low. But Neighbors came right out of his stance and stayed low and got up under you."

The hard work, the tough conditioning, the ability to outlast their opponents in the fourth quarter paid off for Neighbors' teams. The 1958 squad finished 5-4-1, but in 1959 they went 7-2-2. In 1960, it was even better: 8-1-2. By the end of the 1961 season, the Crimson Tide was undefeated and looking back at a three-year run in which they had lost only three games. Heading into their final game—the Iron Bowl against Auburn—the players knew if they beat their rival, they would likely be crowned national champions.

But first things first.

Alabama beat Auburn in '59 and '60, and Neighbors and his fellow seniors very much wanted to make it three in a row. But not only did they beat Auburn the previous two years—they shut them out. And as the game clock wound down, it looked like they would again hold Auburn scoreless.

In the book, *Game of My Life,* Neighbors told the story of this particular game. The Tide dominated all four quarters. With just two minutes to go, they were up, 34-0, and Coach Bryant took out the starters. The guys thought they were done for the day, so they started taking off their helmets and pads. Then Auburn got dangerously close to the goal line, and Coach Bryant yelled for his first team players to return. They did. And they held them. The clock ran out.

"I think he did that so we could talk about it the rest of our lives, how Auburn never scored on us," Neighbors said. "I didn't want to go back in there. I wanted to go home. I had done all I wanted to do that day. [Playing at] Legion Field was like playing on a rock. You got all beat to death out there, legs and elbows all cut up and bruised. It wasn't a fun place to play in November or December. But now, I'm glad we did it."

A fantastic end to a perfect season.

Neighbors, the defensive captain of the national championship team, was named all-America in '61 and won the Jacobs Award as best blocker in the SEC.

Years later, he would be named to the Team of the Decade for the sixties (on both offense and defense!), the Alabama Team of the Century, the Alabama Sports Hall of Fame, the National Football Foundation Hall of Fame, and the College Football Hall of Fame.

But back in 1961, Neighbors wasn't done with football. He got offers from two pro teams, the NFL's Washington Redskins and the AFL's Boston Patriots.

He went to Boston and played four years. Then, Neighbors went to Miami and played four more. Neighbors loved seeing his former college teammates scattered across the fledgling AFL.

"Tommy Brooker was with the Kansas City Chiefs," Neighbors said. "Benny Nelson played for the Houston Oilers, and, of course, Joe [Namath] was with the Jets. We had them everywhere!"

After eight years as a pro, Neighbors hung up his cleats due to injuries. He said he was grateful for the time he had.

"It was a great experience," he said. "I met a lot of wonderful people. It was football, and I loved football. I got an extra eight years."

Now Neighbors was faced with the question that confronts every retired football player. He was thirty years old. What would he do with the rest of his life?

During his college days, Neighbors always thought he'd end up as a football coach. He studied to be a teacher, and in his last year as a pro player, he was contacted by Coach Bryant, asking him to join his coaching staff if he took the Dolphins' head coach position. (As we all know, that never happened.)

While playing pro ball, Neighbors also worked part-time in the brokerage business.

"We all worked in the off-season," Neighbors said. "We didn't make forty million dollars like they do now. Although I'm happy for the guys today. That's a rough business! These guys make enough money now that they don't have to work. Which is good because you know what 'NFL' stands for—'Not for Long.'"

So Neighbors went from part-time to full-time broker. Some forty years later, he's still at it, putting in long hours at the Huntsville office of Wachovia Securities. Neighbors' clients include folks from Tennessee, Georgia, California, New York, and, of course, Alabama (including Auburn alums). His status as a former Tide star hasn't hurt his trade.

"You can't depend on that, though," Neighbors said. "People want to make darn sure that you know what you're doing before you get their money, so playing football has nothing to do with this business."

One well-known Alabama guy who trusted Neighbors with his money was Coach Bryant.

"He was my client from 1969 until he died," Neighbors said. "Coach Bryant liked the stock market. He was real good at it. Sometimes he was demanding. If you put him on something that wasn't too good, he'd get mad about it. For two or three minutes."

So, how did Neighbors go from a guy who hid from Coach Bryant during college and even for a while afterward to a guy who talked to the coach once a week and even, incredibly, bore the responsibility for his money?

"After I retired from football, Benny Nelson and I went to Tuscaloosa for a basketball game," said Neighbors. "We heard somebody banging on the glass door. It was him. He wanted us to come up and see him, so we did. After that, I started calling him, and we built up a relationship. We became friends. I went to games and helped him recruit back when ex-players could. I did what he asked me to do."

Years later, when Neighbors' son Wes, an all-state player at Huntsville High School, was being recruited by Alabama, Neighbors was impressed that Coach Bryant gave him no special treatment.

"Coach Bryant came to our house and came to a game and watched him play," Neighbors said. "He treated him like all the other recruits."

Wes went on to play for Alabama, although he was redshirted as a freshman in 1982. So even though he was on the team, he never got to see playing time under the Bear's watch.

After Coach Bryant died in 1983, Wes told a reporter:

> Of course I was disappointed I didn't get to play under Coach Bryant. For years he meant so much to our family. Growing up, that's all I heard my father talk about, and of course I wanted to play under Coach Bryant. I hope I was able to contribute to Coach Bryant's last team by being out there at practice every day. But I realize his decision to redshirt me was for the best. I'll have a better chance to play because of it.

Wes, who played center for quarterback Mike Shula and others, did play and played well. People often ask Neighbors if he gave advice to Wes, and his son Keith (who later played on the 1992 championship team).

"I made up my mind that I wasn't going to say anything to them about the game unless they asked me," Neighbors said. "So I never did. Sometimes it was hard to do. But I don't think you need to be telling them something all the time. They've got coaches; they don't need me to say anything. So I just bragged on them."

Neighbors has a lot to brag about these days. His family, including his sons and daughter, Claire, all live within one mile of his Huntsville home. The family often spends time at the Neighbors' condo in Destin, Florida. Neighbors and his wife, Susan, have been married forty-five years and have eight grandchildren who love to hear Coach Bryant stories.

Neighbors says he thinks about the coach often, especially when times get tough.

"He'd remind you that you had to have self-discipline, good habits, and a good work ethic," Neighbors said. "When you go astray you need to get back in the groove. Just do the things you need to do."

OZZIE NEWSOME

"Martin Luther King preached opportunity. Bear Bryant gave us opportunity."

— OZZIE NEWSOME

WITH SINCERE APOLOGIES TO DOROTHY AND HER PALS, WHEN IT comes to Alabama football, there is only one Wizard of Oz.

During his four years with the Crimson Tide (1974–1977), Ozzie Newsome was the top college receiver in America. He had the best set of hands Bama fans had ever seen. If a quarterback threw a ball anywhere in his zip code, he was going to catch it. Throwing to Newsome was as good as a guarantee. He was everybody's go-to man and incredibly exciting to watch.

Newsome piled up so many honors (not to mention yards) during his college playing days and in the years that followed that it's exhausting to list them all. But let's give Newsome his due.

In 1976 and '77, he was named all-SEC, earning the distinction of SEC Lineman of the Year in '77. He was a second-team all-American in 1976 and

Photograph courtesy of Paul W. Bryant Museum/The University of Alabama

If a ball was thrown anywhere in his zip code, Ozzie Newsome caught it.

first team (as well as Bama's team captain) in 1977. By the time his college career was over, he was Alabama's all-time career receiving leader (102 receptions for 2,070 yards). In 1994, he was inducted into the College Football Hall of Fame. But perhaps his most treasured accolade came just a few years out of college when he heard that Coach Bryant called him "the greatest end in Alabama history."

"Remember," Newsome said with a laugh, "he said that after I graduated."

Indeed, once their playing days were behind them, many Bama players were pleasantly surprised to learn that the coach they respected, and sometimes even feared, became a different person. Now that the student-teacher dynamic was gone, he was free to dish out compliments for some former players, much to their surprise. Some even found themselves on the receiving end of a full-blown bear hug.

"I got closer to Coach Bryant once I had graduated and left the university," Newsome said. "We could go and sit and talk about taxes and other things. He was a confidante. It wasn't just a player-coach relationship—that was always going to be there—but he embraced me in other areas once I left. There was a trust we had developed so he could let his guard down a little bit. Plus, he was trying to help me because I was dealing with other things in life."

Among the other things in Newsome's immediate post-Bama life was a soon-to-be extraordinary career in the NFL. In 1978, Newsome was drafted in the first round by the Cleveland Browns, the team he played for his entire thirteen-season pro career.

As a tight end he distinguished himself immediately. In his first season he was named the Browns' Offensive Player of the Year, the first rookie to receive that honor in some twenty-five years. He was named all-pro in 1979 and 1984 and went to Pro Bowls in 1981, 1984, and 1985. Browns fans fondly remember "the Streak," when from 1979 to 1989, Newsome caught passes in 150 consecutive games. Ultimately, he caught 662 passes for his club and was inducted into the Pro Football Hall of Fame in 1992.

When Newsome retired, he wasn't ready to leave football entirely, which is why he accepted a position as special assignment scout for his team. Soon thereafter the Browns moved to Baltimore, where they became the Ravens, and Newsome made the move with them. Soon, he was promoted to assistant to the head coach/offense-personnel. Next, he was appointed director of pro personnel and in 1996 became responsible for the team's draft.

Newsome kept climbing. His next stop on the administrative ladder was as senior vice president of football operations. Finally, in November 2002, he reached the top rung when he was named Ravens executive vice president and general manager. He thus became the NFL's first African American general manager and by all accounts, he is doing a tremendous job. Maybe it's partly because Newsome is used to being first.

Newsome was born in Muscle Shoals, Alabama, on March 15, 1958. He was one of the first African Americans to play on an integrated Little League baseball team and one of the first to attend an integrated high school—Colbert County High School in Leighton, Alabama. When he came to the university, black players had been on the roster of Crimson Tide teams for a mere four years. It could have been a negative experience. Newsome says it was exactly the opposite.

"Those four years at the University of Alabama were the best four years of my life," Newsome said. "You were an Alabama football player. There was no black and white."

Bama fans may want to breathe a collective sigh of relief when they find out how close Mr. Newsome came to attending Auburn.

"I had committed to Auburn before the signing date because I had played on a very good high school team and the quarterback, who was a year ahead of me, went there," Newsome said. "They were saying we could be reunited. Plus, another receiver from my area had committed to Alabama, so people were encouraging me to go make my own mark at Auburn."

Then John Mitchell, one of Bryant's assistant coaches and the first African American to play at Alabama, went to see Newsome.

"He was very matter of fact," Newsome said. "He just sold the program. When I visited the campus, the environment they had created down there was so attractive. It was all about winning. It wasn't about selfishness. It was about, if you come here, you will be part of a winning program. Not just winning but a program that is going to be contending for a national championship. That sets you apart from everything."

What sealed the deal for Newsome? It had to be Coach Bryant.

"That's true," Newsome said. "Knowing that the guy leading the team was more popular than the governor himself ultimately made up my mind."

When Newsome first hit the field as a freshman, Coach Bryant was upbeat.

"He was encouraging when I first got there, and then he got hard on me once he realized I had talent. He never allowed a person to become complacent. He used to talk about, 'Let's go out and try to get 10 percent better today.' Can you imagine just working to get 10 percent better? If you do that every day, you are getting a lot better. He wanted you to get to the point that you wanted to strive for that yourself. Which is something you'll use the rest of your life."

Newsome worked hard and quickly excelled on the field. During his freshman year, the Tide was struggling against a strong Florida State team that had won some thirty straight games. In the fourth quarter, Newsome caught a pass that set up the winning field goal.

"To the people in the state that live and die with Alabama football—and that's a lot of people—that was the play that put me on the map," Newsome said. "Or the next year when we beat Penn State in the Sugar Bowl. That's the game fans still bring up. And believe me, they can tell the story better than I can!"

So many memorable games. Newsome was a star, but even when he was a senior and a shoo-in for the NFL the next year, Coach Bryant didn't let up.

"I remember one practice, we had a conditioning task," Newsome said. "You could either run four quarters, or a mile, under a certain amount of time. My intention was to complete it and not be winded or tired. The next day, Coach Bryant was whipping me a new behind because he said I had 'the senior strut.' Doing just enough to get by. So he told me, 'No. You've got to push yourself.' So the next controlled scrimmage we had, he took out the other starters and just kept me in there for about seventy plays."

Photograph by Phil Hoffmann, Ravens team photographer. Used by permission.

Newsome inspects the troops at Ravens camp.

Newsome took this important lesson with him to Cleveland.

"In the NFL, I never became satisfied," he said. "If I led the league in receptions, so what? What am I going to do next year? Am I a complete player? Am I the type of person I need to be in the locker room? You're never satisfied with yesterday. You're always looking to get better for today and tomorrow."

These days, Newsome lives just north of Baltimore in Cockeysville, Maryland, with his wife, Gloria (who he met at the University of

Alabama), and his fifteen-year-old son Michael. His two daughters, April and Teresha, live in Birmingham.

He spends long hours in the Baltimore Ravens front office applying the 10-percent rule and striving for zero complacence as he works to build his team.

"In my business, if you live on yesterday, you become yesterday's news," Newsome said. "This is a highly competitive environment and there's only thirty-two teams. You have to work to get better every day, because if you don't, the rest of the league will catch up with you."

Newsome's drive, on and off the field, grabbed the attention of former Ravens owner Art Modell, who put Newsome in charge of the team's operation in 1996.

"All along, I saw in Newsome a certain maturity, a quality of deliberation before he makes a decision," Modell told a *Baltimore Sun* reporter. "I felt that could translate into running an organization as GM. I took a shot. It wasn't much of a shot."

Newsome is largely credited as the architect of the Ravens' Super Bowl XXXV championship team in 2000. After boasting arguably the best defense in the league in 2006, another Super Bowl visit might be in their sights.

"That's definitely our goal," Newsome said.

Note the word, *our.*

In every Ozzie Newsome interview over the years, there is a common theme. Newsome says "we" a lot more than "me." When asked about his achievements as a player at Bama, he proudly states, "We went 42-6 when I was a player. We won three SEC Championships, won three bowl games. . . ."

When asked about his accomplishments in the NFL, he lists the Browns stats: "We played in the AFC Championship three times…"

Today, even though he is known to be cooperative with the press, he prefers the limelight be directed toward his players. He prefers to be the proverbial man behind the curtain in Baltimore. Surely, his college coach, who he thinks of often, would be incredibly proud.

"I can see now why he did certain things and why he made the decisions he did on a daily basis," Newsome said.

As he sits in his office surrounded by Bear Bryant memorabilia, Newsome becomes quiet when asked how he felt when he learned Paul W. Bryant had passed away.

"Empty," he said. "Completely empty."

Newsome then perks up when asked what his future holds.

"I think I'll go back to Alabama and retire there," he said. "I'll just go and tailgate."

RAY PERKINS

"There is no way that me or anyone else could be like Coach Bryant. I think it would be ridiculous for anyone to try."

— RAY PERKINS

EVERY DIEHARD FOOTBALL FAN KNOWS THE NAME RAY PERKINS. BUT what comes to mind when they hear his name?

Do they remember the Alabama all-American who caught passes from Joe Namath, Steve Sloan, and Ken Stabler? Do they remember the Baltimore Colts receiver who was a favorite target of Johnny Unitas? Do they remember the New York Giants head coach, who in 1981 led his team to the playoffs for the first time since the early sixties? Or do they remember the man who succeeded Coach Bryant as Alabama's head coach?

There's a lot to remember about Ray Perkins.

But Perkins, retired and living in Hattiesburg, Mississippi, with his wife, Lisa, and two young daughters, is not a "let's look back" kind of guy. The only legacy he is concerned with these days is a family one.

Photograph courtesy of Paul W. Bryant Museum/The University of Alabama

Steve Sloan, Coach Bryant, and Ray Perkins in a post-game huddle

"I'm a hands-on daddy," Perkins said. "I'm involved in my two little girls' lives on a daily basis. I drive them both to school every day. They are my life."

Perkins has two sons from his previous marriage, Tony, forty-one, and Mike, thirty-nine, who recently welcomed a son, Tyler, making Perkins a proud grandfather.

Meanwhile, Perkins and Lisa are raising their daughters, Rachael, nine, and Shelby, three, just across the river from Petal, Mississippi, the tiny town where Perkins grew up.

The mellow, content life of taking family outings, playing golf, and dabbling in real estate (Perkins laughs when he admits to devoting a full two hours a week to this endeavor) is a far cry from the hardscrabble existence of Perkins' early years.

Growing up with an alcoholic father and a sick, often bedridden mother, Perkins learned to take care of himself at a very early age. He dropped out of school in the eighth grade to work several jobs, including pumping gas. The owner of the gas station, Marcus James, and his high school coach, Ed Palmer, convinced Perkins to return to school and encouraged him to play football.

"If it hadn't been for football, I'm not sure what would have happened to me," Perkins said.

While Perkins excelled on his high school team, he began to dream of playing for a coach in a neighboring state. He had an uncle who told him if he played for Coach Bryant, he would always win.

"I don't know why but winning was pretty important to me at a fairly young age," Perkins said.

A friend who was a big Alabama fan gave Perkins a 1960 press guide that he memorized and pored over until it was dog-eared and ragged. (Perkins still has it.)

So, when Alabama offered him a scholarship it was a no-brainer. (Especially since Alabama was the only school to do so.) Perkins remembers visiting Tuscaloosa the summer before his freshman year.

"We were out on the practice field and Coach Bryant walked over and said, 'Hello Raymond.' It had been several months since I'd seen him and I was sure I wasn't the only player he had recruited. And he's remembering my name? That really impressed me."

Coach Bryant would go on to impress and inspire Perkins many times. Perhaps he made his most lasting impact on the young player when Perkins was seriously injured during the spring of his freshman year. After a collision with defensive back Billy Piper, Perkins sustained a blood clot on his brain and was rushed to a Birmingham hospital for emergency surgery.

He was in the hospital for nine days. Coach Bryant, who had rented a room in a nearby hotel, was with him every day.

"You talk about making an impression on a young man," Perkins said. "He cared about you. He flat did."

Although his life literally hung in the balance for a few days, Perkins' primary thoughts were about football.

"I was mainly concerned with whether I was going to get to play again," he said. "I didn't give much thought to whether I was going to live or not."

While he recovered from his injuries, Perkins' coaches redshirted him and debated about bringing him back the following season as a fullback, his former position, where he would be sure to take a lot of hits. Defensive coach Gene Stallings suggested switching Perkins, a fast-runner, to receiver.

For weeks, trainer Jim Goostree threw balls at Perkins, who learned to catch while he worked himself back into shape.

"The day they told me I could play again was one of the happiest days of my life," he said.

Perkins played on two national championship teams (1964 and '65) and the 1966 team that was denied the top crown despite what many people believed was the best Crimson Tide team ever. He put up incredible numbers, finishing his all-American career with 63 receptions for 908 yards and nine touchdowns.

But the numbers don't begin to illustrate how exciting a player he was to watch. In a 1966 *Sports Illustrated* article about the thrilling 1965 Alabama victory over much-favored Nebraska in the Orange Bowl, Perkins is described as "stretching, lunging, curling, and diving for 10 receptions for 159 yards and two touchdowns. Possibly the only thing more spectacular than Perkins' touchdown catches was the chain reaction [of soaring rockets and Roman candles] they set off in the end zone."

Pro scouts noticed Perkins' dazzling performances; and in 1967, he was drafted by both the AFL's Boston Patriots and the NFL's Baltimore Colts. Former teammate Joe Namath suggested he get someone he trusted to serve as his agent. Perkins immediately thought of Coach Bryant, who agreed to serve in this role.

"We were at the Sugar Bowl in 1967," remembered Perkins. "Coach Bryant said, '[Colts coach] Don Shula is here and wants to talk to me tonight about your contract. What do you think I should ask for?' I said, 'I thought you were my agent!'

"The next day, Coach Bryant came back and said, 'This is what we got.' I said, 'It looks pretty good.' We ended up signing the contract after the game in my room."

One remarkable detail in this Jerry Maguire moment—Bryant took no percentage. Zero.

Rachael, Ray, Lisa, and Shelby Perkins

"I didn't even buy him a Coke!" laughed Perkins.

After playing for the Baltimore Colts for five seasons, a knee injury forced Perkins to retire in 1972. Highlights of his pro career include two trips to the top; Super Bowl III (the Colts lost to the Namath-led New York Jets) and Super Bowl V (the Colts beat the Dallas Cowboys).

Perkins immediately went into coaching, beginning as receivers coach for a year at Mississippi State. He then returned to the NFL to coach receivers for the New England Patriots, where he stayed for four years. In 1978, he became the offensive coordinator for San Diego, where his team led the division in scoring, with 355 points.

When he first became a coach, Perkins had asked Coach Bryant for some advice. After giving him a wise but fairly predictable checklist (get good coaches, get good players, get them in shape, etc.), he shared what he thought was the most important thing a coach should do.

"He said, make sure they feel like doing it on game day," Perkins said. "I'll never forget that. He did absolutely the best job of getting us motivated and in shape and making sure we felt like playing on game day. When I was a coach, the number-one thing I was afraid of was not having my team in condition to play a sixty-minute ball game. So I think I gained a reputation for working my team too hard because of that. But I made sure at the end of the week they got plenty of rest before game day."

In 1979, Perkins was named New York Giants head coach. Inheriting this team, which hadn't been to the playoffs since 1963, was an enormous challenge. Factor in the relentless media attention and demanding New York fans, and you've got a pressure-cooker situation. But Perkins, who had a talented staff, including Bill Belichick and Bill Parcells, persevered and led his team through three winning (if not Super Bowl-bound) seasons.

Perkins made no secret of the fact that he missed coaching college athletes.

In 1983, he told a reporter, "I like the relationship between player and coach that's peculiar to college. College men are easier to motivate than professionals. In the NFL, you have to go to the greatest player to find the kind of spirit you find in the average college freshman."

In 1982, Perkins got the chance of a lifetime when, after Coach Bryant announced his retirement, he was offered the job as Alabama's new head coach.

"Coach Bryant called," Perkins remembered. "He said, 'Raymond, are you interested in this thing down here?' I said, 'Coach Bryant, I would walk to Tuscaloosa for it.'"

His answer was definitive despite the fact that he, and everyone else, knew that this was an impossible act to follow. Immediately, the comparisons to Coach Bryant began.

"There is no way that me or anyone else could be like Coach Bryant," Perkins said. "I think it would be ridiculous for anyone to try. I don't claim to be similar to him. What I learned from him, I tried to apply in my own way."

Under Coach Perkins' watch, the Crimson Tide went 8-4 in 1983 but notched a losing (5-6) season in 1984. During his final year, 1985, the numbers were back up when Alabama finished 9-2-1. For Perkins, his best memories stem from the relationships he formed.

"The players I coached helped me a lot more than I helped them," he said.

He counts many former players, such as Mike Shula, Kermit Kendricks, Cornelius Bennett, and Walter Lewis, as good friends to this day.

"The best players are often the best people," he said. "Truly good human beings. And the people who had success, winning games and winning championships, went on to become highly successful people later."

In 1986, Coach Perkins left Alabama to become head coach of the Tampa Bay Buccaneers. Obviously, this was a controversial move that displeased a lot of Alabama fans. But Perkins is not a guy to dwell on the past.

"In the coaching business, you make decisions based on the information you have and try to do what you think is best," he said. "At the time, that was the best decision for me and my family."

After four years in Tampa Bay, Perkins returned briefly to college football, when he coached one season at Arkansas State. He then returned to the NFL as an offensive coordinator, first for New England and then Oakland.

After retiring briefly, he returned the following year as an assistant for the Cleveland Browns before retiring for good.

And retirement, according to Perkins, has been very good.

"I'm enjoying it very, very much," he said.

Even though Ray Perkins is not a person to look back, some of the happiest times he has spent in the last few years are during annual reunions with Alabama teammates.

"I treasure those times and those friendships," he said. "We laugh and tell old stories. We can laugh at it today, but we all have a great appreciation for what we went through. If you can cope with what they dished out back then, you should be able to cope with life."

GARY RUTLEDGE

"There's no substitute for hard work."
— GARY RUTLEDGE

GARY RUTLEDGE IS SITTING IN A BIRMINGHAM PHYSICIAN'S OFFICE talking with the doctor. The topic of conversation? Alabama football. The doctor wants to hear about that LSU game way back when. And the Auburn game. He wants the inside scoop on what's happening now. And most of all, he wants to know what Bear Bryant was *really* like.

"Doctors want to talk football all the time," Rutledge said. "Especially during the season. I have to redirect the conversation or I'll never get anything done."

Fortunately, Rutledge is not sick. He's just doing his job as a sales rep for Solvay Pharmaceuticals, the company he has been with for nearly thirty years. He says he doesn't mind talking football with his docs. He is appreciative that they remember him as a quarterback for the magnificent 1973 team, which won the national championship as voted by United Press International (UPI).

Rutledge's father Paul ("Jack") Rutledge first went to the University of Alabama on a football scholarship in 1947 but ended up switching to baseball. He left college his junior year to play pro ball and spent three years in the minors with the Chicago Cubs and the New York Yankees.

Photograph courtesy of Paul W. Bryant Museum/The University of Alabama

Gary Rutledge: the first of two brothers to lead a national championship team

While Rutledge was growing up in Birmingham, his dad made sure that he and his younger brother, Jeff, always had a ball in their hands. A football, a baseball, a basketball—it didn't really matter. But sports was always front and center in the Rutledge house.

"My dad was a really good athlete, and he trained me and Jeff," said Rutledge. "We could play both sports because he taught us skills to be baseball and football players. And we both played basketball for our high schools. And we golfed. We played sports. That's all we did. We don't know how to hunt or fish at all!"

Even though they're only four years apart, Rutledge says he and Jeff were not competitive with each other. As Crimson Tide fans know well, Jeff followed his brother to the Capstone and incredibly, became the second member of the Rutledge family to quarterback a national championship team for Alabama.

"When we both got those scholarships to go to Alabama, our dad was the proudest man you ever saw," said Rutledge. "He and my mom came to all our games for eight years. He was the proudest guy in the world."

When Jeff first hit the practice field at Alabama he had to try to overcome being known as "Gary's brother."

"He got over that pretty quick," Rutledge said. "As soon as he started

Photograph courtesy of Gary Rutledge

Gary and Jeff Rutledge

playing as a sophomore, and then broke Joe Namath's career touchdown pass record, they quickly knew who he was. Now, I'm Jeff's brother."

Before he was "Jeff's brother," Rutledge was an all-around sports star at Banks High School in Birmingham. Football was his favorite sport. As a sophomore, Rutledge shared quarterbacking duties with junior Johnny Musso, who would go on to become one of the best halfbacks ever to play for the Crimson Tide.

"I always admired Gary when we were growing up because he was not a very big guy at all," Jeff said in the book *Bama Under Bear.* "In fact, he wasn't flashy or anything, but he was a competitor and he worked hard and he won."

As a junior and senior, Rutledge was the starter, and by the time graduation rolled around, he had collected all-city, all-state, and all-American honors as well as letters in three sports. He was offered scholarships from other schools, but Alabama was always his only choice.

Rutledge played well on the 1970 freshman team (they went 5-0) and did his duty as practice fodder for the varsity players, but still, in the spring of Rutledge's first year, Coach Bryant made the decision to "redshirt" him, meaning he would sit out a year. Rutledge was disappointed at first, but what he didn't know then was the coach would be unveiling a new offense that year—the wishbone—and Rutledge would be glad to have extra time to learn it.

In 1972, Rutledge was the backup quarterback behind starter Terry Davis. He remembers his first play as a varsity player during his sophomore year.

"It was the first game of the year, and I really wasn't expecting to go in," he said. "I was over there sitting on my helmet, pretty much. They had those tear-away jerseys then, and Terry Davis was trotting off the field with his jersey torn. All of the sudden, they were hollering, 'Rutledge! Rutledge! Get in here!'

"Well, Coach [Mal] Moore gets me on the sideline and says, 'Gary, run a right counter, forty-nine option.' That's the hardest wishbone play ever, where you fake to the right, reverse out and turn your back to the defensive end and pitch it outside. It's my first varsity play, and he makes me run the hardest one.

"I reverse out, the end luckily is not coming at me hard. I run out there and pitch it on the ground. Well, I'm trotting back off the field because Terry is coming back on. So I went running over to Coach Moore and Coach Bryant expecting to get chewed out, reamed out really bad. But then, Coach Bryant just looks at me and says, 'Gary, I just want to apologize for Mal for calling that play.'"

The rest of the year went more smoothly for Rutledge and his team. Despite two disappointing losses at the end of the season (including the infamous "Punt, Bama, Punt!" loss to Auburn), the 10-2 Tide finished the year as SEC champs.

During the summer before the 1973 season began, Rutledge married his high school sweetheart, Kathy Kinney. (Today, they have three kids, Lindy, Stacey, and Brett, who is a senior at Alabama.) In the fall, the newlywed quarterback got down to gridiron business.

All season long, Rutledge alternated as starting quarterback with sophomore Richard Todd. The concept of sharing was difficult for both players to accept at first, but it made for lively competition between two outstanding quarterbacks.

"We got used to sharing the spot," Rutledge said. "I was lucky to start all the games we won. So I played about 60 to 70 percent of the time. Richard and I got along great and complemented each other really well. That's why Alabama was so successful in the seventies. We had great players, and we wore down the other teams because we played so many people."

In 1973, the Crimson Tide finished 11-1 and were crowned national champions. The season's many high points included a thrilling 42-21 win over Tennessee.

"The touchdown to Wayne Wheeler on the first play is probably what fans remember the most," Rutledge said. "Every game that season we ran our first play with the fullback straight up the middle. So we surprised them with a fake and a pass."

Fans also remember Rutledge's impressive 85-yard scoring toss to Joe Dale Harris in the 66-0 stomping of California. (At the time, that was the longest touchdown pass in Alabama history.) They also remember the LSU game, where the Tide traveled to Baton Rouge and (as *Sports Illustrated* put it) "took the Tigers by the tail." *SI* made mention of several of Rutledge's moves, including a fake that turned into an easy score and a flip-pass to George Pugh for a 49-yard touchdown run. They also put him on the cover.

For Rutledge, the most memorable game was The Iron Bowl. The Tide was looking for revenge after the heartbreaking 17-16 loss the previous year. And they got it: Alabama beat the Tigers 35-0.

"When they beat us [the year before], all the bumper stickers said, 'Punt, Bama, Punt!' After that 35-0 whipping we gave them, it was, 'Score, Auburn, Score!' That wasn't my best career game, but it was my most satisfying win."

Something else Rutledge will never forget: the quarterbacks' pre-game walks with Coach Bryant.

"He had a different relationship with his quarterbacks than with the other players," Rutledge said. "He would always gather the quarterbacks together on game day and walk us around, just the five or six of us who were making the trip. If we were staying at a motel, we'd walk around the pool; just the quarterbacks, Coach Bryant and Coach Moore.

"He would say, 'Keep your poise and confidence. If somebody gets in a fight, don't return the punch because that's the one that always gets called. In a crucial situation, put your best ball carrier behind your best blocker on a third-down play. Be calm and cool, but show leadership. Keep command of the huddle. Let your teammates and your linemen know you're in charge.'"

The supreme highs of 1973 were followed by major disappointment for Rutledge, when just one week before the '74 season began, he badly separated his shoulder during a scrimmage. He sat out all but the final two games of the season.

"I was hoping to play my senior year," Rutledge said. "I wanted to play in the Senior Bowl. I wanted to give pro football a shot, but I'm not very big so that probably wouldn't have worked out anyway. But the Saturday before our first game, Coach Bryant always had a big scrimmage. I got tackled and separated my shoulder. It was my right one so I couldn't throw."

According to Rutledge, Coach Bryant came to see him in the hospital and apologized. Since his injury, the coaches changed the policy, and quarterbacks can't be hit in the pre-season scrimmage.

Rutledge played the last two games of the season, although he struggled because his arm was still not 100 percent. While Alabama was in Miami to play in the Orange Bowl, it was announced that offensive coordinator Bud Moore would be the new head coach at the University of Kansas. Coach Moore planned to run the wishbone at Kansas and needed someone who knew it well. He offered Rutledge the position of quarterbacks coach.

Rutledge remembered what Coach Bryant said when he consulted him on his decision. "He said, 'If that's what you want to do, it's an all-consuming job. You've got to want to coach more than anything.'"

Rutledge spent three years at Kansas, but due partially to frustrations from the job and his and his wife's extreme homesickness, they returned to Birmingham in 1978. Rutledge became the head coach at Homewood High School. The team had a poor season, and Rutledge realized he was not cut out to be a coach.

"It just wasn't for me," Rutledge said. "I didn't like the fact that you spend so much time away from your family at night. I didn't like the fact that you could have the best game plan and then the kids don't want to practice hard or they're not as dedicated as you are. I wanted to get into something where I was only responsible for me."

After he quit coaching, Rutledge visited Tuscaloosa one day to watch his brother Jeff and teammates on the practice field. He was standing on the sidelines, when, to his astonishment, Coach Bryant waved at him and climbed down from his coach's tower.

"I'd seen him climb down that tower before but it was usually to tear a guy's head off and jerk him around by his face mask," Rutledge laughed. "But

Photograph courtesy of Gary Rutledge

Brett, Cindy, Gary, and Stacy Rutledge

he made a special trip down and sat on the staircase just to talk to me. It was pretty nice."

During the visit, Jeff told Gary about an opportunity he'd heard about from the team doctor. The president of a pharmaceutical company was looking for a sharp ex-Alabama player to work for his company. Rutledge was immediately offered the position.

"In sales, you work as hard to be as successful as you want to be," he said. "You have to be self-motivated. It's the same as football. There's no substitute for hard work. The pride you had as a player, as an athlete, you've got the same thing here. I like to try to be one of the top reps in my district and in my company. I've been real successful here."

HOWARD SCHNELLENBERGER

"We're on a collision course with the national championship."
— HOWARD SCHNELLENBERGER

HOWARD SCHNELLENBERGER IS A LOT LIKE THE GUY IN THE HOSPITAL operating room holding the paddles over a flatlining patient's chest. He tells everyone to stand back ("Clear!"), puts the paddles in place, and shocks the patient's heart back into action. When the patient leaves the hospital, he is back to his old self. Or sometimes, he's even better than he ever was.

Schnellenberger, who played for Bear Bryant at the University of Kentucky in the fifties and coached for him at Alabama in the sixties, does his reviving on the football field. He is perhaps best known for breathing new life into the football program at the University of Miami, which was on the verge of being eliminated when he arrived as head coach in 1979.

The Miami board of trustees had just voted to give the program five more years before pulling the plug. At his first press conference, Schnellenberger promised that the Miami Hurricanes would not only not be a thing of the past in five years, but that they would win the national championship. And that's what they did.

In 1985, Schnellenberger returned to his native Kentucky to resuscitate the University of Louisville's football program. He admits that when he took the reins at Louisville, due to the fact that they hadn't marked a winning season in thirteen years, his predictions had to be more conservative.

So he declined to fix a year to their goal and instead simply stated: "We're on a collision course with the national championship. The only variable is time."

Even though Schnellenberger had been gone for years, a lot of fans and sports reporters remembered this statement when in 2007 the Louisville Cardinals finished No. 5 in the nation after beating Wake Forest in the Orange Bowl.

Four years after he left Louisville, Schnellenberger accepted a position at Florida Atlantic University in Boca Raton, Florida. At FAU, Schnellenberger would not be expected to revive the football program. Mostly because they didn't have one.

Photograph by Ronald C. Modra. Used by permission.

Schnellenberger: the great resuscitator

Incredibly, Schnellenberger's role as director of football operations would be to start a football team from scratch. And in the spring of 1998, that's what he did. In his tiny office next to the gymnasium pool (there was no football office yet), he set about making calls and recruiting sponsors and alumni boosters for his program. Soon, he'd raised $15 million; and in 1999, the school's board of regents approved FAU's adding football.

Schnellenberger, by now named head coach, shifted his focus to hiring staff and recruiting players. The following August, FAU's inaugural team of 164 players hit the field for its first practice. They played their first game on September 1, 2001.

After competing for four years at the Division 1-AA level and making it to the play-offs in 2003, in 2005, FAU moved to the Sun Belt Conference and the Division 1-A level.

"That was one of my goals when I came here," Schnellenberger said.

The others? "Building a stadium and winning a national title."

Crimson Tide fans sometimes forget that before Alabama claimed Coach Bryant as their own, he briefly belonged to Maryland, Kentucky, and Texas A&M.

When he accepted the position as head coach at Kentucky in 1946, Coach Bryant was only thirty-two years old. He was determined to win, even at a non-football school such as Kentucky. And he did. During his eight seasons with the Wildcats he led his teams to a 60-23-5 record, took them to their first four bowl games, and in 1950 scored a Southeastern Conference championship.

The new head coach impressed his players from the start. When George Blanda, who played for Bryant from 1946 to 1948, first saw him he said, "That must be what God looks like."

As a high school player, Howard Schnellenberger was one of the best linemen in Kentucky. He was highly recruited and was ready to sign with Indiana University when Coach Bryant came to call.

Bryant was not one to come empty-handed: he brought the governor of Kentucky along on the visit. Schnellenberger's dad was impressed, but his mother said it would be wrong to break the commitment to Indiana.

Coach Bryant, who knew Mrs. Schnellenberger was a devout Catholic, returned a few days later with the archbishop of her diocese. The deal was done.

Schnellenberger told Keith Dunnavant, author of *Coach*: "When Coach Bryant goes to war, he doesn't just bring the rifles, he brings the howitzers. That's the lesson I learned that day."

The military metaphors don't end there. According to Schnellenberger, football practices at Kentucky were exactly like boot camp. They were also reminiscent of Bryant's famous Junction Boys training camp, the pre-season session endured by Bryant's first team at Texas A&M at an old military base in the dusty town of Junction, Texas.

"When I saw the *Junction Boys* movie a few years ago, it ticked me off," Schnellenberger said. "I didn't know they were only out there for eight days. We were out there for six weeks!"

As Schnellenberger tells it, before there was a Junction, there was a Millersburg.

"He took us to a military camp north of campus. There were probably 132 freshmen on the bus. Only forty came back."

The Kentucky stories sound strikingly familiar to the scenes from *Junction Boys.* Guys climbing out of windows and sliding down drainpipes to escape in the middle of the night. A rock-strewn field. No water. Collapsing from heat stroke.

Also familiar is the commitment and the bond shared by the players who made it through the experience and stayed with the team.

"He made it so hard," Schnellenberger said. "He was running off the quitters. The ones who stayed were committed."

As he told Dunnavant: "Coach taught me that hard work and sacrifice could get you somewhere in this world. He set the tone for my whole life."

Schnellenberger played for Coach Bryant for two years before Bryant left for A&M. He finished his playing years at Kentucky in 1956 as an all-American tight end under Coach Blanton Collier. He stayed on as Collier's assistant coach at Kentucky for two years then he joined Coach Bryant's coaching staff at Alabama, in the national championship year of 1961.

"That was a real high time to be at Alabama!" he said. "There was no rebuilding going on that year."

As an Alabama assistant coach, Schnellenberger is perhaps best remembered as the coach who recruited Joe Namath. When Joe was a high school senior in Beaver Falls, Pennsylvania, dozens of college coaches were after him.

Namath had committed to Maryland, but when he didn't score the required minimum on the college boards, he was up for grabs. The Alabama coaches snapped into action.

Coach Schnellenberger is still passionate about the game.

Photograph by Ronald C. Modra. Used by permission.

Schnellenberger knew Joe's older brother, Frank, who had been a freshman at Kentucky when Schnellenberger was a senior there. Frank was more like a father figure to Joe and thought playing for Bryant would give him the discipline and focus he needed.

Expecting to stay only one day, Schnellenberger arrived in town with just the clothes on his back. He hoped to hustle Joe out of town before other schools found out he was available. But the visit with his star prospect stretched into a week.

Not only did he have no change of clothes, Schnellenberger was running out of cash.

"Before I left, Coach Bryant went into one of his tin boxes and grabbed me some petty cash," Schnellenberger recalled. "I should have brought more on my own, but I didn't have much extra in those days."

Finally, he convinced Joe to come to Tuscaloosa. Schnellenberger had barely enough money to buy their plane tickets, and when a storm forced them to spend the night in Atlanta, Schnellenberger wrote a bad check for their hotel room.

At breakfast the next morning, Schnellenberger, who had only the change in his pocket, was incredibly relieved when Joe only ordered coffee.

Despite the ribbing his fellow coaches gave him for still wearing the clothes he had on when he departed a week earlier, Schnellenberger breathed a huge sigh of relief when he delivered his charge to the practice field.

As legend goes, Coach Bryant took it from there. He invited Joe to join him on his coach's tower—a first for a player or recruit—and the rest is history.

These days, Coach Schnellenberger doesn't have a coach's tower on his field at Florida Atlantic. What he does have, though, is a balcony that wraps around his second floor office and overlooks the playing field. Many days he and his assistant coaches watch practice from this picturesque spot.

"It's not about watching them," he said. "The important thing is for the players to see us watching them."

Schnellenberger has had his share of visitors join him on his balcony at FAU. One frequent guest is friend and mentor, Coach Don Shula, who lends his name to the Shula Bowl, the annual matchup between FAU and rival Florida International University.

"I'm so lucky in my life to have had four great mentors," Schnellenberger said. "Coach Bryant, Coach Collier at Kentucky, Coach George Allen when I worked for the Los Angeles Rams, and Coach Don Shula."

Schnellenberger was an assistant coach for Don Shula and the Dolphins from 1975 to 1979. He is often asked why Shula was so successful as a coach.

"He knew he was going to be a coach from the time he was a player, so he prepared himself for it," said Schnellenberger.

"As a player on the field, he was the most knowledgeable guy. Not only about the *X*s and *O*s, but he understood what motivates professional players."

Before Coach Shula arrived to begin directing all those winning seasons in Miami, Coach Bryant was offered the Dolphins head coaching job. As we all know, he declined. No one was happier than Howard Schnellenberger.

"He called me when they offered it to him and I said, 'Coach Bryant, please don't take that job,'" Schnellenberger said.

"'You're meant to be a college coach. Kids respond to you. You're very special. If you go to the NFL, it's not going to be the same. It's not going to be as much fun for you.' I don't know if I had a major impact, but I sure tried to talk him out of it."

Although Schnellenberger has coached both in the pros (as head coach of the Baltimore Colts and an assistant for the LA Rams), his major achievements hail from his days as a college coach.

There have been many highs (Miami, Louisville, Alabama, and Kentucky);

and as in any high profile profession, there have been inevitable lows (Oklahoma, and the stints in the NFL).

But what inspires Coach Schnellenberger most about his most recent job? "Everything. Because every day is something new and different."

Even though he is among the oldest college football coaches in the country (currently third-oldest behind Bobby Bowden and Joe Paterno), he doesn't wax philosophical about the "good old days." Nor does he buy into the theory that today's youth are spoiled.

"We try our best to spoil them," he said. "But I see these kids working just as hard as we ever did. Going to school today is so tough. For football players, every moment of their time is taken up. They go to class. They go to study hall. They compete with kids at the top of their class and all this after being up at 5:00 AM for practice. These kids are committed. The founding class had to be leaders from the start. They had no one to look to but themselves. Tell me what's easy about that."

Although he's lost none of his passion for the game or his players, Schnellenberger says he is probably a more understanding coach than he was years ago.

"I had to change a little when I came here because at first, I only had freshmen," Schnellenberger said. "But when they became seniors, then I could hold their feet to the fire."

Schnellenberger is grateful to be writing the last chapter of his working life in Florida. He is often accompanied on the sidelines or one of many campus activities by his wife, Beverlee, who he says is a full partner in everything he does at FAU.

He has three sons (second son, Tim, played for him on the national championship team at Miami) and three grandchildren. And more goals to add to his list: "I want to take my team into the stadium by 2010 I hope," he said. "And either have the University of Miami come in and open the season or Florida State. Then the course would be set toward getting into the Big East Conference."

STEADMAN SHEALY

"You have to be willing to do what everybody else isn't."

— STEADMAN SHEALY

AFTER PAUL W. "BEAR" BRYANT DIED IN JANUARY 1983, THE ENTIRE state of Alabama shut down. His funeral began with a service in Tuscaloosa and a fifty-five-mile-long procession to Elmwood Cemetery in Birmingham for the burial. Some half a million mourners lined the streets along the way, and thousands more crowded around the cemetery that cold, sad day.

Of all the people Coach Bryant knew—governors, presidents, famous football players and coaches, successful businessmen, well-known ministers, as well as scores of regular folks—just one man gave the eulogy in Tuscaloosa.

Steadman Shealy.

"Mrs. Bryant asked me to do it," Shealy said. "Coach Bryant and I had a unique relationship. We talked a lot about the Lord together. He knew I was very devout in my faith, and we'd talk about Jesus and what he meant in his life and my life. A lot of the things people would never know—we talked about. We had a very close relationship."

Shealy was in fact extremely close to Coach Bryant in the last years of his life. He was one of the quarterbacks on Alabama's teams from 1977 to 1979, which finished with two national championships. After graduation, he worked for Bryant as an assistant coach for one year, then stayed on as a graduate assistant while going to law school.

Photograph courtesy of Steadman Shealy

From the gridiron to the courtroom: attorney Steadman Shealy

Much to his surprise, Coach Bryant asked Shealy to handle all his legal affairs while Shealy was still just a law student. Then, in 1982, Shealy co-hosted *The Bear Bryant Show* with the coach after longtime co-host and media relations man Charley Thornton took a job at Texas A&M. Even though he has been gone nearly twenty-five years, Paul Bryant is still a crucial part of Shealy's life.

"There's rarely a day that goes by that I don't think of something he said or did," Shealy said. "He's the best teacher I ever had."

Shealy grew up in Dothan, Alabama, and, naturally, he was an avid Alabama football fan. He played baseball, basketball, and ran track at Dothan High School. He also played football, and as quarterback he led his team to the state championship finals his junior and senior years.

In the spring of 1976, recruiters were literally tripping over each other at the Shealy house. One afternoon, new Auburn head coach Doug Barfield was in the living room chatting with Shealy and his parents, while Georgia Coach Vince Dooley waited in his car in the Shealy's driveway. As Barfield made his case, the phone rang. It was Coach Bryant. Shealy politely excused himself to take the call.

As Shealy related in the book *Game of My Life: Alabama,* Bryant began the conversation with a question.

"What jersey have you always wanted to wear?" Bryant asked.

"Crimson," Shealy answered.

"What's the problem then?" Bryant responded.

The problem was, as much as Shealy wanted to play for Alabama, he knew there were many other talented quarterbacks already there or on their way there. This point was hammered home by suitors from other schools (Mississippi State and several Ivy League universities, as well as Georgia and Auburn) who promised if he signed with them, he would be the number-two guy immediately. Alabama made no such promises. But Shealy took a leap of faith and headed to Tuscaloosa.

"When I got there, I was number nine!" Shealy said. "It was a fight. There was a lot of competition and a lot of athletes. I didn't play or travel as a freshman. Mostly I just got beat on."

Over the years, Shealy has described his freshman year over and over as "a nightmare." Imagine lining up against the varsity defense, as freshmen players do, to square off against powerful vets, many of them with all-SEC or all-American beside their names. It was brutal. But Shealy persevered.

"Those practices prepared me for my sophomore year and got me ready to play from then on," he said. "It taught me that you had to outwork the other guys. It also made me truly appreciate the opportunity to play. I'd been through the battle."

Shealy's first outing as an Alabama player (against Nebraska in the second game of 1977) is something he'd like to forget. With national TV cameras rolling, Shealy attempted a hand-off but ended up losing his balance and falling to the ground for a five-yard loss.

"I stumbled again on the next play and gained a couple of yards or three yards," he said in *Game of My Life.* "I think Jeff Rutledge threw three interceptions in that game, so no one would sit with us on the plane on the flight home [after a 31-24 loss]."

After the team went 11-1 in 1977, Shealy couldn't wait for his junior season. But during spring practice, he badly injured his knee and required surgery. Unfortunately, a major staph infection resulted. Shealy lost thirty pounds and had to fight hard to work his way back.

"I would go into the football building and the coaches were planning the year without me, some coaches not even giving me the time of day," he later told a reporter.

Shealy was determined. Even though he could barely move his knee, the trainers told him he could play if he could manage a 125-degree bend. The night before his physical he tied his knee into position and kept it that way until morning!

What may have helped him more than anything, even more than his intense will to succeed, was his head coach's confidence.

"I always felt like Coach Bryant believed in me," he said. "He knew how I had worked all summer to be able to play, and he had faith in me. That made a difference."

Just four months after having major surgery, Shealy was back and played in eleven of twelve games, sharing quarterbacking duties with Jeff Rutledge throughout his junior (national championship) year of 1978. He became known as the running QB, while Jeff was known as the passing guy. No question, Shealy could do both, but his running was something to see.

Photograph courtesy of Paul W. Bryant Museum/The University of Alabama

Shealy took an on-field leap of faith.

Shealy says he had no problem having to share the job. As he said in *What It Means to Be Crimson Tide:* "Coach Bryant believed in playing men if they had earned it. I probably played about ten snaps a game as a sophomore and about twenty-five snaps a game as a junior, backing up Jeff. And why not play the backup quarterbacks? Everyone needs to play. I'm convinced that when the backup gets a chance, he gives about 110 percent effort."

In 1979, Shealy was front and center. He was the starter, and his incredible team finished 12-0 and once again was crowned national champions.

"The national championship is the standard Coach Bryant set for us," Shealy said. "We won two and should have won three!"

After the perfect season of 1979 and graduating the following year in the top 1 percent of his class, Shealy joined Coach Bryant's staff as an assistant coach. He was having trouble deciding whether to pursue law or a coaching career, when he approached his coach for advice.

According to a 1989 article by reporter Hal Hayes, Coach Bryant answered, "Steadman, I can't and wouldn't ever try to tell you what you ought to do. All I can tell you is, if you think you can't live without football, coach. If you can, don't."

Shealy was relieved.

"I had gone to see him hoping he would answer my question," he said. "Like he did so many times when people went to him for advice, he wound up making me answer for myself. I knew after talking with him what I was supposed to do. As much as I loved the game, I knew I could live without football; live without coaching football."

Shealy was lucky, though. He remained on the Alabama coaching staff as an assistant while attending law school. So basically, he had the best of both worlds. He is grateful for the time he was able to spend with Coach Bryant, which turned out to be the last few years of his life.

"I got closer to Coach Bryant while I was working with him," Shealy remembered. "I was his eyes and ears on the sideline, so I stood by him every game to make sure he knew what was going on from an offensive standpoint."

There's a famous picture of Shealy standing next to Coach Bryant during his 315th victory. Maybe a less well-known image is that of Shealy sitting next to the coach during the 1982 broadcasts of *The Bear Bryant Show*.

"It was awesome to be there, but I was terrible!" Shealy laughed. "I was a twenty-four-year-old kid who didn't know what I was doing. It was fun just to be close to him."

In his role as Bryant's right-hand-guy, Shealy was perhaps the first person to know of Bryant's decision to retire after the 1982 season.

"I hoped it wasn't true," he said. "I wasn't sure he was serious. But then, after we lost to Southern Miss, he walked in and said, 'Well, I think this is it for me.'"

The thought of Coach Bryant retiring was sad. But the reality of his death just one month after his retirement was unthinkable. Shealy was in a tax class when he got the news and left the room abruptly, crying uncontrollably.

He was touched when Mary Harmon Bryant asked him to deliver the eulogy and although it was gut-wrenching to get through it, doing this last thing for Coach Bryant was very healing indeed.

Shealy stayed on as a graduate assistant coach for one year with Coach Ray Perkins, working with a group of quarterbacks that included a young Mike Shula. He then set up his law practice. Today the offices of Cobb, Shealy, Crum & Derrick have offices in both Dothan and Tuscaloosa.

Shealy practices civil law and loves the fact that he spends his days helping people. And yes, he has heard all the lawyer jokes.

"Until you need a lawyer, it's kind of easy to bash a lawyer," he said. "But when you need one, he becomes your best friend."

Certainly, this particular attorney makes a lot of friends and faces new challenges every day.

"A lot of times the enormity of cases is really challenging," Shealy said. "You have to put it all together, and then you present it to the jury and let them decide it. It's just like playing a ball game."

"Coach Bryant always taught the basic principles of life. One of the things he talked about was being willing to do what others are not. I've learned that in the law practice that what sets you apart as a lawyer most of the time is just outworking the other side."

Shealy shares these words of wisdom often with his five children: John David, Robert, Anna Katherine, Shealy Jr., and Jacqueline, a member of the Crimson Tide gymnastics squad.

Ann, his wife of twenty-five years, was also a gymnast at Alabama. In fact, according to Shealy she was the first female athlete on full scholarship at the university.

As good as things are in his life, Shealy says he always strives to get better.

"The thing about Coach Bryant was that he was never satisfied," Shealy said. "He didn't live off what he did yesterday or five years ago. I want to move forward as a father, a husband, a lawyer, etc. Every day I want to get a little better."

STEVE SLOAN

"Steve Sloan is one of the finest people you will ever meet."

— MANY FORMER PLAYERS, TEAMMATES, AND FELLOW COACHES

NEXT TO THE WORD "TEAM PLAYER" IN THE ENCYCLOPEDIA BELONGS A picture of Steve Sloan.

Even though he was an all-American quarterback for the Crimson Tide and led the team to a 9-1-1 national championship in 1965, people often think of this great player as Joe Namath's back-up.

Indeed, when Sloan came to Tuscaloosa as a freshman in 1962, Namath was already a huge star. Then, during his first season on the varsity ('63), Sloan played mostly defensive back, only occasionally filling in at quarterback. But when his opportunity to lead the offense came, he made every snap count.

Toward the end of the 1963 season, Coach Bryant suspended Namath for breaking curfew. Alabama fans held their collective breath as the Namath-less

Photograph courtesy of Paul W. Bryant Museum/The University of Alabama

Sloan made every snap count.

Crimson Tide beat Miami in their last regular season game with No. 2 quarterback Jack Hurlbut at the helm. Then Bryant stunned everyone when he decided to start third-string quarterback Steve Sloan in the Sugar Bowl against Ole Miss on January 1, 1964.

"I was really shocked," Sloan remembered. "I read about his decision in the newspaper. It was my first start at quarterback for Alabama at a bowl game and I was filling in for Joe Namath. Then it snowed during the game. In New Orleans! I'd say I was nervous."

Sloan led his team to a 12-7 victory that day. The next season, he continued to perform his defensive duties until he was needed at quarterback, which turned out to be often due to Namath's frequent injuries.

Then in 1965, with Namath gone on to big bucks and bright city lights in the American Football League, Sloan got his chance to show his stuff. In his quiet, nonflashy fashion, Sloan methodically went about breaking Namath's school records when he passed for 1,453 yards and made 97 completions.

One of the most famous or infamous games in Alabama football history was the '65 Tennessee game. Playing the Vols was always intense, but "the Third Saturday in October," as the game is best known, was especially meaningful to Cleveland, Tennessee, native Steve Sloan, who had been named top player in the state (for both golf and football) by the Associated Press while attending Bradley Central High School.

"I was a lot more into the Tennessee-Alabama rivalry than I was the Alabama-Auburn rivalry," Sloan said. "Having not grown up in Alabama, I didn't know that much about Auburn. Although I learned fast! But being from Tennessee, to me, that was the big game. I knew some of the guys playing for Tennessee, and when I'd go back home in the summer, all the people in Cleveland were Vols fans, so they'd give me a hard time."

That 1965 game ended in a tie. And anyone who knew Coach Bryant knew how much he hated ties. ("That's like kissing your sister," he growled.)

In the fourth quarter, with the score tied 7-7, Sloan was hurt, and in came Kenny Stabler to replace him. In the remaining seconds, Stabler, who thought it was third down, threw the ball out of bounds to stop the clock. But it was fourth down. So the clock ran out. No chance to score. Tie ball game.

"I was the first one back to the dressing room because I was already out of the game," Sloan recalled. "When I got there, the door was locked. I remember thinking Coach Bryant is not going to be happy. He came up and looked around. No one was coming or anything, so he just kind of hit the door with his shoulder and knocked the door in. The lock came off and we went in!"

Once inside, the coach blamed himself for the loss.

"When there was a mistake that appeared to be due to coaching, that really bothered him," Sloan said. "He took full blame for the error. And as it turned out, we got even better that year, so the tie was not as detrimental as it seemed at the time. The door didn't come to that conclusion, though!"

Sloan, who played two years for the Atlanta Falcons after he left Alabama, soon returned to the university to begin what would ultimately stretch into a decades-long coaching career at a string of major universities. In all his years as a coach, he never rammed down a door. In fact, he never even considered it.

"The door would have knocked me down," Sloan laughed. "Coach Bryant had an unmatched level of toughness and charisma. He was a big guy as well, and when you're a big person, too, that seems to make a difference. He was a very dominant person. I just really wasn't that way. I was a little more laid-back."

After a shoulder injury forced his NFL retirement in 1968, Sloan returned to Alabama as an assistant coach. As most Bryant players-turned-coaches found, their relationship changed when they became his colleague.

"As a player, I was scared to death of Coach Bryant," Sloan said. "As a coach I felt a little bit better. But in all those years as an assistant, all I said to him was 'Yes, sir' or 'No, sir.' And if he asked a question, I tried to answer it for him."

But sometimes Coach Bryant wasn't especially receptive to answers from his staff, as was the case the time he called on Sloan during the 1970 Bluebonnet Bowl.

"Part of my job was to call the plays," Sloan remembered. "He didn't talk on the headset much because he thought someone might be listening. Anyway, he came and got the headset and told me we needed to put Ron Durby in the game. Well, Ron was a lineman on the 1964 national championship team. He's a judge now. A super guy!"

One problem, though Durby was not on the roster in 1970.

"You never said 'no' to Coach Bryant," Sloan continued. "But I said, 'Coach, I don't know if we can do that or not.' He had a few choice words he generally used. I said, 'You're right, Coach.' He said, 'I thought you'd see it my way.'"

Sloan never brought it up again.

Photograph courtesy of Paul W. Bryant Museum/The University of Alabama

A methodical, steady Steve Sloan

In 1971, with Coach Bryant's blessing, Sloan accepted a job as offensive coordinator at Florida State. After a year with the Seminoles, he moved on to Georgia Tech.

Then in 1973, he was named head coach at Vanderbilt. According to Sloan, Bryant played a pivotal role in his being offered this position that he wasn't sold on at first.

"Everybody told me not to take the job," Sloan said. "I called Coach Bryant and told him I wasn't going to take it. But he said, 'You're going to take the job.' So I took it! I was only twenty-eight!"

Sloan thus became the youngest college head coach in the country. After inheriting a team that went 3-8 the previous season, Vanderbilt went 5-6 in 1973 (a low point being the 44-0 thrashing by Alabama). Then, in 1974, although they lost to Alabama again (this time by a more respectable 23-10), Vandy stunned the conference by finishing 7-3-2.

Sloan, who was named SEC Coach of the Year, graciously credits his staff, including a young defensive coordinator named Bill Parcells, with the great year: "Sometimes you can get a team of people together even if it's by accident and everything works out. That year, everything blended. I just loved the Vanderbilt experience."

According to Sloan, "If you have a good year, they think you're a good coach." So the offers poured in.

He packed up his wife, Brenda, and his two young sons, Stephen and Jonathan, and went to Texas Tech in 1975. He stayed for three seasons, taking Tech to two bowl games and compiling an overall record of 23-12.

Early in 1977, he visited Coach Bryant in Tuscaloosa. Unknown to all but a very few, Bryant had actually considered retiring in 1978.

"He said, 'Next year I'm going to retire and I want you to take the job,'" Sloan said. "I said, well, that's fine coach. I'll do that. I really should have been more nervous about it than I was." Then, later that year Sloan read in the paper that Coach Bryant had signed a new contract.

"He called me after that," Sloan said. "As far as I was concerned, if he wanted to keep coaching, that was fine. I wanted him to do what was best for him. I figured whatever was going to happen to me was going to happen."

That next year, Sloan moved on to Ole Miss, where he coached from 1978 to 1982. His teams struggled and failed to notch a winning season during his tenure, although Sloan says he learned a great deal and carries no bitterness. He also cites no regret at not getting the chance to follow Bryant as head coach if he had retired in 1978 or after his actual retirement in 1982.

"I never felt bad because I don't feel like I would have been a good guy to follow him," Sloan said. "He was like General Patton. He had a much stronger personality than I had."

Sloan then spent three years as head coach at Duke. After that, he did in fact get the opportunity to return to Alabama in 1987, as athletics director. The experience was a difficult one for a number of reasons. Coach Bill Curry was hired at the same time, and the fans never fully accepted a "Georgia Tech" guy (Curry) as part of the post-Bryant lineage. An uproar in which many fans blamed Sloan ensued when the university agreed to play in Auburn for the first time in decades, and on top of that Sloan and the university president could not get on the same page. So, after just one year, Sloan left Tuscaloosa and briefly returned to Vanderbilt as the Commodores' offensive coordinator.

In 1993, Sloan took another stab at running a major university athletic department when he became athletics director at the University of Central Florida in Orlando, where he remained for almost ten years.

"I really loved UCF," Sloan said. "It was a school with so many dynamics in place. They have forty-seven thousand students! The seventh-largest in the country. The president liked athletics and wanted to fund athletics."

There are definite differences between coaching a football team and running an athletic department. Sloan says he learned many of the skills he needed—such as organization and planning—from Coach Bryant.

"Most businesses have a flow chart," Sloan said. "You have a president, a vice-president, and on down. His flow chart was him and everybody else! But even though he probably wouldn't realize it, he knew the basic principles of management better than any person I knew: organization, leadership, management, and control. He had a lot of skills he didn't necessarily acquire in school."

Although most people think of Bryant as playing the role of teacher in most of his relationships, there was a time when he sought out Sloan to teach him a deeply personal, spiritual lesson.

"He was attending the American Football Coaches Association meeting in Washington," Sloan recalled. "He called and said, 'I want you to fly up here. I want to ask you a question.' I said, 'Coach, could you ask me over the phone?' He said, 'No. I want to ask you in person.' So I flew up there.

"I remember it was so cold with the wind blowing. I make my way up to his hotel room. He's got a bunch of people in there, so he takes me off to a side room. He was interested in the doctrine of grace. In the Christian faith, you don't have to do anything to be forgiven. So I showed him a couple of verses. He said, 'You don't have to earn it? You don't have to work for it?' I said, 'No. It's a gift.' He said, 'OK. I just wanted to understand it.' The whole conversation took fifteen minutes. I walked downstairs, got a taxi, and flew back."

Sloan spent his final four working years as athletics director at the University of Tennessee–Chattanooga. He retired in 2006 and lives in Orlando with Brenda and his terrier, Nicholas.

He plays a lot of golf—usually three days a week—and works at Sanctuary Ridge golf course, running tournaments and doing speaking engagements for the club.

After years of packing and unpacking and getting on and off planes, he and Brenda are happy to mostly stay put in Orlando.

Of course the Sloans have many mementos of Sloan's playing and coaching days, including tributes to the man who Sloan said was like an extra-large father figure to him. But one particular reminder might be missed by the casual observer.

"I have a bear on the back of my license tag," Sloan said. "I picked it because of him. Every time I see it, I say, 'Hey Coach!' I would never say, 'Bear.' Someone would have to hold a gun to my head to get me to do that. And I still wouldn't do it."

KEN STABLER

"Coach Bryant saved me."

— KEN STABLER

ONE OF THE CRIMSON TIDE'S MOST BELOVED FOOTBALL HEROES, Kenny Stabler, was born on Christmas Day 1945 in Foley, Alabama. The guy we affectionately call "the Snake" (a nickname bestowed on him by his high school coach for his twisting, swerving running style) spent his formative years constantly playing sports.

"I was your typical small town, good athlete," Stabler said. "I was a good baseball pitcher; I threw the ball hard. And I was a good basketball player and football player."

Typical? Maybe in the sense that he played football in the fall, basketball in the winter, and baseball in the spring. But young Stabler was anything but ordinary. By his senior year in high school, he had some exciting offers on the table.

"The Yankees offered me $50,000 to play minor league baseball," he said.

"That was a ton of money back then, especially in our house."

Stabler was seriously tempted to accept the offer. He could really help his family with that kind of money. Plus, he loved baseball. ("To this day, I wonder if I could have thrown the ball like these guys do now," he said.)

But there was one small problem. Stabler grew up dreaming of playing football for the Crimson Tide while he and his dad, Slim, listened to Alabama games on the radio. He idolized Pat Trammell, Billy Neighbors, Billy Richardson, and Joe Namath.

Photograph courtesy of Paul W. Bryant Museum/The University of Alabama

Ken Stabler: yet another great quarterback to wear #12

Then, Coach Bryant came to call.

"That was it!" Stabler laughed. "He was so big and had that face that looked like it should have been carved in Mount Rushmore. Coach Bryant was the most imposing figure I had ever seen, next to my father. He looked just like him. They could have been brothers!"

So, Stabler forgot about the Bronx Bombers and decided to head to Tuscaloosa to see if he could pick up where Trammell and Namath had left off.

During his sophomore year of 1965, Snake played backup quarterback behind Steve Sloan. He also logged some playing time at defensive end. It was an incredible season for the Crimson Tide, crowned national champions for the second straight year.

Snake was the starting quarterback in 1966 and the team went 11-0, outscoring their opponents 267-37 along the way. Despite the sting of not being voted national champions, it was an absolutely tremendous year all the way around. Especially for the Snake, who led the team in rushing (397 yards on 93 carries, for a 4.3 yard average, with three touchdowns). He was named

MVP in the Sugar Bowl, where the Tide soundly defeated Nebraska, 34-7. It was a sweet ending to a perfect season.

"I always remember playing Nebraska in the Sugar Bowl," Stabler said. "They were a heavy favorite. They were a much bigger, stronger team than we were. It had been drizzling rain all weekend in New Orleans. A wet field probably favors Nebraska. A bigger, stronger team probably ran the ball a little better than we did. So we're coming out of the locker room walking toward the end zone. It had been raining all weekend, and I swear to God, Coach Bryant stepped on the field and it quit raining."

Divine intervention? Maybe. But what made that game so unforgettable was the fact that despite being outweighed almost thirty pounds to the man, the Crimson Tide could not be stopped.

No question, heading into the '67 season, the Tide was riding high. Everyone, including Stabler, expected him to take the helm and lead his team straight to another national championship season.

Then, during a run-of-the-mill drill at spring practice, the Snake tore cartilage in his knee. Coach Bryant told him to stay off it and not to practice until it was healed.

"I got kind of bored because I couldn't practice," Snake said. "So, I started going to visit my girlfriend down in Mobile. We had study hall from 7:30 to 9:00. I would skip study hall, jump in the car and drive four hours to Pritchard, Alabama, hang out with this girl I was seeing down there for four hours, jump back in the car and drive four hours back to try to make a 7:00 class. But I didn't make many of those."

"Then one day, I got a telegram at my parents' house. It said, 'You have been indefinitely suspended. – Coach Paul W. Bryant.' Then, I got another telegram the very next day from Namath. It said: 'He means it.'"

So, reluctantly, Snake enrolled in summer school. He had to take and pass a lot of tough classes to restore his eligibility. But nothing was tougher than making the long trek into the coach's office.

"It was the hardest thing I've ever had to do!" Snake said. "I was so intimidated by that toughness and fairness about him. You go in his office and that desk is raised and that couch is soft, and you sit way down under his eye level.

"So, I go in there and say, 'Coach, I have done everything necessary to become eligible by SEC standards; my grade point is back up and I want to come back out for the team.'

"He spits his tobacco, then looks me dead in the eye and says, 'You don't deserve to be on this team, get your ass out of here.' I said, 'Well, I am going to come back out anyway, Coach.' He said, 'We'll see.'"

Stabler came to every practice and absorbed all the punishment that was sent his way. He refused to quit. Eventually, Coach Bryant relented. Stabler was thrilled. He figured he had worked his way back and would pick up where he left off after the glorious success of last season. But, not so fast.

"I was excited and got back out there for the first day of practice in the fall," Stabler said. "In practice, your uniform color dictates the team you're on. Red jersey, first team. White jersey, second team. Blue jersey, third team. Orange jersey, fourth team. Green jersey, fifth team.

"Well, Coach Bryant had this thing he would call you when you were out of favor with him—a turd. Been called that a hundred times. So here I was, after being MVP in the Sugar Bowl the year before, and when I get my basket, it had a brown jersey in it. He made me work myself back to the top!"

No question. Coach Bryant was consistent.

"He taught me that no one player is any more important or bigger than the team itself," Snake said. "He treated everybody the same, from the groundskeeper to the bus driver to the president of the school. To him, we were all in it together. We are all the same."

Photograph courtesy of Paul W. Bryant Museum/The University of Alabama

With Snake at the helm, The Tide was riding high.

Years later, we know that Stabler's jersey went from brown to crimson that fall. But Snake didn't know it until the last possible minute.

"We were playing Florida State in the opener," Stabler said. "Joe Kelley started the game. We went three and out. On the second series, we got the ball. I was standing there beside Coach Bryant, waiting to go in. Then, he hit me in the back so hard it knocked the breath out of me. He said, 'Go ahead!'"

So Snake was back. His senior year was indeed another incredible season. Snake credits his coach.

"It was just the way he said things and phrased things," Snake said. "We would always play teams that were bigger and faster, but we always won. I think he outcoached and outmotivated the other guy. We only lost three games in three years, and that was because of how great a coach that he was."

Stabler left his final mark on Alabama's playing field during the Auburn game his senior year. Barely a day goes by when a fan doesn't ask him about his famous play during this game—the Run in the Mud.

"I don't mind at all!" he said. "It means so much to so many people because it was against Auburn! I played fifteen years of pro football, but that's the worst weather that I have ever played in. The field was six inches deep in mud and water. And it was real, real windy. If you look at old pictures, the fans' umbrellas are all turned inside out!

"So, before the game, Coach Bryant says we are not going to throw the ball. We are going to run the ball and control the line of scrimmage. When Auburn screws up its kicking game, we will play for field position and try to do something."

In the fourth quarter, that's just what Alabama did. After Auburn's punter mishandled a snap, Alabama took the ball at their forty-six yard line. On a third-down play, Stabler saw a hole and sloshed right through it.

"Once I started running, I just went straight for that chain-link fence!" Stabler said. Bama won the game 7-3.

Post-Bama, Stabler was drafted by the Oakland Raiders. He meshed perfectly with John Madden's rebellious, love-to-hate-'em renegades, backing up Daryle Lamonica and George Blanda at quarterback his first couple of years.

Photograph by Ronald C. Modra. Used by permission.

Snake Oil: Stabler's NFL career included a stop in Houston.

By 1973, he was the starter, and Snake-led teams visited the championship game five times and beat Minnesota (32-14) in Super Bowl XI.

To this day, Snake holds the Raiders team records for passing attempts, completions, yardage, and touchdowns. He was a five-time Pro Bowler, twice all-pro, three times all-AFC, and twice AFC player of the year. He notched thirty-six 200-yard passing games and, at one point, had 143 consecutive pass attempts without an interception (a Raider record). He also led the NFL in passing touchdowns in 1974 and 1976. (And this guy's not in the Hall of Fame?)

According to Stabler, playing for Coach Bryant at Alabama laid the groundwork for his NFL success.

"He taught us all those lessons, those corny clichés about self-sacrifice and discipline and all those things that go along with teamwork. You're only as strong as the weakest link on the chain. But it's true! If he didn't figure out a way to grab me by the back of the neck and kick me in the ass and make me get back in school, I wouldn't have had a pro football career. There is no question in my mind. I'd be bartending or selling cars or God knows what if it wasn't for him. Coach Bryant saved me."

Although Stabler says he never forgot Coach Bryant's teachings, he admits he sometimes needed a refresher course.

"I was always someone who needed some type of direction; some tough love," he laughed. "In high school, college, and in pro ball. But I was so fortunate to play for so many good people. The closest people to me were my coaches."

Indeed, Snake says the Raiders' John Madden was like a big brother to him and the Houston Oilers' Bum Phillips, whom he played for from 1979 to 1982, was like a grandfather.

After playing his final two seasons with the New Orleans Saints, Snake retired from the NFL in 1984, gathered up all his lessons and football knowledge, and put them to excellent use as a broadcaster. First, he worked for CBS, doing regional games with Greg Gumbel and James Brown. Next, he spent several years working on the *Silver Bullet Stadium Show* for Turner Sports.

Then, Wright Waters, the general manager of the Crimson Tide Sports Network, called and offered him the color analyst's position for the University of Alabama.

"There was something about it that felt really good," said Stabler. "I live in Alabama. My daughters [Alexa and Marissa] were getting ready to go to school at the university, and I was looking forward to being around them. I love being around the team and talking about the team. I thought about it a couple of days and dove on it!"

For Stabler, talking about football for a living comes as easily as breathing.

"I'm an *X*s and *O*s guy, so I watch a football game with my hands under the center," he said. "I try to throw the game at our listeners with a right and a left and an up and a down. Then Eli throws in the wind blowing and the colors and the band playing. The best compliment we get is when someone says, 'Thanks for making us be at the game.' That's what we shoot for."

Over the years, the honors keep coming Stabler's way. He's a member of Alabama's Team of the Century, the Alabama Sports Hall of Fame, and the Bay Area Hall of Fame. (And fans wait for the day when the Pro Football Hall of Fame will be added to this list.)

Photograph by Ronald C. Modra. Used by permission.

Snake can talk some football.

There's one title he particularly treasures: grandfather. His daughter Kendra's twin boys call him "Papa Snake."

Mostly, he loves watching his own family become part of the University of Alabama family. And, he loves watching football.

"I love college football in general," Stabler said. "The healthiness and the cleanliness and the amateurness of it. And Alabama has won more national championships than anybody else. We'll get back to that. It comes from everybody. From the players, the coaches, the broadcast team, the fans. The best way to do it is just simply go win. Winning cures the common cold!"

GENE STALLINGS

"People in Alabama loved Coach Bryant. They just tolerated the rest of us."
— GENE STALLINGS

TALK ABOUT A TOUGH ACT TO FOLLOW. THE HANDFUL OF MEN WHO have succeeded Coach Bryant as head coach at the University of Alabama know, no matter what, you will always be compared to the Bear.

When Gene Stallings stepped into Bryant's long shadow in 1990, expectations were especially high. The comparisons to Coach Bryant were inevitable. But this time it wasn't just speculation as to how the new coach would measure up against the winningest coach in college football history. This time, people were comparing the men.

"There's just one Coach Bryant," Stallings said. "He set the bar, and the rest of us are just trying to do the best we can. I was fond of saying that people in Alabama loved Coach Bryant. They just tolerated the rest of us. I'd step out of my office and I was on Paul Bryant Drive, walking past the Paul

Bryant Conference Center next to Paul Bryant Museum. Down the street is Paul Bryant Athletic Dorm. You drive into Tuscaloosa over the Paul Bryant Bridge.

"There's no comparison. I tried to win some games the way he did, but I never tried to compete with Coach Bryant. I knew my place. I think that's one reason it was a little easier for me to coach at Alabama because it did not intimidate me that he had such a great record and that the people loved him so much. I loved him, too."

Photograph courtesy of Paul W. Bryant Museum/The University of Alabama

Stallings: at home on Alabama's sidelines

The Bryant-Stallings connection goes way back. Stallings, who grew up in Paris, Texas, played for Coach Bryant at Texas A&M. He was one of the famed "Junction Boys" on the 1954 team that Bryant took off-campus and put through a grueling preseason boot camp during his first year as head coach.

Stallings has been asked about his Junction experience many times. Often, he sums up those grueling, hardscrabble days by saying: "All I know is we went out there in two buses and came back in one."

When *The Junction Boys* movie came out in 2002, Stallings said he was disappointed with the result.

"There is a difference between toughness and brutality," he said. "Coach Bryant was tough but he wasn't brutal. The movie portrayed him as a brutal-type man. It showed him kicking a player when he was down. The language was awful. It looked like he didn't care about the trainer and all of us, and that just wasn't true. They worked us hard, but everybody worked hard in those days. We didn't get water, but nobody got water in those days.

"Coach Bryant did care for the player. Those of us who played for him and worked with him wouldn't have loved him the way we did if he was brutal to us. He made us better players and better people. He gave us a little swagger in our walk because we won games and hadn't been winning games. It was like being a Marine. You were proud of the fact that you wore that."

Stallings was one of just thirty-five players who returned to the A&M campus on that legendary lone bus from Junction. After two rebuilding seasons, the squad that bonded at Junction finished 9-0-1 and Stallings was named all-conference and co-captain of his undefeated team.

After graduating with a degree in physical education, Stallings stayed on at A&M as a graduate assistant coach. The following year, Coach Bryant was named head coach at Alabama, and he invited Stallings to join his staff.

"I was thrilled to death," said Stallings. "I was making forty-five hundred dollars a year and thought I had the absolute best job in the world. I loved every minute of it."

Bryant, a strong believer that defense won games, named Stallings defensive coordinator on teams that won the national championship in 1961 and 1964.

Gaylon McCollough, a Crimson Tide player from 1962 to 1964, remembered Stallings making a strong impression on his players.

"He was uncompromising," he said. "That is the one word I would use to describe him. He knew what was the right thing to do, and he was dead set on getting it done that way."

Then in 1965, when he was just twenty-nine years old, Texas A&M invited him back. This time as head coach and athletic director. Stallings said yes.

After he heard the news that Stallings would be following in his footsteps and taking the A&M job, Coach Bryant gave an interview to the *Houston Post:* "It's the first time I've cried in twenty or thirty years," Bryant said. "And believe me, I really did. I cried because I'm so proud that one of my little Junction Boys is going back there to take over. And secondly, I cried because I'm so upset about losing him. Shoot, with Stallings gone, I may have to go back to work. A&M could go back to Rockne and they could not have picked a better man. He will be the best football coach the school ever had and that includes father."

(By "father" Bryant meant himself.)

In his book, *The Legend of Bear Bryant,* Mickey Herskowitz tells a great story about this moment in college football history. A writer named Bob Curran told Herskowitz that he had walked into Bryant's hotel room during the above-mentioned interview, which was taking place by phone. He said Bryant looked really choked up and asked a friend, "What's wrong with Paul?"

"He just lost an assistant coach," the man whispered.

"How old was he?" Curran asked.

"Twenty-nine."

"My God!" exclaimed Curran. "That's awfully young. How did he die?"

"Oh, he didn't die," the friend assured him. "He just went to Texas A&M."

The Aggies struggled during Stallings' first couple of years. Then, in 1967, after losing their first four games, the team regrouped and finished the season with six straight victories, their conference title, and an invitation to the Cotton Bowl.

Their postseason opponent? The University of Alabama.

The week before the game, the two head coaches had a ball playfully baiting each other in the press. When Stallings arrived for a press conference wearing muddy boots and an old dirty cap, Bryant ribbed him, "I refuse to have my picture taken with someone who looks like that." Stallings (who later returned in a tuxedo) shot back, "You taught me to work. I can party after the game."

Stallings would soon have reason to celebrate when his Aggies bested the Tide, 20-16. Bryant evidently took the loss fairly well, evidenced by the fact that he gave his protégé a huge, midfield bear hug and even helped carry him to the winner's locker room. Stallings is surely Bryant's only opposing coach who can make such a claim.

The good times were short-lived, though. In 1972, Stallings was fired from Texas A&M. Supporters say he was working under near-impossible conditions, challenged by recruiting players to an all-male military school during the Vietnam War. True to form, Stallings made no excuses and landed on his feet in the NFL when Tom Landry hired him as an assistant coach for the Dallas Cowboys, where he stayed for fourteen years.

During his tremendous run with America's Team, the Cowboys won seven division titles (1973, 1976–79, 1981, 1985), three conference championships (1975, 1977–78), and played in three Super Bowls, winning it in 1978.

Then, in 1986, Stallings was named head coach of the St. Louis Cardinals.

E. J. Junior, a former Alabama all-American playing for the Cardinals, remembers the day Coach Stallings, who he had never met, arrived in town.

"I went into his office," E. J. said. "He was sitting in the chair talking on the phone. His back was turned. I couldn't see him, but I could hear his voice. When you listen to him, not seeing him, his words and voice reminded me so much of Coach Bryant. It was an eerie feeling! I got a chill."

Stallings' years with the Cardinals, who moved to Phoenix in 1988, were not successful and he was fired in 1989. Again, supporters came to his defense saying he was at the mercy of one of the worst organizations in pro football. Stallings again offered no excuses. "We didn't win," he said.

Then in 1990, Stallings was hired as Alabama's new head coach. He was thrilled. The fans were hopeful. And he had a myriad of supporters, including his former boss in Dallas, Tom Landry:

Photograph courtesy of Paul W. Bryant Museum/The University of Alabama

Under Coach Stallings, Alabama was back on top.

He worked for Bear Bryant, played for Bear Bryant, and he is a lot like Bear Bryant. He's a good, solid fundamentals coach. He knows the game very well, teaches it very well, and expects nothing but the best from the people who he coaches.

I don't know of a better person. He's an exceptional person. He's straight and he's honest. If I had to go to war, he's the one I'd want with me.

Despite all the great expectations, Stallings' first season got off to a rocky start when Alabama lost their first three games. That 1990 squad rebounded, though, and finished 7-5. After starting the 1991 season with a humiliating (35-0) loss to Florida, the Tide truly turned—they went on to win the next twenty-eight games in a row!

The 1992 national championship season was as perfect as it could be. Alabama methodically went about picking off its opponents one by one and capped off the year with a Sugar Bowl victory against heavily favored (not to mention cocky and brash) Miami.

"When you have a team that clicks, as we did in '92, everybody comes away from that experience not only as better players and coaches but as people," Stallings said. "And as far as athletic accomplishments go, winning the national title has to be number one."

The national championship gave Coach Stallings another reason to be compared to Coach Bryant.

Barry Krauss, an all-American linebacker at Alabama from 1976 to 1978, told a reporter in 1992: "He's so similar to Coach Bryant it's ridiculous."

Jay Barker, quarterback on the '92 team, said: "Coach Bryant was a guy I grew up wanting to play for. I feel like out of Gene Stallings I got the next best thing."

True, there were many similarities between these two great coaches and the fact that they worked together and achieved similar results only underscores the parallels. They were both honest, hard-working, relentless, straight-talking, loyal, demanding men. But although people said they were cut from the same cloth, many would agree that the weave of the fabric was a little looser on the Stallings side of the coat.

Photograph courtesy of Paul W. Bryant Museum/The University of Alabama

Cigar chompers Jay Barker and Gene Stallings

Not to say he wasn't incredibly tough. Reporters called him "Wyatt Earp with a whistle" and said he was "tough as rawhide." Players and coaches who worked for him were wary of the Stallings glare, a piercing look he would direct your way if you crossed him or talked back to him. But there were definite differences between these two men.

Linda Knowles, a long-time personal secretary to both coaches, says things were much more hectic around the office during the Stallings era for one main reason: "He was much more approachable," she said. "People would just stop by the office and say, 'I was just passing through and thought I'd say hello to Coach.' He would take the time to stop and speak to them. We just didn't have that with Coach Bryant. People were in awe of him."

Coach Stallings is well known for his charitable work, and while he was head coach, it seemed he could not do enough for the community. Not to say Coach Bryant didn't have a compassionate heart. He did.

Knowles explains: "Coach Stallings was much more involved in community affairs than Coach Bryant. I think that goes back to people being intimidated by Coach Bryant, so they didn't approach him as much."

No question, Stallings ultimately took what he learned from two great coaches—Bear Bryant and Tom Landry—and made his mark as his own man.

In 1996, Stallings retired as head coach, leaving Alabama with a record of 70-16-1. He and his wife, Ruth Ann, and his son, John Mark, moved back to Paris, Texas, where they live on a sprawling ranch that often serves as home base for visits from his four daughters (Anna Lee, Laurie, Jackie, and Martha Kate) and their families. During holidays, there are two dozen people in the house.

Even while he was at Alabama, Stallings was perhaps as well-known and beloved for his title of "father" as he was for the title of "coach."

His son, Johnny, who as an infant was diagnosed with Down syndrome, was a frequent and welcome presence around the football field during his dad's days as boss. No one could mistake the love Coach Stallings had for his son, who in his mid-forties continues to struggle with health issues.

Meanwhile, Gene Stallings continues to give back.

"When you're retired, people call on you to do things because they think you don't have anything to do!" he laughed.

Or maybe, they just feel comfortable asking.

DWIGHT STEPHENSON

"Dwight Stephenson was the best center I ever coached. He was a man among children."
— PAUL W. "BEAR" BRYANT

OF ALL THE GREAT ATHLETES WHO HAVE PLAYED CENTER IN COLLEGE and pro football, many people name NFL Hall of Famer and former Crimson Tide great Dwight Stephenson as the best to ever play that position. Coach Bryant concurred when he famously said, "Dwight Stephenson was the best center I ever coached. He was a man among children."

"That statement follows me to this day," Stephenson said. "When people say things like that, it's a good feeling. But coming from someone like Coach Bryant, it really means a lot. When I was a player, I wasn't sure if he even knew who I was!"

He always deflects the praise to his teammates.

"We'd cover each other," Stephenson said. "It was a team thing. Knowing those guys were doing their job allowed me to go out there and be the aggressive player I wanted to be."

Jim Bunch, who played guard alongside Stephenson on the 1978 and '79 national championship teams at Alabama, attended Stephenson's Alabama Sports Hall of Fame induction ceremony in 1994. "The whole offensive line was there from 1979," Bunch said. "He had us stand up—Vince Boothe, Buddy Aydelette, Mike Brock, and myself—and he talked about each of us for five minutes. That's the kind of guy Dwight is."

Photograph courtesy of Paul W. Bryant Museum/The University of Alabama

According to Dwight Stephenson, it was a team thing.

Whether he's talking about his playing days or his current life as the owner of D. Stephenson Construction, a successful South Florida commercial construction company, Stephenson constantly talks about teamwork.

"Coach Bryant used to say, 'You're only as good as the people around you.' I always try to remember that," Stephenson said.

Stephenson started his company in 1994 after spending a few years investing in and renovating apartment buildings. What he says appeals to him most, other than working with good people, is creating something from scratch.

"Building something, then driving past it knowing you had something to do with it is a great feeling," he said. "It's tangible and concrete. There was nothing there. Someone had an idea. Then you had to gather a team and push it through. You know it's not going to be easy. There are going to be some ups and downs in the process but you persevere. It's a lot like sports."

Stephenson, the second of seven children, grew up in Hampton, Virginia. His dad worked in a shipyard, and his mom worked in the school cafeteria. They were the type of people who never complained and never missed a day's work.

"When my mother retired from her job she had something like three hundred sick days she never used," Stephenson said. "They got up each day and went to work no matter what."

Even though he didn't start playing football until he was a junior, Stephenson won all-state honors at center and defensive end his senior year. When Alabama coaches came to scout two of his teammates from state championship Hampton High, Stephenson got noticed. Despite worrying about attending school so far from home and fearing that he wasn't good enough to play for Bear Bryant, Stephenson signed with Alabama. (Both of his other teammates who had also been scouted went to North Carolina State.)

Stephenson started out at Alabama playing defensive end, before former Crimson Tide star center-turned-assistant-coach Sylvester Croom tried Stephenson out at his former position.

"Coach Croom took about four of us to see if we could snap the ball," Stephenson remembered. "He said, 'If he can't do anything else, he can snap the football.' He didn't know if I could block, he didn't know if I could run, but I could snap."

Turns out Stephenson could do all those other things, too. And he credits Coach Croom with honing his skills.

"I learned so much from him, and I owe him a lot as far as my career goes, believe me," Stephenson said. "He gave me confidence and taught me the game. He talked so much about quickness, explosion. As a player, he was the best center. So, if he told me to do something, I did it."

Coach Croom has often returned Stephenson's compliments over the years. In 1979, he told a reporter, "I'm a Dwight Stephenson fan. Physically, he has strength and quickness. I was a power center, and Paul Crane was a quickness center. Dwight is both."

The compliments continued coming Stephenson's way.

He was named all-American in 1979, all-SEC (three times), and was the winner of the Jacobs Award for best blocker in the SEC. (Later, he was also named to the Tide Team of the Century.) Then, in 1979, he was drafted by the Miami Dolphins.

"I was excited to be going to Miami and playing for Coach Don Shula," Stephenson said. "But I was excited to be drafted by any team!"

Before he was drafted, Stephenson collected more compliments from Coach Bryant, although he didn't hear about it until much later.

"Coach Shula called Coach Bryant to ask him about me and what kind of player I was," Stephenson said. "He tells a story that he thought Coach Bryant was pulling his leg. That I might not have been that good! He thought he might have been trying too hard to sell him on me."

As football fans know well, Coach Bryant was pitching an excellent product. Despite playing only eight seasons, Stephenson was elected to the Pro Football Hall of Fame in 1998.

Once again, Stephenson credits others for his enormous success.

"Coach Shula, like Coach Bryant, knew how to get the best out of people," Stephenson said. "As far as coaches, I've had the best. Coach Bryant and Coach Shula were similar. They were both very organized and very demanding."

Coach Shula, who would admit that he loved Alabama players because of their work ethic, lobbed the credit right back to Stephenson. During 1986, when Stephenson missed just two days out of a possible fifty during the Dolphins off-season training program, Coach Shula told reporters: "If I could tell a young player to learn from one of my veterans, to follow around and copy one player, that player would always be Dwight."

The mutual admiration society extended from coaches to pro players who also hailed from the University of Alabama.

According to Stephenson (and many others), John Hannah, who played for Alabama from 1970 to 1972, is one of the best linemen in history,

Hannah returns the compliment: "I played with a lot of good centers and saw a lot of them, but Stephenson is the best. As a matter of fact, I got killed in a game against Chicago once because of him. I watched Stephenson get up under Refrigerator Perry and flip him. Perry would go on his back! So I went out there and tried to flip the Refrigerator and the only person that got flipped was me! I had to go back to my own style."

Stephenson calls his Dolphins teammate and former Alabama star, Bob Baumhower, one of the best defensive linemen ever to play the game.

He also says that facing nose tackle Baumhower in Dolphins practices made him a better player.

"I had to go against Bob Baumhower in practice every day and I hated it," Stephenson said. "Then, finally, one day I figured out how to play Bob Baumhower. He gets very, very close to my face, right? I had a free hand, you know, the centers do. He would get real close and be ready to come off the football. I just pushed his head down and he hit the ground. He said, 'Dwight, you hurt me, man.' So I did it a couple of times. All of a sudden, he adjusted his stance. He sat back a little bit, and then I could get underneath him, and that's what I was trying to do the whole time."

Baumhower adds to Stephenson's accolades: "Dwight Stephenson was a bear. He was the toughest guy I ever played against, and that made it easier on game day."

Speaking of "easier," Stephenson is among the majority of Alabama players who found NFL practices less demanding than those two-a-days back in Tuscaloosa.

Photograph courtesy of Paul W. Bryant Museum/The University of Alabama

Stephenson strove to be quick and explosive at center.

"At Alabama, we were nineteen-year-olds full of energy, but we used to come off that field and we couldn't move," Stephenson said. "We'd have to go lay down. In Miami, I wouldn't say it was easy, but I found myself working just to make myself feel tired; how I was supposed to be feeling after practice."

Although a knee injury cut short Stephenson's playing days, he packed some incredible, memorable play into only eight seasons. People often ask him what it was like to be positioned in front of Dan Marino for five seasons.

"Playing with him was really fun," Stephenson said. "Especially during his first two or three years, nobody knew how to play us. It was funny. You'd see the cornerback (on the other team) and he was scared. And Marino was full of confidence. He could throw an interception and come back like it never happened. He wouldn't be afraid to adjust and try that play again. He never went into a shell."

With Stephenson protecting him, Marino didn't have to go into any shell—he was already well-protected. During each of his seasons as a starter, Stephenson anchored an offensive line that allowed the fewest sacks in the NFL.

As Marino told reporters, "Because of what I had to concentrate on during a game, it was hard for me to notice Stephenson while he was in there. But I sure noticed it when he was not in there."

Stephenson was "in there" quite a bit. He played in 107 straight games from 1980 to 1987 until the player's strike interrupted his streak. He was named all-AFC and all-NFL five consecutive times, played in five consecutive Pro Bowls, and was named the NFL Players Association Lineman of the Year five years in a row. Stephenson started in two Super Bowls (XVII and XIX) and three AFC championship games for the Dolphins.

In 1985, he received one of his most cherished awards when he was named Miller Lite-NFL Man of the Year for his work on charity and community projects.

Stephenson has lent his time to a long list of worthy causes, including United Cerebral Palsy and the Boys and Girls Clubs. "I tried hard to make a good name in South Florida so one day I could use it," Stephenson said. "We work hard every day to maintain it."

When he says "we," Stephenson is again acknowledging his team—the

Photograph by Ronald C. Modra. Used by permission.

Stephenson takes a break outside his Fort Lauderdale office.

people surrounding him. At the top of that list is his wife, Dinah, who lives with him in their Delray Beach home and works with him handling risk management at his Fort Lauderdale office. "Why do you think it's called 'D. Stephenson Construction'?" he laughed.

The Stephensons have three children, Marshea, a teacher in Tampa, Florida; Dwight Jr., who plays linebacker at Notre Dame; and Dwayne, a journalism major at Missouri.

According to Stephenson, he tries to resist telling his kids too many stories about the good old days and how tough it was playing for Coach Bryant. But there are a couple of points he can't help making from time to time.

"I try to make them appreciative of their opportunities," he said. "I tried to raise them so they won't quit. There are ups and downs no matter what you're doing in life. You've got to hang in there."

RICHARD TODD

"The quarterback gets too much blame when things are going bad and too much credit when things are going great."

— RICHARD TODD

Coach Bryant always spent a great deal of time with his quarterbacks. He took walks with them before games. He often ate with them and had extra meetings with them.

It wasn't unusual to see Bryant with his arm around one of his quarterbacks whispering what appeared to be some top-secret information. Naturally, people assumed he had a close relationship with these guys.

Richard Todd, Alabama's quarterback from 1973 to 1975, has a slightly different take.

"We were always around him," Todd said, "but I don't know if we were close to him. I remember one time being told after practice that Coach Bryant wanted to see me the next morning in his office. I'm wondering, 'What'd I do?'"

Photograph courtesy of Paul W. Bryant Museum/The University of Alabama

Bryant and Todd share the spotlight.

Maybe today a player would ask the coach delivering the message what was on the boss' mind. But back then, you didn't ask questions.

"I was up all night thinking, *What did I do?*" he said. "I thought about anything bad I could have done over the last two weeks. I stayed out late one night. Maybe he found out about it. So, I got there and it was nothing! Something like, 'You did this on that play, and you need to do this.' I said, 'Yes, sir!' and got out of there."

In other words, players didn't usually linger in the Coach's company.

"When he wanted to see you, it was usually bad," Todd laughed. "The less time you spent in his office, the better!"

Most players found it difficult to be completely at ease around Coach Bryant on the field, as well.

"He was intimidating," Todd said. "I used to stutter—still do! I'd be OK at practice, but then Coach Bryant came around, and I'd try to call plays, and I'd be stuttering. I'd have to get our fullback to talk half the time! He was probably saying, 'This is our quarterback? He can't even talk!'"

Richard Todd's dreams of wearing the crimson jersey began early. He was born in Birmingham, but his family moved several times when he was growing up when his school-teacher father found new positions in Bristol, Virginia, and Arkadelphia, Arkansas. The Todds returned to Alabama, spending a few years in Tuscaloosa when his father got his doctorate at the University of Alabama, then moved to Montgomery before finally settling in Mobile where Todd attended high school.

As an eighth grader, he watched ex-Crimson Tide star Joe Namath lead the New York Jets to a Super Bowl victory.

"I was a big Joe Namath fan," Todd said.

Like his hero, Todd liked to throw the ball. So much so, that he briefly considered derailing his dream.

"I actually committed to Auburn," Todd said. "They had Pat Sullivan, who had just won the Heisman Trophy. He was a thrower. And I was a passing quarterback in high school. I could run, but I was more of a passer. And Alabama had just changed to the wishbone."

Todd laughs when he remembers a recruiter from Alabama telling him not to worry about the wishbone.

"He said he thought that if I came to Alabama, Coach Bryant would change the system," Todd remembered. "So, I when I went up to meet Coach Bryant, I said, 'Coach, if I come here, are we going to open it up a little more?' He's puffing on that Chesterfield with no filter, spitting the tobacco, and said, 'We had the best passer you ever met at Alabama' [he was talking about Scott Hunter], 'and we went 6-6. So, if you come here, are we going to change the offense? Nope.'"

Even though it might not have been the exact answer he was looking for, Todd's meeting with Coach Bryant brought his dream back into focus.

"I wanted to play for him," he said. "That's why I went to Alabama."

Good decision. Todd played for incredibly successful Alabama teams. In 1973, with Todd sharing quarterback duty with Gary Rutledge, Alabama scored 477 points, the most in Crimson Tide history, and Alabama was crowned national champs (a divided title shared with Notre Dame).

Although it was difficult to argue with a winning game plan, rotating several players in and out of a position, especially one as crucial as quarterback, was something most players had to get used to.

"If you were a really good player and you wanted to win a bunch of awards, you wouldn't go to Alabama during that time," Todd said. "If he had played Wilbur Jackson, our running back, the entire game that year, he would have rushed for more yards than anyone, ever! And he'd probably still hold that record. Coach Bryant would rush three backfields and play three quarterbacks. We just had so much talent that he substituted a lot and played a lot of people."

Even though Gary Rutledge and Todd were competing for a job, by all accounts they got along very well.

"Richard was fun," Rutledge laughed. "He was big, strong, and fast. I was skinny and slow. We were good friends, and we complemented each other really well."

Partly because so many different players played, the Alabama teams of the 1970's exhibited a great deal of camaraderie. Another reason for the exemplary team spirit?

"We won!" Todd said. "Winning hides a multitude of sins. Everybody tries

Photograph courtesy of Richard Todd

Three Alabama guys at NY Jets camp: Namath, Bryant, and Todd

Photograph courtesy of Paul W. Bryant Museum/The University of Alabama

Todd opens it up.

harder to get along when you're winning. When you're not, there's finger-pointing—I saw that later with the Jets."

When you are as successful as Alabama was during those years, losing is tough. In fact, it's devastating.

"My sophomore year, we lost the last game of the season," Todd remembered. "It was like someone died when we lost! It was horrible."

But winning was the norm, and pro teams sent scouts to Tuscaloosa for a closer look. When scouts were in the stands for practice, Coach Bryant graciously made sure Todd did some throwing.

"When the scouts were down there looking at me, he would have a five- or ten-minute period where we'd just be doing dropbacks," Todd said. "And we never did that! He knew the scouts wanted to see if guys could throw the ball."

The scouts liked what they saw, and the New York Jets drafted Todd in the first round. He found out later that Joe Namath had put in a good word for him.

"Joe had a lot to do with it," Todd said. "My senior year, we probably threw the ball six times a game. They knew I was tough, but could I throw? Joe said, 'Check this kid out. He can throw the ball.'"Joe wasn't just being loyal to a fellow Crimson Tider. He had firsthand knowledge of Todd's talents."He always came back to Tuscaloosa during the summer, and we would work out," Todd said. "We'd get Ozzie Newsome and Bob Baumhower, and I'd run routes for Joe to get myself in shape. Imagine running around catching his passes. That was a blast!"

Todd followed Joe to New York in 1976, and one of his fondest memories came during his rookie year when Bryant visited their preseason camp.

"Someone took a picture of Coach Bryant in the middle, me on one side, and Joe on the other," Todd said. "I still have it. I love it."

After the '76 season, the Jets released Joe, who went on to finish his career with the Los Angeles Rams, and Todd became the starting quarterback. It was a tough act to follow.

"Joe won a Super Bowl, and that's what we were compared to," Todd said. "Which is justified. We struggled for a lot of years. But then we had a couple of good years. The quarterback gets too much blame when things are going bad and too much credit when things are going great."

In 1981, Todd led the Jets to their first winning season (10-5-1) since 1969. The following season, the Jets went to the AFC Championship game but lost a muddy contest to the Dolphins.

One of the biggest challenges Todd faced in New York was the intense media scrutiny, especially when the team was not doing well.

"I handled some things a little different than I would now just from a maturity level," he said. "I wasn't the friendliest guy to the press; that was transparent in the way I acted. It's hard in New York. There are so many papers and so much competition that everybody's trying to get an angle. If you played badly, that's one thing, but they try to get involved in your personal life, which is really none of their business."

Todd played pro ball in an era of changes. Not all of them good. People often ask ex-Alabama guys what Bryant would have thought of players celebrating after they made a good play.

"If he had a player call attention to himself when he did something good, he would take him out!" Todd said. "I played with Mark Gastineau. He's the one who started the Sack Dance, which they've outlawed now. It was horrible."

Todd, who played his last two pro years in New Orleans, prefers watching college football these days.

"Anything can happen," he said. "That's why I love college football. It's not as scripted as pro football. It's always more fun to watch kids play."

Photograph courtesy of Richard Todd

Todd followed Namath as Jets quarterback.

Todd and his family attend most Alabama home games when they're not busy watching another group of Crimson Tide athletes: the men's golf team.

Todd's son, "Gator," is a top-notch golfer for Alabama's highly ranked team and plans to turn pro when he graduates in 2008.

"I don't know where he got his talent," Todd said. "It has to come from his mother's side. I'm absolutely horrible at golf."

Todd, his wife, Lulu, son Jimmy (eleven years old), and daughter Darbi Lou (sixteen) live in Lulu's hometown of Florence, Alabama. Todd commutes to his job in Atlanta, where he is a senior managing director with Bear Stearns, a company he's been with for twenty-one years.

He first interviewed with Bear Stearns while still playing in New York.

"It was the year we went on strike," Todd said. "I was thirty years old, and I realized I wasn't going to be playing football the rest of my life. I thought, *What am I going to do?* I majored in P. E. because I always wanted to be a coach. But then after being around college football and pro ball for eleven years, it was the farthest thing from my mind."

Before the interview, Todd was nervous. "I thought, *I'm a P. E. major! What if this guy has all these business questions?*"

Richard Todd and his son Gator

As it turns out, they talked a lot of football that day. The executives at Bear Stearns liked how Todd interacted with people. When he retired from pro football in 1985, he went into sales for them. He worked in New York for two years, then transferred to Atlanta, where he has been ever since.

Richard Todd doesn't claim many regrets. But during his frequent visits to Tuscaloosa, where he enjoys reminiscing with his ex-quarterbacks coach (and current athletics director) Mal Moore, he can't help but feel a little wistful.

"I wish I had known Coach Bryant longer is all I have to say," Todd said. "It would be fun to be an alumnus and go down there and talk to him after practice. You could bring up old stories and he'd probably bring up ones you'd never heard. I'd have liked that."

PAT TRAMMELL

"Pat Trammell was the
favorite person of my life."
— PAUL W. "BEAR" BRYANT

PAT TRAMMELL PACKED A LOT OF LIVING INTO HIS SHORT, INCREDIBLE life. On the football field, he was a tough, tenacious, unbeatable quarterback who led the Crimson Tide to a national championship (Coach Bryant's first at Alabama) in 1961.

In the classroom, he was a star student, who had the grades and the discipline to attend and complete medical school. After graduation, he set up a dermatology practice in Birmingham. But all too soon, Dr. Pat Trammell was gone. He died of cancer on December 10, 1968. He was just twenty-eight years old.

Trammell, the son of a doctor, grew up in Scottsboro, Alabama. He was a standout athlete at Scottsboro High School. He was the most valuable basketball player in the state of Alabama his senior year, but football was his passion.

Photograph courtesy of Paul W. Bryant Museum/The University of Alabama

Tough, tenacious Pat Trammell

He was named all-County, all-state, all-Southern, and all-American for his gridiron efforts.

When Trammell arrived on campus in Tuscaloosa in 1958, he was part of Coach Bryant's first recruiting class at the university. He was incredibly confident from the start. According to Richard Scott, author of *Legends of Alabama Football*, Coach Bill Oliver remembered Trammell standing with a bunch of fellow recruits who were talking about what positions they were going to play. "Well," Trammell said, "y'all can just forget about quarterback. I'm going to be the quarterback."

Cocky? Maybe. But Trammell had the goods to back it up and soon established himself as the definitive team leader. In a 1968 game program article, Coach Bryant explained: "Pat was a pretty mature young man for his age. He was one of those people that you might say kind of vibrated leadership. When he walked into the room, you knew he was the leader."

Steve Sloan, who played quarterback after Trammell's reign, said, "He was a real bright guy. Trammell and Coach Bryant were so similar. Trammell had this level of toughness and leadership that went with Coach Bryant's philosophy at that time. He was just the perfect guy to play quarterback."

The quarterback is often considered the team leader. He calls the plays and handles the ball more than any other player. But Trammell took this concept a step further. Players talked in his huddle at their own risk. No one doubted that he was in charge. Sometimes, even Coach Bryant played second fiddle to Trammell.

"He was the only guy I knew that would talk back to Coach Bryant," teammate Billy Neighbors said. "They'd send in plays and if Trammell didn't want to run it, he wouldn't run it. He would just say, 'We are not going to run that. They don't know what they're talking about.'"

Jack Rutledge, Bryant's longtime assistant coach and a player on the '61 squad, saw Trammell's rebellion firsthand.

"Coach Bryant would eat lunch with the quarterbacks," Rutledge said. "Then on game day, the team captains that were appointed that week would eat lunch with them, too. I was captain against Mississippi State that particular week.

"So the relationship we had with Coach Bryant, you know, you are not saying anything," Rutledge said. "You're sitting at the table eating and hoping the meal will get over in a hurry. But Trammell is just sitting there eating like he normally does. Then Coach Bryant takes out a pen and drew a little thing on his napkin. He slides it in front of Trammell and says, 'Pat, what do you think about that play?' Trammell keeps eating and says, 'I don't think that will work worth a damn.'"

Even though the coach folded up that particular napkin and stuffed it in his pocket, there were no hard feelings. By all accounts, Trammell and the coach were extremely close. As coach and quarterback, they spent a lot of time together. They ate together. Took the ceremonial walk around the field before the game together. But Coach Bryant wasn't one to put up with dissension. Mostly, Trammell got away with contradicting his coach because more often than not, he was right.

"I have never known of a smarter player," assistant coach Jimmy Sharpe told a reporter in 1968. "He had the greatest insight into a play and what it was trying to accomplish. If it broke down, Trammell knew where it broke down without seeing the film. He had a tremendous memory. No matter what the situation, you had no doubt that whatever play Trammell called was the right play."

Many of his former teammates and coaches say that Trammell was so adept at making the right call because he always knew everyone's assignment. And if you missed that assignment, Trammell would give you hell for it.

Pat Trammell didn't just talk the talk. During his three varsity seasons, Alabama lost only three games. And it may not be a coincidence that Trammell was sidelined with injuries during those particular games.

Although tremendously effective where it counted—on the scoreboard—Trammell's playing style was not flashy. There were more quick pitches, quick kicks, and a short runs than dramatic long bombs. His form was not picture-perfect. When asked about Trammell's style several years after the 1961 championship season, Coach Bryant told reporters: "As a quarterback, Trammell had no ability. He was not a great runner, but he scored touchdowns. He didn't pass with great style, but he completed passes. All he could do was beat you."

The ability to win. That's what mattered on the football field. In the process of leading his team to the title in 1961, Trammell racked up many impressive stats, including passing for 1,035 yards (a team record at the time) and finishing the season with only two interceptions. He led the Crimson

Photograph courtesy of Paul W. Bryant Museum/The University of Alabama

Who's in charge here? Trammell and Coach.

Tide in scoring in both 1960 and '61. He was all-SEC and an all-SEC academic selection in 1961 and finished fifth in Heisman Trophy voting.

Many people thought Trammell would tuck this list of achievements under his arm and head straight to the NFL. Then, during a trip to New York City, where Trammell and Coach Bryant were attending a MacArthur Bowl presentation, the opportunity for a pro career presented itself when Trammell met Green Bay Packer Coach Vince Lombardi. The (other) legendary coach asked Trammell if he would be interested in playing for the Packers.

Trammell's answer? "Hell, yes."

Then, Coach Bryant intervened and told Lombardi that Trammell was not going into the pros. He was going to med school.

"He's not good enough to play pro football," Bryant said.

Trammell later laughed about this comment, speculating that Coach Bryant wanted him to become a doctor so, like a proud papa, he could boast to recruits about his ex-player turned doctor.

Indeed, Trammell went to medical school. Then, sadly, not long after he set up his practice in Birmingham where he lived with his wife, Baye, and their young son and daughter, Trammell discovered he had a tumor.

He immediately called Coach Bryant to tell him the news. In his autobiography, Bryant described how he felt.

"My stomach turned over," he said. "If I had been standing up, I'd have probably dropped to my knees."

Trammell and Baye flew up to New York City so Trammell could be treated at the Ewing Clinic. A few days later, Bryant followed. Joe Namath and Trammell's former teammate Ray Abruzzese picked Bryant up at the airport and drove him into town.

It was a cheerful scene in Trammell's room. Lots of joking and kidding. Finally, Baye, Joe, and Ray left, and it was just Trammell and the Coach, who told the doctor he planned on staying for a while. According to Bryant's autobiography, the doctor left and returned with a bottle of Jack Daniels Black.

He said, "Coach, Pat can't have anything to eat, but he can have some of this. I'll put it right here on the dresser, and you and Pat can have a little party, and he can tell you what he really thinks of you. And it probably won't be what you think he thinks."

Bryant remembered that Trammell was in feisty form, telling him several times, "Goddamit, Coach, shut up. I been listening to you for ten years, now you listen to me."

The next day, Trammell had surgery. The doctors told him they "got all of it" and everyone, including young Dr. Trammell, was very positive about his future.

After his return to Alabama, Trammell talked openly about his illness. "I had a lot of self-pity when I found out about it," he told a reporter, "but regardless of the outcome I can never complain. I've done a lot of thinking, and I've been so fortunate. This has really made me count my blessings."

In the fall of 1968, Trammell brought his young son, Pat Jr., to visit Tuscaloosa, where they stayed in the Pat Trammell room. Coach Bryant invited them to ride on the team bus back to Birmingham for the Iron Bowl. But his heart was heavy because before they made the trip, Trammell told him that the cancer had returned.

The Crimson Tide beat Auburn 24-16 and back in the locker room after the game, the team was celebrating, whooping and hollering.

Team captain Mike Hall then climbed up on a trunk and pulled Trammell and his son up with him. The room went silent as Hall presented them with the game ball.

"We knew he was sick," Hall said. "It was pretty damn emotional. Just about everybody was crying."

The following week, Trammell was in the hospital again, and Coach Bryant went to visit him. "Shouldn't you be out recruiting?" Trammell laughed.

The next day, Trammell went into a coma. He died several days later on December 10, 1968.

The guy who was synonymous with the words "tough" and "tenacious" couldn't beat this ugly disease. And it broke Coach Bryant's heart.

"This is the saddest day of my life," he said.

According to Allen Barra, author of *The Last Coach,* Trammell's funeral was a huge event attended by teammates and bold-faced names such as Auburn's Shug Jordan. Even Governor George Wallace and President Richard Nixon sent condolences. And Coach Bryant, who wept openly, escorted Trammell's mother to the service while his wife, Mary Harmon, accompanied Trammell's father.

Coach Bryant later said, "Pat Trammell was the favorite person of my life." What a testament to an incredible man.

Coach Bryant and several of Trammell's teammates (Tommy Brooker, James A. Sharpe, Joseph K. Sims, and Billy Neighbors) found a way to honor Trammell's legacy and keep his spirit alive when they established the A-Club Foundation immediately following Trammell's death. This charitable organization, which thrives to this day, assists the families of former University of Alabama athletes during times of hardship with funds for education, medical emergencies, and other pressing needs.

"It all started because Coach Bryant wanted to make sure Pat's kids were taken care of," said Billy Neighbors, who still works with the foundation.

A few years later, Coach Bryant took the giving spirit a step further. With an initial gift of $1 million, he established a separate scholarship fund for the children of all of his former players. Some 750 students have attended the university on these scholarships, beginning with Pat Trammell Jr. According to Allen Barra, Coach Bryant kept a close watch on his charge.

"The only negative thing about the scholarship is that once a quarter I had to take my grades to him," said Pat Jr. "I wasn't as smart as my dad, and if I made Bs and Cs he'd get mad at me and tell me my dad never made a B the whole time he was in college."

Pat Jr., a financial planner who lives in Birmingham with his family, has great memories of Coach Bryant, who never forgot his (or his sister's) birthday and often invited him to stand on the sidelines at Alabama games.

Of course Pat Jr. still has fond memories of his father as well, and every year he pays tribute to him when he presents the Pat Trammell Award at the football team's senior banquet. Recent recipients of the award, given to a player for excellence in athletics, academics, and character, have included Andrew Zow, Antonio Carter, and Matt Miller.

In the 1982 book, *Bama and the Bear,* Trammell's widow, Baye, summed up the relationship between her late husband and Coach Bryant: "I feel that their relationship began as one of pupil and teacher. I saw Pat's feelings grow from awe and fear of Coach Bryant, to determination to please him. I think it eventually got to the point where they could read each other's minds—they were really on the same wavelength, and in many ways they were a lot alike.

"It was mainly a matter of their love for the game and their study of it at night, not only physically but intellectually as well. And I think their personalities, in a way, were alike as well. They both intimidated people a little bit until you got to know them, and then you'd realize that intimidation sometimes comes from something you don't understand.

"Coach Bryant was an unbelievable motivator, a good and sensitive man who allowed his feelings and friendship to spill over to the men who played for him."

TOMMY WILCOX

"I knew that if I could make it at Alabama, I could make it anywhere."

— TOMMY WILCOX

WHEN PEOPLE ARE WITNESSES TO HISTORY, THEY OFTEN DON'T REALize it until much later. Tommy Wilcox was present for several major milestones at the University of Alabama during his stint as a player for Coach Bryant. And he was well aware of every one of them.

The first came in 1978. Wilcox was a redshirt freshman but watched as his team won the national championship. In 1979 Wilcox was a starting defensive back when the Crimson Tide won another national championship.

Then, in 1981, the world watched as Coach Bryant set about tying, then breaking, Amos Alonzo Stagg's record as the winningest college football coach in history. (Wilcox was a major contributor to both events.)

Next came the grand finale, when Wilcox played in Coach Bryant's final game before he retired. And then came the poignant postscript, when Bryant passed away suddenly the following year. Wilcox was honored to be one of eight men to serve as a pallbearer at his funeral.

"There are thousands and thousands of players who deserved to do what I did," Wilcox said, "and for Mrs. Bryant to pick me, it was an honor."

That's a whole lot of history for a guy from Harahan, Louisiana.

When he was growing up, Wilcox and his dad watched football on TV, but somehow he found himself drawn to the wishbone-playing Crimson Tide rather than his dad's alma mater, Tulane, or even their rival, LSU.

"I said to myself, if I ever get the chance to play for Alabama, I'll take it," he said.

In high school, Wilcox played strong safety as a freshman, then switched to quarterback. His senior year, he led his team to the state championships. To his delight, the Alabama scouts noticed. Other schools were competing for Wilcox's talents and tried to convince him he would never play at Alabama since the roster was so deep. Wilcox took that as a challenge.

"That was a slam in my competitiveness," he said. "I felt that I could play at Alabama. And more important, I knew that if I could make it at Alabama I could make it anywhere."

Photograph courtesy of Paul W. Bryant Museum/The University of Alabama

Tommy Wilcox jumped at the chance to play for the Crimson Tide.

When Coach Bryant offered him a scholarship, Wilcox enthusiastically accepted.

When he arrived in Tuscaloosa, his enthusiasm was somewhat dampened though, when he was redshirted his freshman year.

As a redshirt quarterback, he played on the scout team, leading the offense in practices against the likes of Marty Lyons, Curtiss McGriff, Rich Wingo, and Barry Krauss—guys who would become synonymous with the Goal Line

Stand. Although it was satisfying (but painful!) to play this important role, Wilcox wanted to play in college football games that counted.

More frustration was brought on that summer when he became academically ineligible to play football. Plus, he was homesick. And he had injured his ankle. Feeling it would be a struggle to get his grades up and fight his way into the starting lineup at the same time, Wilcox decided to head for home. When he didn't show up for fall practice, Coach Bryant made a trip to Louisiana.

According to *Legends of Alabama Football*, Coach Bryant called Wilcox from the airport and asked him to meet him at a nearby Hilton. They went to his room and he pulled two chairs out from the table so he and Wilcox would be sitting close to each other, face-to-face.

"He said, 'Boy, what's your problem?'" Wilcox recalled. "I started talking and sort of looking around the room and he said, 'Wait a minute, boy. When you talk to me, look me in the eyes!'"

He listened to Wilcox and said he understood his problems and concerns.

"He said, 'If you'll do what I think you'll do and come back to school and work hard and you'll get after folks like I think you will, I think you have the chance to be an all-American before you leave Alabama,'" Wilcox said. "Needless to say, I was back at school in three days."

Despite the fact Wilcox had missed the first week or so of fall practice, his teammates welcomed him back. To his surprise, though, he was still playing on the scout teams, and this time he was getting pounded on both offense and defense. In over a week's time, he never left the field.

This wasn't going to be easy.

"I took some punishment," Wilcox said in *What It Means to Be Crimson Tide*. "I never came out of scrimmages. I had to stay after practice. And I was thinking, *This isn't what we talked about in that hotel room.*"

It wasn't long, though, before Wilcox had proved himself and earned the opportunity to play, even though it wasn't at his anticipated position. Coach Bryant told Wilcox he had a choice: play No. 2 quarterback behind starter Steadman Shealy, or switch over to defense and start right away.

"I told him, 'Coach, I sat out all last year and got the heck beat out of

Photograph courtesy of Paul W. Bryant Museum/The University of Alabama

Wilcox gets busy in the secondary.

me,'" he said. "I want to play. I don't want to sit on the bench anymore. Wherever you want me to play, I'll play."

So Wilcox got busy in the secondary as a strong safety and turned into one of the most successful defensive players ever to play for Alabama. He was named SEC Freshman of the Year in 1979, all-SEC in 1980, and all-American in both 1981 and 1982. He finished his career with 243 tackles, 10 interceptions, and 25 pass breakups.

And despite his success as a defender, he did get a chance to play quarterback—once. During the 1979 season, during a match-up against Mississippi State, Alabama found itself with all three quarterbacks (Gray, Jacobs, and Shealy) injured at the exact same time. Enter Tommy Wilcox. He took only three snaps before returning to his day job. And he didn't seem to mind a bit.

In a 1979 interview, Wilcox told reporter Kirk McNair, "If I get a shot at quarterback in the spring, I'll take it, but I'm really happy where I am. I want to play wherever Coach Bryant thinks that I can help the team. I'm just grateful to be able to contribute."

And contribute, he did.

As a four-year starter, Wilcox's great plays (interceptions against Auburn and Mississippi State) and great games (returning home to beat LSU) are many. But one game sticks out for him. And it's one of those above-named milestones: Coach Bryant's 314th win to tie Coach Stagg's all-time victories record.

"It was against Penn State," Wilcox said. "We went in there and played great football and got a big lead at halftime, but they came back in the second half and drove right down the field to a first down at about our seven yard line. We held them on a couple of runs, then they threw a pass on third down and we were called for interference, giving them a first down at our three. They rammed at us four times from the three, but we stopped them four times and held, and we went on to win."

So, after Alabama made its second successful Goal Line Stand against Penn State in two years, Coach Bryant had his 314th win.

"We were all running off the field in jubilation that we had just stopped them," Wilcox remembered. "Coach Bryant, as the defense was coming off, he stepped on the field, took his hat off and tipped it at us, as if to say, 'A job well done.' That's something I had never ever seen him do before, and to this day that's still a big moment."

After he left Alabama, Wilcox played for two years in the USFL (for the Chicago Blitz) before a serious neck injury forced his retirement in 1984. After quitting pro football, he returned to Tuscaloosa to complete his degree in public relations. When he got his diploma, he and his wife, Mary, his high school sweetheart, made Tuscaloosa their home, and he immediately put his PR skills to work as a pharmaceutical sales representative.

Business was good for over a decade until at the end of the nineties, when the company he worked for was sold and Wilcox was laid off.

"That was just one of those tough times," Wilcox told a *Bama Magazine* reporter. "I had a family, a car payment, a house payment, and no job. I just tried to think about what Coach Bryant used to say about how tough times don't last but tough people do.

"That's the thing about athletes. When we get down, we're fighters. For the most part, we know how to deal with adversity. Coach Bryant taught us to continue on when things go bad. He taught us more than football—he taught us about life."

True to form, Wilcox persevered and after twenty years in the business, continues to work as a pharmaceutical sales rep for Bristol Myers Squibb. In addition, Wilcox, an avid outdoorsman, is living many a man's dream by hosting his own fishing and hunting TV show, *Tommy Wilcox Outdoors.*

At first, the show, which is syndicated on FOX, featured primarily fellow SEC greats, including other former Alabama players such as Wesley Britt, Sylvester Croom, and Barry Krauss. "I figured that since just about everybody loves both football and the outdoors, if I could bring those two passions together, people will watch," Wilcox said.

A particularly popular episode was the Auburn-Alabama pheasant hunt. As the show evolved, Wilcox expanded his guest list to include celebrities outside of football, such as country music superstar Hank Williams, Jr., and NASCAR's Nextel Cup champion, Tony Stewart.

Wilcox grew up hunting and fishing in Louisiana but says he prefers the variety of fish and game found near his Tuscaloosa home. Another reason for sticking around Tuscaloosa? His daughter, Kristi, is a student at the University of Alabama. (Her younger sister, Kacie, might follow.)

Wilcox doesn't hide his excitement about her decision to attend the college closest to home and closest to his heart.

"I'm tickled to death!" he said. "I'm just glad she decided to stay close. They say you've got to give them a little space and let them try their wings and fly. But there's a difference between flying to another tree and flying to a different forest."

BIBLIOGRAPHY

Barra, Allen. *The Last Coach.* New York: W.W. Norton, 2005.

Bolton. Clyde. *The Crimson Tide: A Story of Alabama Football.* Huntsville: The Strode Publishers, 1972.

Book, Randall. *Bama and the Bear.* Springville, UT: Cedar Fort, 1983.

Briley, John David. *Career in Crisis: Paul Bear Bryant and the '71 Season of Change.* Macon, Ga.: Mercer University Press, 2006.

Bryant, Paul W. and John Underwood. *Bear: The Hard Life and Good Times of Alabama's Coach Bryant.* Boston: Little, Brown and Company, 1974.

Dunnavant, Keith. *Coach: The Life of Paul "Bear" Bryant.* New York: St. Martin's Press, 2005.

Ford, Tommy. *Bama Under Bear.* Huntsville: The Strode Publishers, 1983.

Herskowitz, Mickey. *The Legend of Bear Bryant.* New York: McGraw-Hill, 1987.

Hester, Wayne. *Century of Champions: The Centennial History of Alabama Football.* Birmingham: Seacoast Publishing, The Birmingham News, 1991.

Hicks, Tommy. *Game of My Life Alabama, Memorable Stories of Crimson Tide Football.* Champaign, Ill.: Sports Publishing, 2006.

Krauss, Barry and Joe M. Moore. *Ain't Nothing But a Winner: Bear Bryant, The Goal Line Stand and a Chance of a Lifetime.* Tuscaloosa: University of Alabama Press, 2006.

McNair, Kirk. *What it Means to Be Crimson Tide: Gene Stallings and Alabama's Greatest Players (What It Means).* Chicago: Triumph Books, 2005.

Peterson, James A. and Bill Cromartie. *Bear Bryant: Countdown to Glory, A Game by Game History of Bear Bryant's 315 Victories.* Champaign, Ill.: Human Kinetics Pub, 1983.

Reed, Delbert. *Paul 'Bear' Bryant: What Made Him a Winner.* Northport, Ala.: Vision Press, 1997.

Schoor, Gene. *100 Years of Alabama Football.* Marietta, Ga.: Longstreet Press, 1991.

Scott, Richard and Jay Barker. *Legends of Alabama Football.* Champaign, Ill.: Sports Publishing, 2004.

ABOUT THE AUTHORS

BROADCASTER ELI GOLD is best known as The Voice of the University of Alabama's Crimson Tide, where he has provided the exciting play-by-play for twenty years. In addition to his Bama duties, this Brooklyn-born, longtime Birmingham resident also hosts *NASCAR Live*, a weekly, nationally syndicated radio call-in show. Gold is considered one of the most versatile broadcasters in sports, having done call-in programs and play-by-play for arena football, NFL, professional baseball, and NHL on radio and television. His many honors include four Alabama Sportscaster of the Year awards.

M.B. ROBERTS is the author of fourteen books, including *Reflections of the Game: Lives in Baseball* and *Brooks & Dunn: The Honky Tonk Truth*, both collaborations with her husband, longtime *Sports Illustrated* photographer Ronald C. Modra. She has collaborated on several projects with Eli Gold, including *Crimson Nation* and *From Peanuts to the Pressbox*.